WORKING WITH ANGER

WORKING WITH ANGER
A CONSTRUCTIVIST APPROACH

Edited by

Peter Cummins
Coventry Teaching Primary Care Trust

John Wiley & Sons, Ltd

Other Wiley Editorial Offices

John Wiley & Sons Inc., 111 River Street, Hoboken, NJ 07030, USA

Jossey-Bass, 989 Market Street, San Francisco, CA 94103–1741, USA

Wiley-VCH Verlag GmbH, Boschstr. 12, D-69469 Weinheim, Germany

John Wiley & Sons Australia Ltd, 42 McDougall Street, Milton, Queensland 4064, Australia

John Wiley & Sons (Asia) Pte Ltd, 2 Clementi Loop #02–01, Jin Xing Distripark, Singapore 129809

John Wiley & Sons Canada Ltd, 22 Worcester Road, Etobicoke, Ontario, Canada M9W 1L1

Wiley also publishes its books in a variety of electronic formats. Some content that appears in print may not be available
in electronic books.

Library of Congress Cataloging-in-Publication Data

Working with anger : a constructivist approach / edited by Peter Cummins.
        p.   cm.
    Includes bibliographical references and index.
    ISBN-13: 978-0-470-09049-7 (cloth : alk. paper)
    ISBN-10: 0-470-09049-9 (cloth : alk. paper)
    ISBN-13: 978-0-470-09050-3 (pbk. : alk. paper)
    ISBN-10: 0-470-09050-2 (pbk. : alk. paper)
    1. Anger.   2. Constructivism (Psychology)   3. Personal construct theory.   I. Cummins, Peter.
    BF575.A5W67 2006
    152.4′7—dc22   2005016321

British Library Cataloguing in Publication Data

A catalogue record for this book is available from the British Library

ISBN-13 978-0-470-09049-7 (hbk)   978-0-470-09050-3 (pbk)
ISBN-10 0-470-09049-9 (hbk)   0-470-09050-2 (pbk)

Typeset in 10/12pt Times and Helvetica by TechBooks, New Delhi, India
Printed and bound in Great Britain by TJ International Ltd, Padstow, Cornwall, UK
This book is printed on acid-free paper responsibly manufactured from sustainable forestry
in which at least two trees are planted for each one used for paper production.

For Sally, Matthew and Simon who have lived with the production of this book. And for my mother, Maeve, who would have vicariously enjoyed the whole production.

CONTENTS

ABOUT THE EDITOR

Peter Cummins trained in Clinical Psychology at the Crichton Royal Hospital in Dumfries, Scotland, from 1974–76. There he was introduced to Personal Construct Psychology by his new head of department, Millar Mair. He has been involved with PCP ever since. He went on to train in Personal Construct Psychotherapy at the Centre for Personal Construct Psychology in London, gaining his diploma in PCP Psychotherapy in 1988. He has worked within the British NHS since 1976, at Bexley Hospital, then Maidstone and since 1995 he has been Head of Adult Psychological Services in Coventry. All his clinical work has been with working-age adults. For the past eight years he has specialised in working with angry and violent people who have managed not to be sent to forensic services.

LIST OF CONTRIBUTORS

Robert W. Adelman, *Clinical Psychologist, P.O. Box 860, Malakoff, Texas 75148, USA.*

Diane Allen, *Chartered Counselling Psychologist, Adult Psychological Services, Gulson Hospital, Gulson Road, Coventry CV1 2HR, UK.*

Peter Cummins, *Consultant Clinical Psychologist, Adult Psychological Services, Gulson Hospital, Gulson Road, Coventry CV1 2HR, UK.*

Rudi Dallos, *Course Director, Plymouth University Clinical Psychology Doctorate, University of Plymouth, Drake Circus, Plymouth, Devon PL4 8AA, UK.*

Bhavisha Dave, *Assistant Psychologist, Adult Psychological Services, Gulson Hospital, Gulson Road, Coventry CV1 2HR, UK.*

Tammy Dukewich, *Merrimack College, North Andover, Massachusetts 01845, USA.*

Chris J. Laming, *School of Humanities, Communications and Social Sciences, Monash University, Churchill, Victoria 3842, Australia.*

Larry M. Leitner, *Department of Psychology, Miami University, Oxford, Ohio 45056, USA.*

James C. Mancuso, *Deceased.*

Michael F. Mascolo, *Merrimack College, North Andover, Massachusetts 01845, USA.*

Melissa A. Maras, *Center for School-Based Mental Health Programs, Department of Psychology, Miami University, Oxford, Ohio 45056, USA.*

Marc D. McLaughlin, *Center for School-Based Mental Health Programs, Department of Psychology, Miami University, Oxford, Ohio 45056, USA.*

Heather Moran, *Consultant Clinical Child Psychologist, Children and Adolescent Mental Health Services, Gulson Clinic, Gulson Road, Coventry, CV1 2HR, UK.*

Carl E. Paternite, *Department of Psychology, Miami University, Oxford, Ohio 45056, USA.*

Dina Pekkala, *Clinical Psychologist, Adult Psychological Services, Gulson Hospital, Gulson Road, Coventry CV1 2HR, UK.*

Harry Procter, *Consultant Clinical Psychologist, Taunton, Somerset, UK.*

Christopher J. Reiger, *Center for School-Based Mental Health Programs, Department of Psychology, Miami University, Oxford, Ohio 45056, USA.*

Gina Selby, *The Ship Inn, Ash Hill, Newbury, Berkshire, UK.*

Graeme Sutherland, *c/o Peter Cummins, Gulson Hospital, Gulson Road, Coventry CV1 2HR, UK.*

Jill C. Thomas, *Department of Psychology, Miami University, Oxford, Ohio 45056, USA.*

Bill Warren, *Associate Professor, Faculty of Education and Arts, University of Newcastle, Callaghan, NSW 2308, Australia.*

PREFACE

This book began as a result of my trying to deal with a clinical problem. The service that I manage was being asked more and more frequently to work with people who had anger problems. We had no one within the service with any expertise in this area. In a supervision group run by Fay Fransella I was able to begin to explore a personal construct perspective on anger. I began running an anger group in May 1997 and first presented a paper on anger at the International PCP conference at the University of Washington in Seattle in July 1997. Within six months of starting to work with anger, I was subpoenaed to a local court to give reasons as to why I had declined to accept a referral. Anger, I discovered, can be a very political issue to deal with, as it is a frequent reason for court proceedings, both for domestic problems and the wider issues of public behaviour. As I began to develop a framework for working with anger, I became aware of issues which seemed to appear again and again for the people I was asked to work with. This book is an effort to provide a coherent set of answers to these issues which repeatedly arise.

When I began, the only structured response I could find was that on anger management from a CBT perspective. I then discovered the work of Averill who had developed a social constructivist view of anger in 1982. He defined anger as a socially constituted syndrome (a transitory social role) which includes the person's appraisal of the situation. For Averill, a constructivist view emphasises the social origins and current functions of anger: 'Anger is a social product, not simply a byproduct' (1982, p. 63). Averill, however, is a social psychologist; most of his research involved university undergraduates and it does not address the clinical issues of working with anger.

The first question I struggled with was what sort of treatment approaches could be developed within a constructivist perspective. Chapters 1 and 2 are my own answer to this. In Chapters 3 and 4 two other constructivist practitioners describe their answers to the same question. I was particularly interested in the fact that we all independently developed group-based treatments. Inevitably, however, there are some people who, for a number of reasons, are not suited to group-based approaches. In Chapter 5, Jill Thomas and Larry Leitner explore the individual treatment of anger. Since many of the experiences which lead to angry adults derive from childhood, I often wonder what would happen if the person had been seen as a child. In Chapter 6, Heather

Moran explores ways of doing just this, describing her way of working with children and anger. In Chapter 7, Rob Adelman both makes a case for REBT as a constructivist approach and takes us on to a slightly older group in his description of a programme aimed at working with adolescents.

The second half of this book represents an effort to answer the questions about what is actually going on within anger. The first question is to explore what it is actually like to be angry. In Chapter 8, Graeme Sutherland presents a powerful description of the reality of living with anger. In 'Mr Angry' he begins by describing the realities of angry behaviour that he and his immediate family had to cope with. He goes on to elaborate where the invalidation underlying his anger was derived from and his struggle both to reconstrue his behaviour and to alter it. He presents a real-life example of how family structures lead to the development of anger, a question addressed in Chapter 9 by Harry Proctor and Rudi Dallos. In Chapter 10 the question of why 80 % of our referrals are male, and whether they differ from female referrals is addressed by Bhavisha Dave et al.

At a clinical level we have noticed that again and again people told us how their relationship with their parents (usually their father) was disrupted between the ages of 8 and 12. This was commonly due to parental separation, but could be due to physical illness or depression leading to a lack of relationship. This distinct pattern left me wondering just what developmental issues children are working on at this particular age. In Chapter 11 Mike Mascolo et al. set out to answer this question.

While home is the key place for children, the second place for them is school. Many of our clients remember either being humiliated at school (often because of literacy difficulties) or being angry and aggressive which resulted in being excluded from school. In Chapter 12, Paternite and colleagues explore what happens in school and present possible alternative constructions. They then provide a framework for validation which would prevent young men growing up angry.

After about a year of working with anger I came across a quote that said that what mattered was to get angry with the right people, in the right way, at the right time. This described perfectly what I was trying to achieve with the people I was working with. I was very surprised to discover that this quote was from Aristotle's *Nicomachean Ethics* which dates from *c.* 324 BC; 2,300 years ago and anger was already understood. This philosophical contribution is described in Chapter 13 by Bill Warren who has taken on the 'daunting task' (Taylor and Novaco, 2005) of delineating the contribution of philosophers.

And, finally, we come to the critical question, does any of what we do actually achieve real change? In Chapter 14, Pekkala and Dave have carefully evaluated the Coventry Anger programme. They have very deliberately used mainstream assessment techniques so that these results can be contrasted with other studies in the anger literature.

The elements of constructivist theory described in Chapter 1 are common to all the contributors to this book. All would accept Averill's (1982) observation that 'one of the orienting assumptions behind a constructivist view is that emotional syndromes are maintained within the social system because they serve a function'. Each of them in their own way has developed an understanding of anger based on constructivist principles.

REFERENCES

Aristotle (1969). *The Nicomachean Ethics*. Trans. D. Ross. Oxford: Oxford University Press.

Averill, J. R. (1982). *Anger and Aggression: An Essay on Emotion*. New York: Springer-Verlag.

Taylor, J. L. & Novaco, R. W. (2005). *Anger Treatment for People with Developmental Disabilities*. Chichester: John Wiley & Sons.

ACKNOWLEDGEMENTS

I would like to acknowledge the inspiration I received from Miller Mair as a trainee, which has stayed with me for nearly 30 years. My raw enthusiasm was encouraged by the late Don Bannister and shaped and developed by the supervision of Helen Jones, and later, Fay Fransella. In particular, it was with Fay's help that I first began to develop a PCP-based approach to anger and was encouraged to develop this book.

The Coventry Anger group, Comprising Diane Allen, Bhavisha Dave, Dina Pekkala and Matt Wilcoxson, have contributed greatly to the evolution of this volume.

I would also like to acknowledge the contribution of my office manager, Angie Morris, who has tried hard to protect my time to allow the production of this book. Claire Ruston at Wiley has very gently but clearly achieved me almost meeting my agreed deadlines.

Finally, I want to acknowledge the hidden contribution to this book of many of the people I have worked with over the past eight years, in particular L. S. and J. E.

THE CONSTRUCTION OF EMOTION

Peter Cummins

When I 'Googled' 'Anger,' I was told that there were 6,190,000 references. The first of these that I looked at (angermgmt.com) told me that one in five Americans had anger management problems! Given that the latest estimate of the American population is 294,353,630, this means there are a lot of angry people in the USA!! The UK has a population of nearly 59 million. I have not found any similar estimate of prevalence; if we were to assume a similar rate to the USA, then we also have a lot of angry people in this country.

It is certainly true that referrals for anger are the second most common reason for referral in the service I work within. This is true despite the fact that there is not a formal diagnostic category for anger. As Novaco (Novaco and Welsh, 1989, p. 40) points out, 'While anxiety and depression are clinical conditions; anger (like fear and sadness) is an emotion'. The existing approaches to anger frequently acknowledge that anger is an emotion, and then appear to forget the implications of this in a maze of cognitive approaches and techniques. By far the most dominant approach is the cognitive behavioural therapy (CBT) approach, of which Novaco is a leading proponent. The CBT approach is almost always called Anger management. This is despite Novaco's (1998) own acknowledgement of three layers:

1. General clinical care for anger.
2. Anger management.
3. Anger therapy.

General clinical care for anger identifies it as a clinical need and addresses it through 'counseling, psychotherapeutic and psycho pharmacological provisions including client education, support groups and eclectic treatments without a formal intervention

Working with Anger: A Constructivist Approach.
Edited by Peter Cummins. © 2006 John Wiley & Sons, Ltd.

structure' (Novaco, Ramm & Black, 2000). I think that this level should also include skills required by all staff to deal with people, e.g. the receptionist dealing with an angry person or inpatient ward staff dealing with everyday anger. The second level, that of Anger management, is usually a fixed length group which is run along psycho educational lines; people are taught the model and encouraged to integrate it into their daily lives. The third form, that of Anger therapy or Anger treatment (Novaco et al., 2000) acknowledges that there can be more to anger than management. As Novaco et al. put it, 'Anger treatment is distinguished from these other levels of intervention by its theoretical grounding, systematization, complexity and depth of therapeutic approach. It is best provided on an individual basis and may require a preparatory phase to facilitate treatment engagement'.

The problem is, however, that the wider world and, in particular, the criminal justice system have adopted the idea of anger management. This comes up in all parts of the social care/justice/professional system. People often attend anger management courses in prison. Family courts have become keen on insisting that people complete anger management courses before they are allowed access to their children or their partner. Doctors who lose their temper at work in stressful situations are told by their disciplinary hearing that they should attend an anger management programme. Social Services often require parents to attend anger management courses if they are to be allowed to retain parental rights to their children. Laming describes a similar pattern, in Australia, in Chapter 3 of this book. Probably due to this popularity we now have Hollywood in on the act, in the film called *Anger Management*.

It is very difficult to get acknowledgement of anger therapy, the dominant ideology is that of anger management. Even after nearly seven years of telling referrers that we run a 'Working with anger group', almost without exception people are referred for 'Anger Management'. This idea, that you can learn to manage your anger in short-term courses, can cause real problems. This is particularly true when we see people who have already been through an anger management programme. (For obvious reasons, I rarely see people who have had a successful experience of anger management.) What I do see are people like Sam who told me 'I have had anger management and it was crap'. When I asked him about this, he described a day programme he had attended in prison. I asked him what made him think it was crap and he replied, 'I knocked a screw [prison officer] out the following day'. This may be a reasonable assessment of limited success in anger management! A careful reading of Novaco's own work makes it very clear that much of what is described as anger management would not meet his basic requirements. As Taylor and Novaco (2005, p. 24) comment: 'There is a wide variation in "anger management programmes" which are now marketed commodities'.

Mr X has been in trouble with the law since childhood. He has been arrested many times. Some of his arrests include assault, embezzlement, carrying offensive weapons and rape. He has not served any jail sentences. The psychiatric assessment concluded, 'He has no emotion as emotion is a sign of weakness. I believe he poses a signif-icant risk to others and he openly stated that he is naturally inclined to violence'.

The conclusion of this report was that the best answer was anger management. Our conclusion was that he belonged in the forensic services! This referral sums up a common current perspective on anger that, even in the extreme, it can be treated by an anger management programme.

PERSONAL CONSTRUCT PSYCHOLOGY AND EMOTION

In a previous work (Cummins, 2003) I have challenged the common misunderstanding that personal construct psychology (PCP) is a cognitive theory which does not deal with emotion. At the heart of PCP is Kelly's focus on abandoning the distinction between cognition and emotion. As Kelly (1991, p. xii) summarises it, 'There is no ego, no emotion, no motivation, no reinforcement, no drive, no unconscious, no need'. There is little written in the personal construct literature directly about anger. There is, however, a significant literature on PCP and emotion. (I have previously summarised this literature in Cummins, 2005). For me, the key paper was McCoy's 'A reconstruction of emotion' (1977). There is also a provocative paper by Don Bannister (1977) 'The logic of passion', in which he challenges the whole way in which emotion is dealt with within PCP, and Viney's *Images of Illness* that discriminates between images of anger which 'take the form of mild irritation which encourages those who experience it to deal promptly with some annoyingly discrepant aspects of their lives' and a second kind of anger which 'take[s] the form of wild outbursts against the people and events of one's world' (1983, p. 37). Davidson and Reser (1996) look at the cultural nature of construing. In looking at the experience of aboriginal youth, they note that where social links break down, the 'emotional state appears to have elements of extreme anger and loss'. Kirsch and Jordan (2000) quote Catina and Schmitt (1993) as stating that 'emotional behaviour is seen as an indicator of the state of a person's construct system'. They go on to use a system of categorising constructs into categories of emotion. The most common construct category at the beginning of treatment was that of rage/anger.

If I add in papers by Fisher (1990), Mascolo (1994; Mascolo & Mancuso, 1990), Katz (1984), and Mahoney (1988), then I have covered the available PCP literature. There is also an interesting book on emotion from an existential perspective written by Strasser (1999), which has a chapter on anger. In this, Strasser describes a clinical case where anger originated in the person's childhood experience of being disregarded as a person. This view fits very well with my previous suggestion (Cummins, 2003) that the most useful definition of anger is that: 'Anger is *an* emotional expression of invalidation'. I need to emphasise the *AN* as there are, of course, many other possible responses to invalidation. As Fransella (2003, personal communication) has pointed out, 'one can invalidate another's construing and make them very happy'. However, the people referred to us have not been made happy!! The most common statement they make is, 'I do not understand what my anger is about – I just get angry about silly things'. Again and again, I have to point out that what makes you angry is not silly, rather, what they mean is that they do not understand their own construing.

This position of getting angry about silly things often makes self-reporting anger very difficult as people are unwilling or unable to identify anger episodes. As I will describe in Chapter 2, this means that I always try to interview a significant other, usually a partner, as part of the assessment procedure.

PCP AND ANGER

There are six key concepts within PCP which are critical for the understanding of anger. These are anticipation, invalidation, hierarchy, hostility, permeability, and sociality. In this chapter I only have the space to focus on these. An introduction to PCP is given by Kelly (1970); a fuller account of PCP is available in Dalton and Dunnett (1992) in the *International Handbook of Personal Construct Psychology* (Fransella, 2003), in the practitioners' version of the handbook (Fransella, 2005) and in Rossotti, Winter and Dimcovic (forthcoming).

Anticipation

Central to personal construct psychology is the idea of anticipation. Kelly's fundamental postulate on which he developed the rest of PCP states that 'A person's processes are psychologically channelised by the ways in which he anticipates events' (1991, p. 32). Our whole way of being is derived from our capacity to construe our past, present and future. When this process is interrupted or interfered with, we end up unable to satisfactorily construe the events we are confronted with. When this happens, we may be invalidated. 'Validation refers solely to the verification of a prediction, even if what was predicted was itself unpleasant' (Kelly, 1991, p. 111) (see later section on invalidation). There are, of course, many possible responses to this inability to construe (which may lead to invalidation), anger is but one of an array of possibilities. Where the reaction is anger, all that is immediately seen is the emotional expression described as anger. The underlying argument is that this emotional expression can be understood as signifying change or resistance to change, and that emotions therefore are expressions of constructs. The language here is difficult as Kelly was quite explicit about the need to abandon the emotion–cognitive construct dichotomy in favour of trying to understand 'emotion as forms of transition'. As Bannister puts it:

> At such times we try to nail down our psychological furniture to avoid change or we try to lunge forward in answer to challenge or revelation by forcefully elaborating our experience. It is at such times that our conventional language most often makes reference to feeling.
>
> (1977, p. 27)

Bannister goes on to point out that Kelly's definitions of transition try to make us recognise that we can only understand the person from within, in terms of the why, from their point of view. To understand my anger, you have to understand my understanding of WHY I get angry (see the later section on sociality). The first step (i.e.

trying to understand me) is to remind ourselves that constructs are not verbal labels. A construct is an act of discrimination. Some acts of discrimination may not have a verbal label. Most of us will have had the experience of trying to decide which of two actions to take, e.g. shall we go to the cinema or the pub? We cannot decide, saying we do not care which we do. We toss a coin to decide. The coin says cinema; we then realise that we really want to go to the pub. The construct was there but had not been able to be verbally realised until the forced choice made this possible. This experience of 'not verbally realised constructs' is at the heart of working with anger. The most common statements made by people when I first meet them are: 'It just happens, I just get angry over silly things, I don't know why'.

What they are often saying is that either they do not have verbal labels for their particular constructs on anger or they have not been able to access these constructs. This reliance on verbal labels is one which can also be seen in much of the personal construct literature. Because we rely so heavily on verbally labelling constructs, PCP itself has been labelled a cognitive theory. As Bannister points out:

> It may be that our failure to argue about "EXPERIENCE" using construct theory has impoverished the theory... If this is true, then it is only when we seriously undertake explorations of our own and other people's experience and behaviour in terms of constructs like guilt, aggression, anxiety, hostility that we will begin to understand their meaning and their content.
>
> (1977, p. 33)

It often takes real commitment by both therapist and client to make construing accessible. For example, Gavin tells me that he just woke up angry and proceeded to assault two people during the course of that day. Careful questioning got us nowhere. He had had a good day the previous day, had gone to bed happy, he just woke up angry. At times like this, the therapist has to hold their nerve. After several interactions regarding the previous day/days, what was happening that week, how things were at work, etc., he finally said, 'Well, there was one thought that came to mind when I woke up. This thought was "Why can I not have a lie in?"'. It became clear that this simple thought triggered off a significant and well-elaborated set of constellatory constructs that triggered the emotion of anger. According to Kelly: 'A Constellatory construct is one that links itself together with a defined set of other constructs. Stereotypes are a good example of this, e.g. where all we are told is that I am Irish, but we immediately make a set of assumptions based on this one fact' (1991, p. 108).

Invalidation

As mentioned earlier, Kelly suggests that invalidation is linked to the verification of a prediction. He goes on to describe how validation affects the construct system at various levels. Constructs which are 'functionally closest to the constructs on which the original prediction was based being most affected by validational experiences' (Kelly, 1991, p. 111).

In the Experience corollary, 'A person's construction system varies as he successively construes the replication of events' (1991, p. 50), Kelly suggested that our understanding varies as we deal with our constructs being validated and invalidated. If I never change my view, e.g. that all people who come to the door are dangerous, then all that happens is that I behave in exactly the same way over the years. I never get to find out if the situation outside the house has changed. If I do test it out and find that there is no longer danger, then I can move on: 'A succession of such investments and dislodgements constitutes the human experience' (Kelly, 1970, p. 18). The clinical problem comes where such investment is continually invalidated, e.g. I decide to risk trusting someone and I am let down. The crucial diagnostic issue is the level of invalidation. Many of the people who are referred to us have experienced fundamental invalidation of core constructs in their childhood. This is most commonly derived from the behaviour of their parents. Again and again, we found that something had happened to damage the parental relationship (mainly with their father) between about 8 and 12. This included abandonment following divorce, physical violence (often extreme), or in some cases major depression or other illness which meant that no one was there to validate them. Even after 30 years in clinical psychology I still find myself deeply shocked at the extreme level of physical violence described by some of the people I have worked with. It is common to find that anger was the way that the person found of surviving traumatic experiences in childhood. This often involved a violent relationship with their parents (usually but not always their father). Their anger was the way that they maintained a sense of anticipation of survival apart from the demands of the parent. It is very common to find that the situation was resolved by the child physically assaulting the parent as soon as this became physically possible (the youngest I have come across was a man who described how he knocked out his father, when he was aged 12). In other words, their anger was a result of being invalidated by their parent(s). Their anticipation was that one day they would physically triumph over the parent (be validated); failure to keep such an anticipation would have led to further invalidation, which in turn can lead to further anger. Emotion and invalidation, then, are at the heart of understanding anger. These people often go on to react to any invalidation in a similarly violent way. The only way that they are confident of gaining respect is through violence. This demand for respect can be triggered off by the most unlikely event. As previously described these events may be dismissed as 'just silly things'. They are also often seen as justified, e.g. he had no right to use that space (see Chapter 8 on Mr Angry). It is here, as described below, that laddering can be a critical clinical tool.

Hierarchy

In his organisation corollary, Kelly stated that each person's construct system was hierarchically organised. This means that there are some constructs which are superordinate, i.e. they are more central to the person.

As I will describe in more detail later, the key to working with anger is to unpack the person's construing. The crucial tool to do this is laddering (Hinkle, 1965). This procedure is nicely described by Fransella, Bell and Bannister as 'essentially a structured interview' (2004, p. 40). Laddering is the process which 'aids the person to generate superordinal high level constructs . . . the question WHY when applied to constructs leads the person to higher level values' (Epting, 1984).

Together with an assistant I went to talk on anger to a Coventry University MA course. One of the course participants uttered the classic line, 'I just get angry about silly things'. I asked her for an example. She replied, 'I really get angry when my partner leaves the toilet seat up'. The following was completed as a group exercise:

Leaves the loo seat up--Listens to me

Respects me

Loves me

This then becomes clear. What is actually happening is that she begins by being irritated about a typical piece of male behaviour, leaving the toilet seat up. She tells him that this irritates her. He does not acknowledge her irritation by changing his behaviour. Each time she comes in to the toilet, she sees that he has left it up again, in other words, he has not listened to her, which she begins to construe as not listening to her as he does not respect her. And if he does not respect her, then he cannot love her. Loving is superordinate to 'respects me' and 'listens to me'. The crucial aspect of love highlighted by Epting (1984, p. 52) is that 'the loving act is always in a direction that is intended to complete us as a person'. In this case, the act of leaving the toilet seat up was interpreted as anything but completing her!! Here is the source of the invalidation. Within the idea of hierarchy is another key idea of Kelly, that of regnancy (Kelly, 1991, p. 355; Cummins, 2003). This suggests that people can go from relatively unimportant constructs directly to core constructs while skipping all intermediate stages, e.g. Gavin gets very angry when his partner will not conform to his expectations. By laddering this construct, in five levels, I got to his core construct of insecurity. It then became very clear that his insistence on her fulfilling his expectations was directly linked to his own fear of his deep-seated insecurity.

Hostility

The hostile person tries to force the evidence to fit their anticipations. If you do not appear to love me, then I will MAKE you love me. I will make you tell me that you love me (even when all the evidence would suggest that there is no loving relationship). It is only when this hostility ceases to work that the person is open to the possibility of reconstrual. It is very common to talk to people who are in their second or third relationship and who say 'I always thought that it was [the others] who were responsible for the failure of the relationship, but they cannot all be wrong, I am finally accepting that it must be me'. As Epting puts it, 'the core of the hostile person is involved in this enterprise . . . the job of the therapist often focuses around the question of what is being invalidated and what makes this invalidation impossible for the person to bear just now' (1984, p. 52). This is particularly true of younger people. We have often found that we do not make much impact on 20-year-old people who have yet to acknowledge their own role in their anger.

Permeability

A permeable construct is one that allows for new information to be included within the construct. A classic and common example of an impermeable construct is one that says: 'If you disrespect me then I must physically beat you up'. If it becomes permeable, then I can accept that you may not have meant to disrespect me and that there may be other ways of responding other than immediate violence. The idea that the disrespect was not intended is not available within an impermeable system.

> The clinical psychologist . . . comes to understand fully why his client behaves in the way that he does and what changes in therapy are most likely to be extensively and spontaneously elaborated, rather than literistically and dutifully performed at the behest of the therapist.
>
> (Kelly, 1991, p. 127)

These therapy changes depend on the permeability of the person's constructs, 'here is his rationale for "doing things on his own; here is the framework of 'emotional insight'"' (1991, p. 127). The struggle for people with anger is to allow for permeability while still keeping their construing system functional. This change is often extremely difficult, I can recall clients who were physically sick the first time they walked past someone who disrespected them, without being violent to the disrespectful person.

Sociality

The sociality corollary focuses on how we relate to the other: 'To the extent that one person construes the construction processes of another, he may play a role in a social process involving the other person', (Kelly, 1991, p. 66). Kelly suggests that the critical issue is how I understand how YOU see the world. 'If I am to anticipate you, I must take some chances and try to sense what you are up to' (Kelly, 1970, p. 24). So if you are frequently angry and physically violent, then the question is, 'What are you up to?' This question then allows that 'you would find that something beyond your overt behaviour was being taken into account and you might revise your investments (in this behaviour) accordingly' (1970, p. 25). Too often people are taken at the face value of their behaviour and not any further. This process is one which diagnostic systems such as the *Diagnostic and Statistical Manual of Mental Disorders* (American Psychiatric Association, 1994) encourage when they seek to record the overt behaviour. I recently saw two people with the same diagnosis of anti-social personality disorder. I asked them both the same question: 'If someone in the anger group said something that annoyed you what would you do?' The first person replied that other people had no right to say anything that might annoy him and therefore he would teach them not to be disrespectful (by assaulting them). The second person replied that he had learned in prison that other people had the right to a different viewpoint from himself and that he would try to understand this different viewpoint.

The lack of sociality in the first person, and the impermeable nature of his construing, made us decide that it would be too risky to put him in a group. The second person, by contrast, could use a group experience. Both of these people met the same DSM criteria, but the presence/absence of sociality is therapeutically more important. Laming also gives some illustrations of sociality in Chapter 4.

DIAGNOSIS

It is this capacity to differentiate between people with the same DSM categorization that makes the PCP emphasis on anticipation (described earlier in this chapter) so important. As Winter points out, 'In PCP psychological disorders are classified in terms of the way in which the client makes sense of his or her world rather than using conventional diagnostic categories'. (1992, p. 3). How the person makes sense of the world is tested out on a daily basis. The person behaves in a certain way and may or may not have their world-view validated or invalidated. Using his metaphor of 'man the scientist', Kelly suggested that the experience of validation or invalidation will either confirm the person's construing or force them to change. There are of course many situations in which the person does not change.

Kelly goes on to point out that it is more useful to look at what the person is actually doing than to rush in to give a diagnostic label. I can either say that Peter Cummins is lazy and spends all day in bed because he is not motivated to do anything. OR I can say that Peter Cummins seems to get a lot out of spending time in bed, I wonder why. I can either say that Peter Cummins is angry and therefore his behaviour has to be understood in the context of his anger, or I can try to understand what his behaviour means or achieves.

To begin with, of course, very few people that come to see me have any real idea of what their behaviour means (this is discussed further above). This is the real struggle in working with people referred for anger problems, what sense do they make of what is happening to them? This is one of the key places where conventional anger management programmes over-rely on construing being immediately accessible to the person.

Getting to understand how the person construes their behaviour is often only part of the task. It is just as important to identify what the people who are close to them think is going on. These people, parents, partners, friends, work colleagues have often spent a lot of care and energy in trying to confront the person with the consequences of their actions, to little avail. It is not uncommon to find that partners have ended the relationship as they were unable to tolerate the consequences of angry outbursts, or they were concerned about the effects these episodes were having on the children. This failure in relationships is one that the angry person is often aware of. It is common to find that the person has come on the insistence of their partner. 'S/he told me that if I did not do something about my temper/anger, then the relationship is over. S/he is the third relationship that this has happened to; I have to accept that maybe it is something that I am doing'. The PCP stand-point is well summarised by Winter (1992, p. 6) 'The apparent failure of some individuals to modify their construct system in response to their validational fortunes is not inconsistent with Kelly's theory and indeed the theory is able to predict which individuals and which of their constructs are most likely to be resistant to invalidation'. The most resistant constructs are usually core constructs. These are usually not immediately obvious, hence the importance of the concept of regnancy.

A final concept that has helped me to make sense of what happens within our groups is that of first- and second-order change: first order change is where the approach aims to 'work directly on the symptoms in order to diminish them and produce more agreeable, less symptomatic conditions within the SAME view of reality' (Ecker & Hulley, 1996, p. 8). This seemed to me to be the aim of many of the anger management programmes which our group members had previously experienced. They were, in effect, told that they were stuck with their anger and that controlling it was the best that they could hope for. They were taught a series of techniques, to aid them to control their anger.

The contrast is to change the angry person's view of reality: second-order change. In Ecker and Hulley's words: Second-order change aims to 'usher the client into an alternate view of reality that does not include producing the symptoms' (1996, p. 8). As our anger groups progressed, I noticed again and again that group members had fewer and fewer examples of angry episodes to report as the weeks went on. Indeed, at times they were almost guilty that they did not have more anger to report. It was as if the anger had melted away. They did have changes to report, just not as much anger. I realised that we were fostering the conditions for second-order change within the group. If invalidation is at the heart of anger, then providing the right conditions for revalidation should 'provide an alternative reality' which did not require the level of anger previously experienced. With these key concepts, together with my colleagues I have developed the Coventry Working with Anger programme. This is described in Chapter 2.

REFERENCES

American Psychiatric Association (1994). *Diagnostic and Statistical Manual of Mental Disorders*. 4th edn. Washington, DC: APA.

Bannister, D. (1977). The logic of passion. In D. Bannister (ed.), *New Perspectives in Personal Construct Theory*. London: Academic Press.

Catina, A. & Schmitt, G. M. (1993). Die Theorie der persönlichen Konstrukte. In J. W. Scheer & A. Catina (eds), *Einführung in die Repertory Grid-Technik*. Bern: Huber.

Cummins, P. (2003). Working with anger. In F. Fransella (ed.), *International Handbook of Personal Construct Psychology*. Chichester: John Wiley & Sons.

Cummins, P. (2005). The experience of anger. In D. Winter & L. Viney (eds), *Personal Construct Psychotherapy*. London: Whurr.

Dalton, P. & Dunnett, G. (1992). *A Psychology for Living*. Chichester: John Wiley & Sons.

Davidson, G. and Reser, J. (1996). Construing and constructs: personal and cultural. In B. Walker, J. Costigan, L. Viney & B. Warren (eds), *Personal Construct Theory: A Psychology for the Future*. Sydney: APS.

Ecker, B. and Hulley, L. (1996). *Depth Oriented Brief Therapy*. San Francisco: Jossey-Bass.

Epting, F. (1984). *Personal Construct Counselling and Psychotherapy*. London: John Wiley & Sons.

Fisher, D. D. V. (1990). Emotional construing: a psychobiological model. *International Journal of Personal Construct Psychology*, *3*, 183–203.

Fransella, F. (2003). *International Handbook of Personal Construct Psychology*. Chichester: John Wiley & Sons.

Fransella, F. (ed.) (2005). *The Essential Practitioners Handbook of Personal Construct Psychology*. Chichester: John Wiley & Sons.

Fransella, F., Bell, R. & Bannister, D. (2004). *A Manual for Repertory Grid Technique* (2nd edn). Chichester: John Wiley & Sons.

Hinkle, D. N (1965). The change of personal constructs from the viewpoint of a theory of implications. Unpublished PhD thesis, Columbus, OH, Ohio State University.

Katz, J. O. (1984). Personal construct theory and the emotions: an interpretation in terms of primitive constructs. *British Journal of Psychology*, *75*, 315–327.

Kelly, G. A. (1970). Behaviour as an experiment. In D. Bannister (ed.), *Perspectives in Personal Construct Theory*. London: Academic Press.

Kelly, G. A. (1991). *The Psychology of Personal Constructs*. London: Routledge.

Kirsch, H. & Jordan, J. (2000). Emotions and personal constructs. In J. W. Scheer (ed.), *The Person in Society*. Giessen: Psychosozial-Verlag.

Mahoney, M. J. (1988). Constructive metatheory: II. Implications for psychotherapy. *International Journal of Personal Construct Psychology*, *1*, 299–317.

Mahoney, M. J. (1991). *Human Change Processes: Notes on the Facilitation of Personal Development*. New York: Basic Books.

Mascolo, M. F. (1994). Towards a social constructivist psychology: the case of self-evaluative emotional development. *Journal of Constructivist Psychology*, *7*, 87–106.

Mascolo, M. F. & Mancuso, J. C. (1990). Functioning of epigenetically evolved emotion systems: a constructive analysis. *International Journal of Personal Construct Psychology*, *3*, 205–222.

McCoy, M. M. (1977). A reconstruction of emotion. In D. Bannister (ed.), *New Perspectives in Personal Construct Theory*. London: Academic Press.

Novaco, R. W. (1998). *Anger Workshop*. Dublin: Trinity College Press.

Novaco, R. W., Ramm, M. & Black, L. (2000). Anger treatment with offenders. In C. Hollin (ed.), *Handbook of Offender Assesssment and Treatment*. Chichester: John Wiley & Sons.

Novaco, R. W. & Welsh, W. N. (1989). Anger disturbances: Cognitive mediation and clinical prescriptions. In K. Howell & C. Hollins (eds), *Clinical Approaches to Violence*. Chichester: John Wiley & Sons.

Rossotti, N. G., Winter, D. A. & Dimcovic, N. (forthcoming). *Personal Construct Counselling and Psychotherapy: A Practical Guide*. Chichester: John Wiley & Sons.

Strasser, F. (1999). *Emotions: Experiences in Existential Psychotherapy and Life*. London: Duckworth.

Taylor, J. & Novaco, R. W. (2005). *Anger Treatment for People with Developmental Disabilities*. Chichester: John Wiley & Sons.

Viney, L. (1983). *Images of Illness*. Melbourne, FL: Krieger.

Winter, D. A. (1992). *Personal Construct Psychology in Clinical Practice*. London: Routledge.

2

THE TUESDAY GROUP

Peter Cummins

THE CLINICAL DIAGNOSIS

Recent publications indicate that referrals for anger are growing for many psychological therapy services (O'Loughlin, Evans & Sherwood, 2004). I was particularly interested in this paper as it also suggests that 'therapy-style group interventions, are not seen as helpful' (p. 18). O'Loughlin et al. report that even when they offered a psycho educational anger management class, only 44 % of referrals attended at least one session. They do not clarify the percentage of referrals that completed the three-week course. The conclusion of this paper was that the most that could be offered was to provide a limited number of psycho educational groups. This sense, that people referred for anger are very difficult to work with, probably underlies the fact that it is not uncommon to find that psychological services often decline to accept anger referrals at all. I have heard this refusal justified with the statement that 'anger is not a mental health problem'. This position is easier to adopt, given that there is no direct psychiatric diagnosis of anger, nor is there a DSM categorisation for anger on its own. This reluctance to engage with the problem of anger is often reflected in the actual referral. The referrer is often at pains to emphasise that the person referred is 'a pleasant man, who deserves a chance', or 'a woman who has been driven to her violence'. These referrals are always phrased to the effect that the person requires 'anger management'. This decision (that anger management is the appropriate course of action) often now comes from the referred person's own network, and not the referring professional, i.e. the person presents themselves to the referring agent (usually the family doctor) asking for anger management. This means that the assessment of whether in fact the central problem is that of anger is a crucial first step.

Working with Anger: A Constructivist Approach.
Edited by Peter Cummins. © 2006 John Wiley & Sons, Ltd.

ASSESSMENT OF ANGER

There are several possible formulations of anger. These include:

1. Post traumatic stress disorder (PTSD).
2. Situational anger.
3. Core anger.
4. Workable anger.

PTSD

PTSD is a relatively common reason for referral to our anger service. An increase in arousal is of course one of the criteria for the establishment of PTSD but this is often not deciphered by the referrer. As Taylor and Novaco (2005) comment: 'It is astounding that in the field of post traumatic stress disorder (PTSD), anger has been given little priority'. A careful history will elicit the fact that the anger problem has a definite onset which then turns out to be linked to a particular event. For example, Mr A., who was referred because of his anger which was a problem since he had his face slashed. It transpired that this had occurred at work due to an industrial accident, and since then he had been having flashbacks, and waking up angry. He has a variety of other problems, all of which confirmed the diagnosis of PTSD. What alarmed people of course was his anger, not his flashbacks/nightmares, and therefore he ended up being referred for 'anger management'.

In another example, Mr B. was referred for anger management because he had assaulted his father and sister. Again, a careful history elicited the fact that he had only been angry in the last eight years. At that time he had been the victim of two armed robberies within the space of 12 months. It became clear from the range of other symptoms he described that the correct overall understanding of his difficulties was within PTSD rather than anger. Laming (Chapter 3) gives another range of reasons as to why people are inappropriately referred for anger problems.

Situational Anger

Here it can be the wrong person who is being referred. The person describes themselves as never having had an anger problem until . . . This is often a new relationship with someone who has a history of past violent relationships. It is not uncommon to see someone whose relationship has ended by the time we see them. They describe how their anger has ceased since the relationship ended; they often come to the assessment as part of their attempt to understand why they 'became angry'. This is where Kelly's concept of Sociality (see Chapter 1) becomes a prominent part of the process of reconstruing the person's anger. A common consequence of such situational anger

THE TUESDAY GROUP 15

is that the person comes to psychological therapies because they have been labelled as someone to whom it is not safe to grant access to their children because of the anger which led to the ending of the relationship.

Core Anger

Core anger is involved in the situation where it becomes clear that without the anger the person could not anticipate surviving, for example, Mr C. who was referred because of his anger. When I asked him what would happen if I removed his anger, he immediately began to tell me about his previous long history of agoraphobia. It was very clear that for him his anger was a preferable way to be, rather than be trapped back within the four walls of his room. The central issue to be approached was that of his anxiety rather than his anger.

A second common core anger is the perception that without anger the person would be a wimp who would be walked over. I have often been told by clients who live in tough areas that without their angry reputation/posture, they would be attacked within their neighbourhood.

A third core anger is where the person lacks any sociality. I asked Mr D. what would happen if someone said something that made him angry. He replied, 'They've no right to say anything that might make me angry' (it was up to others to know what he found unacceptable).

In the situation of dissociative anger the person only feels real when they are angry. This is usually not something they are able to directly acknowledge. Any attempt to focus on the role that anger plays for them leads to them becoming scared and resistant to change. Their core constructs, i.e. those that 'stabilize the person's own sense of himself or herself as a person' (Epting, 1984, p. 46), are all linked to anger.

Workable Anger

The people with workable anger are the people whom we think we can usefully work with. We have four main criteria:

1. That the person themselves agrees that they have a problem with anger.

It is not at all uncommon for people to say that, in their view, they do not have an anger problem. They often take the view that:

(a) The problem is other people's anger, not theirs.
(b) They are frustrated, not angry, e.g. Mr E. was referred for 'anger management' by the court and his family doctor. When I talked to him about his anger he was

quite clear that he was frustrated, not angry. He then described how he was being prevented from seeing his children by his ex-wife. He had responded to this by forcing his way into the house to see the children. My report suggested that access to the children, which could be supervised at a specialist contact centre, would be a better first option rather than anger management.

(c) They like being angry. It is anger that gives them status and power. They only came to assessment because of pressure either from family, courts or social services.

(d) They cannot imagine not being angry, it is part of their core identity (see section above on core anger).

2. That their anger is not single focused.

If a person says that they only ever get angry with their wife, then it is usually more helpful to see this as a relationship issue and to see the couple together. We frequently have people referred to us by other counselling agencies who are concerned about the level of anger being expressed within the relationship. If the anger is only expressed to their children, then it may be that parenting classes would be more appropriate. The people we do best with in the group programme are those who get angry in many different situations with a wide range of people.

3. The person is safe to work with.

Working with this client group is often working on the edge and safety is a crucial issue for both parties. People are often very honest about how safe they are, e.g. when I asked Mr F. what would happen if someone in the group said something to upset him, he replied 'If I am upset I lose it, I do not know what I would do, I might have to go for him'. It is sometimes clear that the person is not safe to put into a group but could be worked with individually. The key issue is that the person has the capacity to cope with the therapeutic encounter without becoming violent. Working at the edge inevitably means there will be times of great tension in the therapy room. At times, the therapist will get things wrong, sometimes without realising it. For example, I saw Mr G. who had a history of intense physical abuse as a child and a history of anger and violence as an adult. He told me about certain non-verbal gestures his father used to make. When in therapy I referred to one of these gestures while physically repeating it, Mr G. stopped, went silent, eventually looked at me and said, 'That was too close' and walked out of the room. He sat in our waiting room and after a few minutes agreed to come back to my office. We then reflected on what had happened. He again told me that I had gone too close and that he was extremely close to assaulting me before walking out. My initial assessment that he had the capacity to control himself, fortunately, turned out to be accurate. This incident became a crucial part of the next stage of therapy and the development of his trust in me, the first time he had ever trusted anyone.

4. The problem is psychological in origin.

We had to introduce this criterion when we saw someone who said, yes, he did have an anger problem, yes, it was with a wide range of people, yes, he could restrain himself enough not to be dangerous, and the problem was due to his diabetes being out of control. The only relevant answer was to suggest that he returned to the diabetic clinic.

THE TUESDAY ANGER GROUP

Initially, I offered a semi-open group as described in Cummins (2003). This format, although successful, was not able to cope with the number of referrals received. The addition of more staff time allowed us to add a 10-week group format in addition to the semi-open group. Our idea was that anyone who completed the 10-week format and needed more could then go on to join the longer-term group. We found that at most one person from each 10-week group wanted/needed more. This meant that we did not have sufficient people to continue the open format group. We have therefore changed to solely providing 10-week groups, a format which allows us to provide up to four groups per year, with at times two groups running in parallel.

The gender of these groups has depended on the referral pattern. We have run groups which were all male except for the female co-therapist and groups which were equally divided between male and female. Recently two female colleagues have endeavoured to set up a group for women only, however, despite sufficient referrals, the reality was that very few women were suitable to join an anger group (see Dave et al., Chapter 10 for a further discussion of this).

People initially referred are assessed using the four criteria described above. They also complete CORE and the STAXI assessments (see Pekkala and Dave, Chapter 14, in this volume, on evaluation). Where necessary, assistance is given to them to complete these assessments. Assuming they are thought suitable for the group, we then meet them again immediately before the group begins to clarify their and our expectations.

We offer up to 10 places in each group. Every time we have run the programme we have ended up with 7/8 participants on the first evening. We have never lost more than 1 participant in each 10-week programme. In the current group, at the time of writing, we have had 100 % attendance for 6 out of the 7 weeks, with only 1 of the 7 group members missing 1 week. This is in sharp contrast to the drop-out rates reported by other people (O'Loughlin, Evans & Sherwood, 2004).

GROUP FORMAT

As far as possible we rely on group work and (dependent on the group) try not to use written work. Up to half of the people we take into the group have at least some problems with literacy. We have found through experience that for many of the group members, asking them to keep anger diaries and providing them with handouts are a waste of time. We would find ourselves half-way through a handout only to realise that several group members had already folded it away, as they could not read it. Homework tasks were rarely done, the excuses often being of the 'dog ate it' variety. I have explored this issue of literacy in greater depth in Cummins (2005). As described in this chapter, we rely on the use of a flip chart and the three key techniques of:

1. Drawing scenes on the flipchart.
2. Repetition.
3. Constant use of examples within the group, using previous group members' experience to validate this.

Description of the Session Work

In session one, we introduce people to each other and set the ground rules. These are the conventional rules of group therapy, respect for each other, confidentiality of what is said within the group, the importance of regular attendance, etc. We then ask people to pair off and tell their partner the story of how they have ended up in the group. We gradually rebuild the group and get each person to introduce their partner. We also provide a set of anger principles which are very similar to those described by Chris Laming (see Chapter 3). We do not set any restrictions on topics discussed except to acknowledge that we have learned that the most contentious area to allow discussion of is that of football. There have been two occasions in nearly eight years when I seriously thought that the group was going to erupt into a physical fight. On both occasions the disputed topic was that of the relative success of particular football clubs!

In session two, we get the group to work through the advantages and disadvantages of anger using Tschudi's (1977) ABC structure. Similar use of this technique is described by Laming (Chapter 3) and Selby (Chapter 4). It involves getting people to first of all define anger and its contrast:

A. ANGER   vs Calm, wimp, sad, ignored, happy
B. Disadvantages of anger vs Advantages of being calm, wimp, etc.
C. Advantages of anger   vs Disadvantages of being calm, wimp, etc.

I have previously described the use of this framework in Cummins (2003), where a fuller description of its application to anger can be found.

In sessions three and four, we develop each person's genogram, on a flip chart with the whole group. We have found that these sessions often become the central focus of the whole 10 sessions, with group members making frequent references to the issues raised by their and other group member's genograms. The importance of these sessions is reflected in the allocation of two sessions for this topic. Group members have commented on the emotional demands of these sessions and of their frequent reflection on the issues raised, particularly if they have to wait until the second genogram session to complete their own family.

The themes which emerge include the transmission of violence through the generations, the central role often played by grandparents in providing refuge, and the consequent desolation experienced on the death of these grandparents. Another central focus is the absence or death of one parent at critical times in childhood (see Chapter 11 by Mascolo et al. for a discussion of the development of anger in childhood) and the ways in which siblings have coped with similar issues. The other dominant theme to emerge is the setting of families within a context, e.g. a group participant said to another group member, 'I thought my family was f***** up until I saw yours'. This comment was actually heard as very supportive and helpful by the recipient, as it allowed him to look at the degree of difficulty he had had as a child with a fresh perspective, i.e. it was not totally his fault.

In session five, we look at sociality. I have already described this concept in Chapter 1. The group session is devoted to getting people to try to understand differently events which have provoked them to anger. A typical issue which often comes up in the group is that commonly called 'road rage'. A group member will describe how someone drove in a way which the group member interpreted as disrespectful, e.g. Mr H. described how a BMW had refused to let him pass. He interpreted this as 'a flash bastard in a posh car trying to show me who is superior'. As the discussion proceeded, it became clear that Mr H. had not even got a good view of the driver. When my co-therapist Dina suggested that the BMW could have been driven by an old lady who was not looking, Mr H. was almost speechless. He struggled to interpret the other's behaviour in a new way. This session is one where the group process can often be seen at its best. While other group members could understand Mr H.'s initial opinion, they could also begin to give him other viewpoints. Mr H. was far more willing to listen to them than he ever would have been to listen to a professional view. He built on this, and the following week reported that he had been driving down the road to his house, when a taxi a little way ahead of him stopped in the middle of the road. His immediate thought was, 'How bloody typical ... ', however, before he'd finished the thought, he found himself wondering if maybe there was a reasonable reason for the taxi driver's behaviour. As Mr H. started to ponder this new perspective, a person with crutches got out of the taxi. Mr H.'s sense of achievement, that he'd not resorted to verbal abuse, sounding his horn or throwing something, was wonderful.

In session six, we look at provocation. We use Proctor's (1985) bow tie technique to elaborate on how provocation can arise and be exacerbated by the person's behaviour/thoughts. This asks the person what they were thinking:

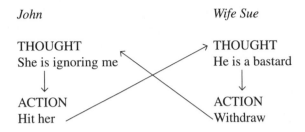

John   Wife Sue

THOUGHT   THOUGHT
She is ignoring me   He is a bastard

ACTION   ACTION
Hit her   Withdraw

This process can be repeated several times, using different coloured pens on the flip chart, so that several cycles are elicited, e.g. after Sue withdraws, John feels even more ignored and proceeds to start smashing furniture, which Sue will not be able to ignore. Sue responds by walking out which leaves John even more rejected, and so on. We try to repeat this procedure for as many incidents as possible, derived from the actual experience of group participants.

In session seven, we look at self-esteem. The vast majority of people we see with anger problems also have low self-esteem. Their sense of invalidation (i.e. they feel that they have been treated without respect) is invariably rooted in their low self-esteem, and their response to that invalidation often reinforces the low self-esteem. All too often, group members find they have lost the moral high ground when they lose their temper. We highlight this cycle of low self-esteem using examples the group members bring and, using laddering, help them unpack what is behind their anger response. Ms A. described to the group how her partner was not interested in her description of what had happened in the previous anger group. This made her very angry and she hit him.

There was clearly a construct:

Listens to me.....................does not listen to me.
The next level was:
Cares about me.....................does not care about me.
Which went on to:
I am valued..........................I am not valued.
Which became:
I am worthwhile.....................I am worthless.

Her anger was the emotional expression of this invalidation, which was focused on her lack of self-esteem.

In session eight, we look at what is required to forgive. One of the key issues for people with anger problems is the growing awareness of the damage that has been caused to their immediate family/friends by their angry outbursts. As they begin to reconstrue their own anger, they often become overwhelmed by a sense of guilt and shame about their past life events. There is often a particular focus on the damage that they have caused to their children; damage which they are only too aware echoes the damage that they themselves experienced in their own childhood.

Before session nine, group participants are asked to review their group experience so far and to identify key issues for them which they would like the group to revisit, either for clarification or amplification.

Session ten is taken up by an overall review of the group, a repeat of assessment tools and a focus on the future.

In addition to these 10 weeks, we also offer a one-off group session for the partners of group members. This has been taken up by up to four partners. It provides an opportunity for partners to review the cost to them of their angry partner. It also allows them to begin to come to terms with the changes that the group has facilitated in their partners. Common themes are the partner's anger that:

1. They have tolerated their partner's behaviour for so long.
2. Now that they see that change is possible, why did the angry person not change much sooner?
3. A sense of loss of their children's childhood (and a sense of loss that they have had to spend all their time protecting the children rather than being normal parents).
4. A real anxiety that the change may not last.
5. A pride in their partner that they have had the courage to confront the problem and do something about it.

GROUP PROCESS

We are very clear about the efficacy of this programme (see Chapter 14 by Pekkala, on evaluation in this volume). Again and again we have had examples provided as early as weeks two and three of a group participant's behaviour changing. In our current group, in week two, one participant reported that their wife had commented that 'they sure work fast in that group' (in reaction to his not becoming angry in a particular situation). It is equally clear that we do not focus directly on techniques of anger management. Indeed, by about week five, it is common for group participants to have little in the way of angry episodes to report.

Central to the understanding of what is going on within the group is the idea of validation. Kelly (1991, p. 110) defined this as 'a person commits himself to anticipating a particular event. If it takes place, his anticipation is validated. If it fails to take place, his anticipation is invalidated'.

Most group members begin the group with a long history of invalidation, as mentioned earlier. They are surprised to meet other people who have histories which they perceive as similar to their own. They are even more surprised to discover that the other group members have reacted to situations in ways that are very similar to their own responses. Thus begins a process of validation which has never happened to them before. This validation comes from the most unexpected group interactions. As described earlier the comment that 'I thought my family was f***** up but yours is much worse' was heard by the recipient as being very validating. It is also the first time that many group participants have met others who have been in prison, who have been convicted of assaulting partners, or who have had a succession of relationships, which have often resulted in children with whom they have lost contact.

In the initial part of each group meeting we begin by asking people how their week has been. Although this can be time-consuming we found that this was an important part of the group. Initially at least, there had often been incidents during the week which needed some time spent on them within the group. This meant that we learnt that we had to be careful to ensure that every group member 'reported in' each week. Within two or three weeks of the group starting, it becomes common for group participants to describe how their interactions during the week were affected by something that has been said at a previous group by another group member. This process was nicely summed up for me when towards the end of a 10-week group one participant said to me 'Peter, I don't mean to be insulting, but I have learned far more from other people in this group than I have from you and Dina [my co-therapist]'. This is the live version of what Llewellyn and Dunnett (1987, p. 251), mean when they say

> The group provides an opportunity for participants, including the leaders, to explore the implications of their particular construct systems, to examine the implications of specific pre-emptive or Constellatory constructions, and to bring to the group results of experiments taking place both inside and outside the group setting.

As already mentioned, as this process develops, something curious begins to happen: the number of angry incidents reported within each week began to diminish, to the extent that at times people were almost apologising for the lack of 'material'. People began to describe how their lives were changing in significant ways. A memorable example of this was when a group member told us that his 6-year-old daughter had come and sat on his lap. Previously she had been too afraid of his reactions to risk coming so close to him. It seemed clear that she had been checking him out regularly and deciding that it was too risky to approach him. Clearly when he began attending the group, something in his behaviour/attitude changed, which told her that it was now safe to sit on him. He was very moved by this change, which in turn set off further changes in his relationship with his daughter. For the first time he began to feel that he was being a 'proper father' and not simply repeating the experiences of his own childhood. Social Services had been involved with this group participant because of the degree of anger in the house. When during the week on self-esteem the group participant was asked what three things he was proud about in himself, he responded, 'That my wife and children now find me approachable'.

From such validation the person begins to be able to reconstrue the events that occur to them. They stop interpreting everything as forms of invalidation, and develop new ways of dealing with situations. They begin to develop a much more functional sociality, i.e. they become better able to develop alternative ways of understanding other people's actions. They often bring these changes to the group for further validation. These changes are tested on a day-to-day basis, e.g. towards the end of one group a group member was in a pub where someone had insisted on invading the table he was standing at and ultimately had knocked over the group member's drink. He was with his wife and brother, who anticipated the worst, i.e. violence. Instead he turned to the perpetrator and said, 'You're really lucky, six weeks ago you'd have left here on a stretcher. As it is, you're a careless prat'. The perpetrator walked off to other people's laughter. Our group member experienced a sense of validation far greater than he had experienced from previous violence. This was accentuated by the validation of a very pleased partner who did not have to cope with the all too familiar sequelae of his violence. This validation is reflected in the change in CORE scores described by Pekkala in Chapter 14 of this volume.

SUMMARY

I have suggested that anger is an emotional expression of invalidation. Over time, the logical follow-on from this has become apparent, i.e. can this invalidation be challenged? If it can be challenged, then what effect would this have on the person's anger? The Tuesday Group and several significant individual patients have taught me that invalidation can indeed be challenged. When it is successfully challenged, the anger does indeed begin to disappear. The group process as described above is a powerful way of challenging invalidation and thus creating the conditions necessary for 'second-order change' (see Chapter 1).

REFERENCES

Cummins, P. (2003). Working with anger. In F. Fransella (ed.), *International Handbook of Personal Construct Psychology*. Chichester: John Wiley & Sons.

Cummins, P. (2005). The experience of anger. In D. Winter & L. Viney (eds), *Personal Construct Psychotherapy*. London: Whurr.

Epting, F. (1984). *Personal Construct Counselling and Psychotherapy*. London: Wiley.

Kelly, G. A. (1991). *The Psychology of Personal Constructs*. London: Routledge.

Llewelyn, S. & Dunnett, G. (1987). The use of personal construct theory in groups. In R. A. Neimeyer & G. J. Neimeyer (eds), *Personal Construct Therapy Casebook*. New York: Springer-Verlag.

O'Loughlin, S., Evans, J. & Sherwood, J. (2004). Providing an anger management service through psycho educational classes - and avoiding therapy. *Clinical Psychology, 33*, 17–20.

Procter, H. (1985). A construct approach to family therapy and systems intervention. In E. Button (ed.), *Personal Construct Theory and Mental Health*. Beckenham: Croom Helm.

Taylor, J. L. & Novaco, R. W. (2005). *Anger Treatment for People with Developmental Disabilities*. Chichester: John Wiley & Sons.

Tschudi, F. (1977). Loaded and honest questions: a construct theory view of symptoms and therapy. In D. Bannister (ed.), *New Perspectives in Personal Construct Theory*. London: Academic Press.

3

SHEDDING VIOLENT EXPRESSIONS OF ANGER CONSTRUCTIVELY

Chris J. Laming

INTRODUCTION

Many men who are abusive or violent construe anger as the cause of their behaviour, and in so doing use it as an excuse. The notion of 'anger management', rather than changing behaviour, is promoted by the legal and medical professions, and in the magistrates' courts. Hence anger is often blamed for abuse or violence, the behaviour is pathologised, and the violent person is regarded as 'sick' (which, by the way, could not really be his fault because 'he was so angry that he did not know what he was doing'!). This approach of 'anger management' is not helpful in enabling an abusive man to recognise and accept his responsibility for his behaviour, and to develop his ability to choose constructive alternatives that do not harm others. Blaming anger for the abuse also increases the possibility that women who have been abused will become more threatened at the evident 'cop-out'. It is this denial of responsibility that increases the likelihood that the man will be abusive or violent again 'down the track'.

SETTING

This chapter describes how one Australian programme in rural Victoria, uses personal construct theory in an attempt to enable men who have been violent or abusive, to change, so that women, children, and others might be safer. The programme is called the Men's SHED (Self Help Ending Domestics) Project, is known as 'Shed', and is based at a community health centre. The Shed started in 1994 at the request of local social workers supporting women and children in abusive relationships, looking for

Working with Anger: A Constructivist Approach.
Edited by Peter Cummins. © 2006 John Wiley & Sons, Ltd.

a constructive intervention for men to change their behaviour (Laming, 2000a). The men who attend the Shed are identified, by themselves, or by others as being abusive or violent, as well as often being angry. As a result, 'Shed' is referred to as a 'Men's Behaviour Change Program' rather than as an 'Anger Management Program', and its core intervention strategy is educational groups for men (Laming, 1998). This chapter is about the Shed behaviour change groups.

STRUCTURE

There are two group programmes in Shed. First, there is a semi-structured, ongoing group which meets weekly and is open to new participants, and to men who want to return after some time for a 'refresher' course. The second group is a closed 12-week programme, called the Men's Responsibility Program, the members of which are drawn from the weekly ongoing group. Both the groups are co-facilitated by a social worker and psychologist. The co-facilitator's role is to ensure that "there is a general climate of validation of construing within the group" (Viney, 1996, p. 159) as well as challenging abusive beliefs (Russell, 1995). The participants gather for the groups in the evening at a community health centre, where it is relatively anonymous. Some of the men have travelled up to 100 km to get to the group. Some are there as part of a court order, although most are there (reluctantly) of their own free will, with varying degrees of pressure from others. Before proceeding, it is worth looking briefly at the two distinct groups: the Men's Ongoing Group (MOG) and the Men's Responsibility Program (MRP).

MEN'S ONGOING GROUP

During the initial assessment session the man is normally invited to attend the open Men's Ongoing Group as soon as possible. There is no waiting period for this group, and most men are able to attend within a few days, some even attending on the same day as their initial assessment. For a man who has been abusive or violent at home, it is important for him to be able to access a Men's Behaviour Change Program promptly because there is a limited 'window of opportunity' in which most men are ready to accept that they need to change (James, Seddon & Brown, 2002; Laming, 2000a). There is still some degree of remorse and regret for their abusive actions, the memories of which are still fresh in their minds. For their family's safety it is important that such men have access to programs that might enable them to change. Many men who attend Shed find themselves outside their range of experience, in a situation that they have never been confronted with before. In this time of transition, they may well experience anxiety, threat, hostility or guilt, and this can help to prepare them to change (Fransella, 2003, p. 222).

The group setting is fairly informal, lasting two hours with a break at half-time. The meetings begin with a reminder of what the group is about, referring often to the 'agreement sheet' (see below), to reinforce key points. Certain group understandings/expectations are also stressed. For example, that what is shared is confidential ('what's said here stays here') except in the case of a man making threats; that the group is not about judging others or being judged but rather about supporting one another in a change process and challenging collusion which minimises the seriousness of men's abuse.

Following the preamble, the men begin to 'check in' with accounts of how their week has been, what they learnt from the previous session, and whether it has helped them remain non-violent. In the case of a man attending for the first time, this can be a daunting experience, and many men have related in the group that 'coming through the door tonight was the hardest thing I have ever done'. Many men attending this intake group also express surprise that they are 'not the only ones', that there are other men in similar situations to them. During this semi-structured ongoing group, a number of Personal Construct Theory exercises, strategies and 'tools' are used to enable the participants to see the possibility of constructive alternatives to violent or abusive behaviour, and to make those changes. These 'Shed tools' will be looked at later in the chapter.

When men move on from this open group, the Men's Ongoing Group, into the structured, closed, 12-week Men's Responsibility Program, the numbers in the former drop. Over the years there has been an ebb and flow in the size of the ongoing group, and generally the participants tend to prefer smaller numbers (6–10 members) rather than larger (14–18 members). The largest group has had 22 members, which necessarily meant that the 'check-ins' were short and contained. For some men, such a truncated process is frustrating, given what is at stake for them as well as for their families, while for other participants it might offer the chance to avoid adequate disclosure of their abusive behaviour, and the opportunity for honest feedback from others.

MEN'S RESPONSIBILITY PROGRAM

This 12-week programme has run three times a year, with the participants in the men's ongoing group eligible to apply. Attendance for at least three sessions of the men's ongoing group is a prerequisite for entry into this group programme that has a structured curriculum. The Men's Responsibility Program also runs once a week for two hours, and is closed to new participants once it commences. This programme looks at types of violence, issues of power and control, strategies to remain non-violent, family background issues, male socialisation, anger control, self-esteem, alcohol and other drug abuse, and the effects and ramifications for victims of violent behaviour. The numbers for the Men's Responsibility Program have varied, though 6–8 participants seems to be the preferred range, with the men in larger groups generally dropping out during the 12 weeks, until that number is reached. The Men's Responsibility Program is co-facilitated by a male and a female, according to 'best practice' principles (Younger, 1995, pp. 4/7), while the Men's Ongoing Group is co-facilitated by two males.

RATIONALE

Groups are arguably the most effective way for a person to develop more constructive alternatives to dysfunctional behaviour (Kelly, [1955] 1991; Dunnett, 1988; Williams, 1989; Winter, 1992; Viney, 1996). In the Shed the co-facilitators experience the group process as giving men a chance to experience and learn constructive alternatives to their abusive and violent behaviour and this perception is supported from other sources (Jenkins, 1990; Younger, 1995; Russell, 1995; Houston, 1998; Laming, 1998; Winter, 2003a; Winter, 2003b; Cummins, 2003):

> For many of the men, their involvement in the group is the first time they have ever talked about their abusive/violent behaviour, the first time they have heard other men talk of their own abusive/violent behaviour, also as we often say, being challenged by their peers (other men) is far more powerful than being challenged by the facilitators . . . another important feature of the group is that it creates a non-judgemental and confidential (but not collusive) environment.
>
> (Davies, personal communication, 2001)

On the one hand, the group provides a place of support, and on the other, a place of challenge. It is keeping the balance between these two poles that is the art of facilitating such a group. In order to facilitate the process better, the 'agreement sheet' is used, in which the underlying philosophy of the Shed programme is stated in simple language.

Shed Philosophy – Agreement Sheet

The philosophy of the group revolves around a number of key concepts or constructs which have been agreed upon by the participants over the years and added to. This is known as the 'agreement sheet' by the Shed men and includes the following:

1. Men are not born violent.
2. Men's abuse or violence is learnt and can be unlearnt.
3. Each of us is responsible for our attitudes and behaviour and for its effects on others.
4. Respect means treating the other person the way I would like to be treated.
5. Our abuse or violence is often used to get us what we want.
6. Men often use denial, excusing, minimising or blaming to justify their abusive behaviour.
7. Our abuse or violence often scares or terrifies our partner and children.
8. We have a choice to behave violently or non-violently.
9. There is more to us than our violent behaviour.
10. Anger is often used by men as an excuse to be abusive or violent.
11. Alcohol and other drugs do not cause violent behaviour, they do limit our control and so when we choose to abuse alcohol, we choose the possibility that we may be violent.

At the start of the group the above philosophy is distributed in the form of an agreement sheet which the participants refer to during the course of the session. The participants use the 'agreement sheet' to remind each other about why they arc in the group, and as a way to get back on track. As they usually put it, to 'cut the crap, and stop the bullshit, and get fair dinkum' or, 'just call a spade a bloody shovel'. For example, the participants will challenge a man who is minimising or justifying his abusive behaviour or is construing himself as the victim and attempting to elicit sympathy for 'poor me', rather than taking responsibility for his abusive behaviour.

RESPONSE-ABILITY

The concept of 'response-ability' is central. In the Shed project it is used in the sense of the 'ability' to respond or to choose ... if you like. It is how we express Kelly's 'Constructive Alternativism';

> we have alternatives available to us with which we try to make sense of (or construe) each other, ourselves and the world swirling around us ... no one need paint himself into a corner ... no-one needs to be completely hemmed in by circumstances ... no one needs to be a victim of his biography.
>
> (Kelly, [1955] 1991)

Hence 'response-ability' as we use it in the Shed Project means that I do have a choice about how I construe my relationship and how I respond to my partner. I do not have to paint myself into a macho corner that defines a 'real man' as one, whose main repertoire in resolving conflicts is to use his anger as a way to intimidate and get what he wants. I do not have to continue to be the victim of an abusive childhood in which, for example, I learned that male to female violence is 'normal' for a man to use to get what he wants. At the same time it is apparent that the Shed men's readiness to accept 'response-ability' is closely linked to the implications of change for them; this idea is echoed elsewhere (Cavanagh & Lewis, 1996, p. 109).

PARTICIPANTS

The men who attend the groups have generally grown up in rural Australia, and about half of them are unemployed. Those who do work are coal miners, electricity industry workers, timber workers, dairy farmers, tradesmen, and an occasional professional. Many of the men's lives are dysfunctional at this time, with issues of alcohol and drug abuse, depression, family break-up, unemployment or illness being common. About a quarter of the men have a criminal history, and Protective Services are often involved to ensure the safety of children in a family violence situation. Their intervention, especially if it involves removing the children from the home for safety reasons, usually results in significant resentment by those men involved. This is reflected in their use of such terms as 'Rottweilers' for social workers who are responsible for this intervention for children's safety.

REFERRALS

Many of the men have been referred to the Shed Project by these same social workers from 'Child Protection'. Other referrers include the Magistrates' Court, the alcohol and drug service, family doctors, police, and community agencies, or support programs for women. 'Self-referral' often happens when men realise how much is at stake, and what they could lose by their continuing abusive or violent behaviour. It is probably true to say that at first no man wants to be in the group and that there are various levels of resistance, reticence, and hostility. Kelly's concept of hostility (2003, p. 18) is particularly relevant here. In talking about hostility, Bannister notes that it is important to facilitate change 'not by assaulting each other's central beliefs but by helping each other to construct alternatives, beginning with areas of peripheral contradiction. Thus we may gradually replace a central belief without the need for hostility' (1970, p. 31). In order to enable a referred person to take up the challenge of changing abusive beliefs, it is crucial to support him in that change, and one of the ways of doing that is to relativise his abusive behaviour. In other words, reminding the man that his abusive behaviour is only a part of who he is, not the whole of him, and that there is more to him than the abuse. In this regard, it is often useful for the man to be reminded of how major areas of dysfunction in his life, at present, are probably a direct consequence of his abusive behaviour.

In this way, the man is challenged to change his abusive behaviour because it is poisoning the rest of his life, for example, affecting his relationship with his children who are scared of him, his wife, who trusts him less and less, his health because he is unable to sleep well, and so on. Since many referred men present for the first assessment with a very negative self-image which often leaves no room to see positives about themselves, it is important to situate their behaviour in a relative context which allows for change, at the same time not to minimise the seriousness of what they are doing. Again, Bannister uses an apt metaphor for this:

> which compares the problem of life to the problem of rebuilding a ship while at sea. If we have to rebuild the ship while sailing it we obviously do not begin by stripping the keel. We use the strategy of removing one plank at a time and rapidly replacing it so that, given good fortune, we may eventually sail in an entirely new ship. (1970, p. 31).

Many men who are referred feel that their 'ship' is already sinking, and that the things that they hold most dearly are under imminent threat. Hence, part of the referral and assessment process is to recognise and address that low self-esteem, in order that the man might be more effective in changing his abusive behaviour.

LOW SELF-ESTEEM

The men's self-esteem is usually rock bottom, in stark contrast to the crass arrogance many portray. In the Shed they seem able to meet and construe things in a similar way, and to realise that 'I am not the only one like this'. In so doing, they are able to build commonality, on safe and familiar ground where they feel at home, and are hence more open to be challenged about their abuse, and encouraged to change. They learn to listen and understand and regard one another in a way which permits alternative construction of how others see their reality (sociality) (see Chapter 1). To put it another way, in the Shed groups the men are given an opportunity to practise seeing the world through the eyes of others, 'sit in another person's space' and to learn problem solving and negotiation skills.

It is worth noting that for men attending the Shed their constructs around macho/machismo behaviour that help drive their abuse or violence are usually very strong, and yet are often juxtaposed with a very poignant sense of their own perceived inferiority. Consistent with the findings of Russell (1995), men who attend the Shed 'often see themselves at the centre of the universe, and display a sense of "superiority" to and "detachment" from their partner/family' (Davies, personal communication, 2001). This is also related to the issue of 'men's convenience', in which they use tactics of power and control to get what they want (Pence and Paymar, 1993; Russell, 1995). To the extent that a man's low self-esteem might lead him to feel sorry for himself and not take responsibility for his behaviour, on the one hand, or be lacking in any real sense that he can change, on the other, it is important to both challenge and support him to see himself differently. Putting it another way, to help him to see alternative ways of looking at himself and his relationships, and to see that the way he behaves with others is a choice, which he is able to change if he chooses. Kelly ([1955] 1991) calls this 'Constructive Alternativism'.

MACHO BEHAVIOUR

I once received an email from a colleague in Edinburgh who runs behaviour change groups for men on probation, using Personal Construct Theory (Macrae & Andrew, 2000). He mentioned how a visiting worker from Nicaragua stood up in a workshop and said, 'Machismo is Eucalyptic . . . it towers over everything so that nothing can grow beside it, it sucks out the nutrients and its roots are deep. We need to pull it out by the roots'. As someone who lives in the land of 'the gum tree' (Eucalyptus), I find this metaphor very apt, and would add that the Eucalyptus also drips a substance from its leaves that suppresses any other nearby growth. Being 'macho' is like that because it poisons any other life around it and stifles the relationship. At the same time my co-facilitator noted that a Eucalyptus easily blows over because the roots are shallow! And so the metaphor continues.

In contrast to the 'macho' image, the experience in the groups is that generally the men who attend are hard on themselves. For example, they often see themselves as failures, and at the same time, paradoxically, often cling tenaciously to the belief that they were justified in their abuse. They are usually angry, resentful, suspicious and hostile. 'Hostility is defined as the continued effort to extort validational evidence in favour of a type of social prediction which has already proved itself a failure'

(Kelly, 2003, p. 18). It is precisely this continual seeking to convince others (and themselves?) that they have a right to be abusive, despite all types of evidence to the contrary, that is defined as 'hostility' by Kelly.

In these apparently contradictory constructs there is also strong evidence of fragmentation (Kelly, [1955] 1991) in their construction system. On the one hand, a man might be struggling with the way he sees himself and his life, his relationships and what he sees as 'failure', and on the other he insists on controlling his family and using bullying tactics to get what he wants. It is almost as if he is able to feel like his life is not so 'out of control' precisely by controlling others, by whatever means. On the surface he is 'in control' and pretending all is well, while underneath he is hurting, scared, and struggling. The image that comes to mind, and one which we use often in the groups, is of a well-built man treading water, with one arm above his head waving, smiling, and 'in control', while under the water his legs are frantically kicking to stay afloat, and the other arm cradles a teddy-bear!

ASSESSMENT

In the initial assessment process the man is asked blunt questions by the Shed facilitator, about his behaviour, designed to get him to 'look in the mirror' and perhaps begin to construe his abusive behaviour in a different way. A favourite question asked by one of the co-facilitators during assessment is:

> How would you respond if a complete stranger walked in off the
> street and started treating your wife/partner the way you do?

The general response to this question is: 'I'd rip his f***ing throat out'.

FOLLOW-UP QUESTION:	'Why would you do that?'
RESPONSE:	'Because what he is doing is wrong!'
FOLLOW-UP QUESTION:	'So what makes you different? What gives you the right to . . . ?'

In response to this last question, many of the men break down crying (Davies, personal communication, 2001).

As part of the assessment process the man is asked to write a self-characterisation (Kelly, 1991, p. 239), or character sketch, as a way to begin getting the man to express what are the things in his life which have most meaning, and to see how his abusive behaviour makes sense for him, in relation to the rest of his life (Houston, 1998, p. 30). One way to do this is to ask the man: 'How do you want to be remembered as a father/husband by your kids/wife?' and 'What do you have to do to achieve this?' Again, this is inviting the man to see his abuse/violence from a different perspective (Davies, personal communication, 2001).

The very hearing of the questions about specific abusive behaviours enables a man to reflect on his relationship in a new way, and in addition, it is usually the first time that another man has put these sorts of questions to him, rather than colluding with his excuses. The aim is to listen credulously (Kelly, 1991, p. 174); subsuming his constructs in order to engage the man in a process of loosening some of his abusive beliefs, attitudes, values, in order to tighten onto non-abusive and respectful ways of relating. 'This is consistent with best practice in any clinical intervention – it is crucial to understand whatever meaning the client gives to his own behaviour' (James et al., 2002, p. 3). Assessing the meaning a man gives to his abusive behaviour is important in understanding how it fits with his view of the world and his relationships, and how he might engage in change, not just in theory but in actual practice (Houston, 1998, p. 28).

During the Shed assessment the man is presented with an abusive behaviour check-list and invited to take it home and rate himself on a five-point scale. In addition, he is given a sheet with destructive behaviours down the left-hand side and con-structive alternatives drawn from the literature (Pence & Paymar, 1993; Russell, 1995), down the right-hand side and invited to gauge and mark where he might be on a continuum from one to the other. Wherever possible, the man's part-ner is also invited to be part of the process and fill in similar ratings about the man, but independently, and in such a way that her safety and well-being are protected.

Before coming to the first ongoing weekly group the men often anticipate something completely different to what happens. The experience of coming itself usually loosens their personal constructions about being alone, and they have a strong sense that others are in the same boat. Many group participants report that they have found it helpful to be able both to hear other men's stories and also to be able to tell their own story without being criticised or judged and condemned.

EXPERIENCE CYCLE

There are various possible phases in a man's coming to the Shed group. At first, many are reticent, resistant and embarrassed at coming, and they often anticipate the worst because they have not had previous experience of a men's group. They usually arrive with this anticipation, being very nervous and anxious. Indeed, many men have already made up their minds that coming to Shed will be a waste of time, but that they will go through the hoops to keep 'her' (or the magistrate!) happy. When a man does actually make it to the group and begins to engage with the other participants in a facilitated process, it can be a challenging process and one which he is likely to react to with more or less hostility, depending on how much his abusive attitudes and behaviour are part of his core construing. Some men remain hostile and refuse to engage.

Participants in Shed are asked to 'look in the mirror', honestly regard their behaviour, identify what 'abuses' others, and to see things from their (abused) perspective. Kelly refers to this in his Sociality corollary which states: 'To the extent that one person construes the construction processes of another, he may play a role in a social process involving the other person' (1991, p. 66). Being in a facilitated group process with other men in a similar situation allows a man the opportunity to begin making another meaning out of what is happening and what he is doing, and hopefully he will begin to opt for alternative ways of behaving that are no longer destructive of others, or of himself. If this is what starts to happen, then the man will reassess his original anticipation of the group, since it has been disconfirmed, and this will lead him to a constructive revision of the group and its usefulness to him, and perhaps to his continuing to attend. A parallel process is that the man will hopefully start an Experience Cycle (Kelly, 1970, p. 26) on the basis of the new alternatives and choices he will encounter within the group about how he can behave in his relationship. This is accelerated to the extent that he has, with him in the group, others who are on a similar journey, intent on non-violence. In this the facilitator's role is to help them 'keep their eye on the ball', and not to get collusive, distracted or complacent, or to allow participants to think that they have got it already fixed.

A CONSISTENT MESSAGE

A consistent message is essential when trying to address and prevent the continuation of men's violence and abuse at home. Men need to hear that they are responsible for their own actions and attitudes and, conversely, women who are victimised need to consistently hear that they do have a right to safety and well-being and that they are not to blame for the abuse. This consistency is ideally reflected in the response of whomever the person comes into contact with: friends, family, the magistrates, court officials, the police, doctors, social workers and solicitors, to mention a few, and it represents a superordinate construct or over-riding principle of the SHED programme.

The superordinate construct here is one which we as society deem overriding many other personal preferences, and it is that: 'each of us has a right to be safe and to be treated with respect, and hence each of us has a duty to protect that same right of others, especially in regard to those generally less able to physically protect themselves, the young, the old, the sick, and often women'.

THE INVITATIONAL APPROACH

An 'invitational approach' is used in the Shed groups and modelled by the facilitators and the more experienced participants as a way to encourage the men to gradually trust the group as a possible venue to explore alternative constructions:

> [Kelly] proposed an invitational mood, in which the speaker takes responsibility for attributing qualities to events, and invites the listener to consider an interpretation of

the event without precluding alternative interpretations. Casting a proposition in an invitational mood suggests that the subject remains open to a range of possibilities.

(McWilliams, 2003, p. 79)

Group members are encouraged to start to 'take on board' other men's stories and suggestions, and then go away and reflect on them as homework. For the group participants, homework is an important component of the programme where significant learning can occur, profound changes can take place and constructive alternatives can be discovered (Davies, personal communication, 2001).

In the group the credulous approach (Winter, 2003b, p. 15) allows for the myriad different stories to be taken at face value and to be treated with respect (which is different from colluding with the abusive behaviour). In this way the narrow construing which epitomises the men's stereotyping of behaviour is challenged and an alternative construction is explored. By inviting the group participants to tell their story and its meaning for them, and by them feeling listened to 'credulously', with an open mind, and not judged, there arises the possibility of them learning to see that it is alright to feel scared, to feel 'out of control' and not coping, and that they are not alone in that 'space', that there are others with them who are struggling with the same experience.

It is from such a scenario that 'Jack', who came to the group initially belligerent and in denial about the effects of his abuse on his wife and children, learned to see himself differently. In his case the 'aha' experience occurred when he was relating to the other members of the group how he was beaten by his father as a child of seven, how he felt, and how the memory of that event, the look on his father's face, the tone of his voice, the words he used, suddenly reminded him of a recent episode of his own violence to his son, and how his behaviour mirrored that of his father to him. He had never made that connection before, and it was mainly because he was listened to with a credulous attitude (Kelly, 1991, p. 121) by the other group members who attempted to see the world through his eyes, that he was able to loosen his narrow construing about his behaviour as justified (because his son had been naughty), and reconstrue it as abusive and destructive. By being listened to with respect, not judged and stereotyped, 'Jack' was able to open his mind to the possibility of changing the way he regarded his own behaviour, and his personal constructions around relating.

SHED TOOLS

There are a variety of Personal Construct Theory techniques that can be used in a behaviour change group for men who have used violence or abuse against women and children. The participants are asked to do a 'self-characterisation' for homework and the content is used to elicit constructs that become the basis of ongoing interaction in the group. A checklist of 'destructive-constructive alternatives' have already been supplied as part of the assessment, these represent alternative poles of constructs which the individuals in the group are invited to explore with a view to elaborating their personal constructions to include possible responses other than abuse or violence when they become angry.

Part of this process is a self-assessment sheet in which the participants are asked to mark on a continuum where they believe they are situated. For example, a continuum which has 'intimidating' at one end and 'non-threatening' at the other might be used to enable a man to see that he is in fact quite intimidating to others at times, while not being absolutely intimidating all of the time (Laming & Fontana, 2003).

Laddering is also used in the groups, though less frequently, and with due caution regarding the person's readiness to both undertake the exercise and to 'take on board' what it might reveal to him (Viney, 1996). Another PCT technique used in the Shed groups is a simplified version of Kelly's Fixed Role Therapy (1991, p. 244) which we call 'Take a hike, Harry'.

As an example of this, let us take 'Jack' again. As a result of telling his story in the group and making the connection between what he felt as a small child when his own father was abusive, and what his own child might feel like now as a result of his own abuse, he is asked to name three behaviours of his that he would like to change. The following behaviours were identified, as were alternative, non-abusive behaviours that he would like to replace them with, and these were written on the white board.

ABUSIVE BEHAVIOURS	NON-ABUSIVE ALTERNATIVES
Scaring his children by threats.	Talking to them with affection.
Verbal abuse to his family.	Communicating with respect.
Using 'put-downs' to attack his wife.	Recognising her contributions and building her self-esteem.

Next, 'Jack' is asked whether the three alternative behaviours are 'doable' or whether they are too idealistic. Group discussion ensues in order to fine tune the alternatives and to suggest practical examples of how they can be demonstrated in the way that 'Jack' means them. It is important that 'Jack' agrees and identifies with non-violent alternatives and their practical application. Next 'Jack' is invited to briefly role-play these alternatives in the group, followed by further suggestions from the participants. When 'Jack' is satisfied with the alternative 'persona', he is invited to give him a name, let's say he chooses 'Bill'. Now 'Jack' is to instructed to go out of the room, send the abusive 'Jack' on a holiday for three weeks, and then come back into the group as 'Bill', and remain as 'Bill' for the next three weeks, keeping a small card with him to remind himself of the three 'non-abusive alternatives' that now represent behaviours which personify the new 'Bill'. He is told not to disclose to anyone outside the group that this is what he is doing, but rather to play the role of 'Bill' as best he can, reminding himself of the behaviours during the day, and observing the reactions of others to the new 'Bill'.

When 'Bill' returns to the group the following week and reports on how his children are already less scared of him as a result of him taking time to play with them, and not yelling at them, it reinforces in the group the notion that change is possible. Difficulties are addressed, other practical ways of expressing the non-abusive alternatives, are explored, and ways that have been tried, and not worked, are discarded. At the end of the three-week period 'Bill' is asked whether he wants 'Jack' to return, the answer is always in the negative! 'Jack' chooses to remain the new 'Bill' and to continue to reconstruct his behaviour non-abusively. This is the exercise we call 'Take a hike, Harry', though in this case it is take a hike 'Jack'.

The ABC Technique (Tschudi, 1977; Cummins, 2003) and the Experience Cycle (Kelly, 1970), are also both used frequently in the groups to enable participants to elaborate the meanings they make of what they are doing. These techniques are often instrumental in freeing them from tight construing which has hemmed them in and cornered them so that they feel trapped and unable to change.

EMOTIONAL ILLITERACY

There is a high degree of emotional illiteracy on the part of many men attending the SHED groups. They are often unable to name the feelings they have in a given situation. They have usually been brought up to regard such feelings, and the articulation of them, as something that is not what a 'real man' does. 'Real men' are self-contained and stand on their own feet, and don't have emotions, and hence do not grow up learning the words for them because they never have permission to communicate like that. 'Only girls talk about what they feel. What are ya anyway, a girl? A Sheila?' Apart from the ludicrous nature of this comment, it reinforces the lower status allotted to 'girls' by the patriarchal construction of society that benefits males.

The expectations, then, for a boy growing up in an environment where such is the prevailing attitude, are that he does not express emotions, he certainly does not express anything that detracts from the image of a 'real man', and that he does not try to communicate at this level with anyone. As a result, many boys and men become locked into an identity which does not allow for the expression of what they really feel, and dictates how they 'must' be. Someone referred to this expectation as 'mustabation'!

HUMOUR

Often humour is used in the role-plays, as a way of making fun of the ludicrous justifications some men give for their abuse, and getting them to laugh at themselves, in order to then arrive at a constructive revision. This playful attitude is important at times in helping to loosen tight construing and is juxtaposed with the seriousness of the issues and the high stakes involved. Indeed, play and humour are important elements of the therapeutic process especially when using something like 'Take a hike, Harry' (Fixed Role Therapy) (Epting & Nazario, 1987, p. 284). Humour is used in the group to both relativise some of the positions taken, and also to counter some of the over-seriousness. When used appropriately in the group, humour can enable the alteration of constructs which otherwise seem impermeable and 'set in concrete'. Often a man who is attending the group has a whole construction system which supports, not only his use of abuse, but also the notion that it is in fact he who is the victim and that he is justified in whatever action he takes, on the grounds that, for example, 'she did the dirty on me', or 'she pressed my buttons', or 'she pulled my strings', or 'she deliberately winds me up'.

When a man is tightly construing himself as the victim, and endeavouring to elicit a sympathetic and supportive response in the group, the use of humour can allow for an immediate loosening of his construction to include the possibility of seeing it differently. Not 'laughing at' him, but 'laughing with' him. This clearly needs to be carefully judged by the facilitator so as to be constructive in its outcome rather than destructive, both for the individual and for the group as a whole.

Humour can also allow the deflation of what a person has created as a constellatory, all-embracing construct, 'bigger than Ben Hur' and literally larger than life, into something which is relative to other constructs in his life. In this way 'the problem' as he construes it, can be relativised and reconstructed.

Australian humour is often dry and self-deprecating and there is a need for vigilance by the co-facilitators to ensure that the humour and jokes are enabling of change for the group and can be sustained by the individual men, given their fragility and vulnerability at times. The key is that the group operates within a milieu of respect (that is, treating another the way I would like to be treated), safety, support, honesty, and confidentiality ('what is said here stays here'). It is obviously important that the participants do not feel judged, put-down, or criticised by others. Indeed, it is common for men attending the group to be very self-critical and to construe themselves, in their words, as 'arseholes'. Humour often helps them listen better to things that are difficult to hear.

METAPHORS AND SIMILES

As is evident from the above, not only is humour a useful tool to use in a behaviour change group, but so are simile and metaphor. Metaphors alluded to in the Shed groups include 'the journey', in which we all struggle and stumble at times, and have a chance to help each other to travel further; 'climbing the mountain' in which, as we climb, sometimes lose our footing and roll down a ways before picking ourselves up and continuing the climb again; resting when we need to, and getting another perspective on our lives from the view up there; worth the effort; 'the shed' as a place where men feel at home, where they can think about life, their relationships and do a bit of calm reflecting on their behaviour; 'the paddock' in which there is a fence down the centre with her half and his half and a gate joining the two, and the choice of respecting the other's space or not (Clark, 2001); 'the shock- absorbers' where there is no more give and take in the relationship, and no more benefit of the doubt given, it is like a vehicle in which the shock absorbers are worn right down and whenever there is a rough patch on the journey together, metal jars on metal, and makes for a rather uncomfortable ride!

The metaphor of the 'clockwork soldier' is used in response to a man who says 'she winds me up' and, similarly, a man who says 'she pushes my buttons' is asked: 'Are you a "tamagochi"?!' (a Japanese toy). Another relevant metaphor in this neck of the woods is 'the greenhouse effect' which is used to refer to a man who scares or intimidates, or physically abuses his family so that what he causes at home is likened to a dairy herd who are stirred up (by yelling or hitting) prior to milking and the result is that the milking-shed is splattered with cow shit, giving a 'greenhouse effect'! 'The boiler' is often used in the groups to illustrate the build up in pressure that a man might experience if he does not find healthy, constructive ways of expressing his frustration, resentment, anger, since every boiler has a limit to the amount of pressure it can sustain. Boilers also need periodic 'shut-downs' to allow for scouring so that they remain safe and do not explode, like the man who 'goes bush' or takes 'time-out' because he chooses to keep his emotions in check, or 'let off steam'.

In terms of the techniques used in the Shed, several metaphors are used to describe them. 'The mirror' is used as a symbol for the man undergoing an assessment for abusive or violent behaviour, where he is encouraged to disclose the reality of his life and to 'look in the mirror' and state what it is that he sees there that he would wish to change regarding the way he relates to his wife and children. 'The jigsaw puzzle' is used to help the man sift through the bits of jigsaw puzzle which put together to make up the picture of his life as he perceives it. This metaphor is used as a way to help him identify distortions, or 'bits that do not fit the picture'. 'Hemming out' is the opposite of being 'hemmed in' or trapped. 'In prison' is the metaphor used to illustrate the feeling of being trapped, caught, stuck, not knowing how to get out. Connected with this is 'the handcuffs' where the participants 'handcuff' themselves to each other in pairs by making string handcuffs, from which they are encouraged to try and extricate themselves without succumbing to frustration and feelings of helplessness . . . there is a way out of every bind or fix, it is just a matter of finding it.

A powerful simile is that of the pointing finger. One finger of the blamer's hand is pointing at the person being blamed and three fingers are pointed back at themselves! Often in the group we use this depiction to remind the participants that blaming usually says far more about the blamer than about the one being blamed.

COLLUSION

Together with such tight construing about his justification for being abusive, the man will also have a related construct about his righteousness, and hence he construes his emotion as righteous anger, which any reasonable person would feel. By the way, this 'poor me' construing has probably taken years to elaborate, on the basis of ever greater anticipations of what works for him, and what does not. A man using such construing has more than likely grown up in a family in which the same dynamic was perhaps used by one or more of his parents, and he has adopted the same behaviour, manipulative but effective, in so far as it bolsters up his construction that it is he who is hard done by. Such a man will most likely also cultivate as friends, 'mates' who do not challenge this construction, but indeed collude with it, both because it is what their 'mate' wants to hear, but also because it connects the superordinate societal constructs around patriarchy and being macho.

Our experience in running the groups is that generally it is 'the battlers' of this world who are more honest, and it is often men who work in professions who have most to gain (and lose) by maintaining a position of moral indignation at the proposition that they are the ones who are really responsible for their abuse. A whole series of abusive beliefs or constructs are often employed to reinforce such a position and in order for the behaviour to change, these must be challenged (Russell, 1995).

SUMMARY

Over the past 10 years the Shed Project has assessed over 750 men, and this probably represents close to half that number being 'advised' to attend, or being given an informal referral. There is a high drop-out rate as men progress through the programme. For example, of every 100 men who are referred from various sources, we have anecdotal evidence that indicates only half (50 men) make an appointment and present for an assessment. Of those 50 men, who are assessed, only about 25 choose to attend the open intake (Men's Ongoing) group. Of those 25 men, only 12 will opt to do the 12-week closed Men's Responsibility Program. Some of these 12 will return periodically to the Men's Ongoing Group, or do another 12-week Men's Responsibility Program when they recognise, or are reminded, that they are slipping back into old abusive habits, and need a 'refresher' course.

The reasons for the drop-out rate do not rest entirely with the men referred. Other reasons could include inappropriate referrals, in which men are referred to the programme because it is the only 'men's programme', even though what they require is a group for separated men, or a group for men who have been sexually assaulted in childhood, or a parenting programme, rather than a men's behaviour change programme like Shed. Other reasons for the drop-out rate might be that the man has been incarcerated, that he has moved interstate, or that the travelling time in this rural area precluded further attendance. It is also true that the methods and structure of the group process do not suit all men, and hence they drop out, despite a willingness to change.

It is not easy for men to deal with changes they are challenged to make to their ways of relating to the world, and especially in relationships. Meaning-making (Leitner et al., 2000) based on abusive forms of behaviour witnessed and learnt when young, easily become part of a person's construct system and are hard to change. The drop-out rate given above is one indication of the difficulty involved in confronting and changing men's abusive beliefs and behaviour, and at the same time there is hope gained from the growing realisation of the importance of men taking responsibility for what they do, and in the existence of programs that enable men to look at their behaviours, and to change any 'destructions' to 'constructions'.

In terms of the 'drop-out rate' from the time of referral to attendance at the structured 12-week programme, there is some evidence to suggest that change already begins to occur from the time of assessment onwards. That is, in the very asking of questions, alternative behaviours are proposed as possible, and rationalised, destructive behaviour that has been absolutised, is relativised. Construing is loosened and non-abusive alternative constructions of behaviour become possible. A man who comes to the assessment full of denial about his violence, when questioned, may begin to see that the way he behaves is indeed, abusive, and that if he stops 'pointing the finger', he can see that he is making choices about how he relates, and that he can change those, that he is 'response-able'.

Similarly, men attending the ongoing group, who do not progress to the Men's Responsibility Program, may make all sorts of changes towards relating not abusively, even though they have not taken the next step. In this way, we can see that the 'drop-out rate' is not as clear as would appear, and that the real test of the efficacy of Shed is whether a man ceases to act abusively, whether as a result of assessment, the Men's Ongoing Group, or attending the structured Men's Responsibility Program. It is the men's partners and children who are the best judges of whether change for their good has occurred, and it is important to include their feedback in any evaluation process.

In conclusion, the Shed groups use a variety of Personal Construct Theory techniques such as self-characterisations, construct elicitation, laddering, ABC technique, experience cycle and fixed role therapy. Men who attend the groups are listened to in a non-judgemental way and are invited to explore alternatives to their violent and abusive behaviour. Anger is relativised as one of a number of emotions that we all can learn to express non-abusively and non-destructively, for others and for ourselves.

REFERENCES

Bannister, D. (ed.) (1970). *Perspectives in Personal Construct Theory.* London: Academic Press.

Cavanagh, K. & Lewis, R. (1996). Interviewing violent men: challenge or compromise. In K. Cavanagh & V. Cree (eds), *Working with Men.* London: Routledge.

Clark, A. (2001). Getting together at the gate. *Psychotherapy in Australia, 7*(3), 24–29.

Cummins, P. (2003). Working with anger. In F. Fransella (ed.), *International Handbook of Personal Construct Psychology.* Chichester: John Wiley & Sons, pp. 83–94.

Dunnett, G. (ed.) (1988). *Working with People.* London: Routledge.

Epting, F. & Nazario, A. (1987). Designing a fixed role therapy: issues, techniques modifications. In R. Neimeyer & G. Neimeyer (eds), *Personal Construct Therapy Casebook.* New York: Springer, pp. 277–289.

Fransella, F. (ed) (2003). *International Handbook of Personal Construct Psychology.* Chichester: John Wiley & Sons.

Houston, J. (1998). *Making Sense with Offenders: Personal Constructs, Therapy and Change.* Chichester: John Wiley & Sons.

James, K., Seddon, B. & Brown, J. (2002). *'Using it or Losing it': Men's Constructions of their Violence towards Female Partners.* Sydney: Australia Domestic and Family Violence Clearinghouse. (website: http://www.austdvclearinghouse.unsw.edu.au)

Jenkins, A. (1990). *Invitation to Responsibility.* Adelaide: Dulwich Centre Publications.

Kelly, G. (1970). A brief introduction to Personal Construct Theory. In D. Bannister (ed.), *Perspectives in Personal Construct Theory.* London: Academic Press. pp. 1–30.

Kelly, G. (1991). *The Psychology of Personal Constructs,* (vols 1 and 2). London: Routledge.

Kelly, G. (2003). A brief introduction to Personal Construct Theory. In F. Fransella (ed.) *International Handbook of Personal Construct Psychology.* Chichester: John Wiley & Sons, pp. 3–20.

Laming, C. (1998). SHED Tools – constructive alternatives to harmful behaviour. In *National Forum on Men and Family Relationships.* Canberra: Commonwealth Dept. of Family and Community Services, pp. 343–350.

Laming, C. (2000a). The SHED Project: a rural intervention project to prevent men's violence against women and children. In W. Weeks & M. Quinn (eds), *Issues Facing Australian Families.* 3rd edn. Sydney: Longman, pp. 307–315.

Laming, C. (2000b). Developing group alternatives for reconstructing personal behaviours. In K. Taylor, C. Marienan and M. Fiddler (eds), *Developing Adult Learners: Strategies for Teachers and Trainers.* San Francisco: Jossey-Bass, pp. 253–257.

Laming, C. & Fontana, M. (2003). Men's behaviour change programs in a regional and rural context. Paper presented at the Rural Social Work Conference, Mildura, Australian Association of Social Workers.

Leitner, L. M., Faidley, A. J. & Celentana, M. A. (2000). Diagnosing human meaning making: an experiential constructivist approach. In R. A. Neimeyer and J. D. Raskin *Constructions of Disorder.* Washington: APA.

Macrae, R. & Andrew, M. (2000). The use of personal construct theory in work with men who abuse women partners. *Probation Journal, 47*(1).

McWilliams, S. (2003). Belief, attachment and awareness. In F. Fransella (ed.), *International Handbook of Personal Construct Psychology.* Chichester: John Wiley & Sons, pp. 75–82.

Pence, H. & Paymar, M. (1993). *Education Groups for Men Who Batter: The Duluth Model.* New York: Springer.

Russell, M. (1995). *Confronting Abusive Beliefs: Group Treatment for Abusive Men.* Thousand Oaks, CA: Sage.

Tschudi, F. (1977). Loaded and honest questions: a construct view of symptoms and therapy.

In D. Bannister, (ed.), *New Perspectives in Personal Construct Theory*. London: Academic Press.

Viney, L. (1996). *Personal Construct Therapy:* A Handbook. Norwood, NJ: Ablex.

Walker, B., Costigan, J., Viney, L. & Warren, B. (eds) (1996). *Personal Construct Psychology: A Psychology for the Future*. Melbourne: APS.

Williams, T. (1989). *The Passionate Technique*: *Strategic Psychodrama with Individuals, Families and Groups*. London: Tavistock/Routledge.

Winter, D. (1992). *Personal Construct Psychology in Clinical Practice*. London: Routledge.

Winter, D. (2003a). Stress in police officers: a personal construct theory perspective. In J. Horley (ed.), *Personal Construct Perspectives on Forensic Psychology*. Hove: Brunner Routledge, pp. 121–142.

Winter, D. (2003b). A credulous approach to violence and homicide. In J. Horley (ed.), *Personal Construct Perspectives on Forensic Psychology*. Hove: Brunner Routledge, pp. 15–53.

Younger, B. (1995). *Stopping Men's Violence in the Family*: *A Manual for Running Men's Groups*. Melbourne: V-Net Inc.

4

TIME AND TOOLS?: TOOLS OR TIME?

Gina Selby

INTRODUCTION

Rage is more prevalent in our society than ever before. Mental illness is increasing. Potentially the two together make a dangerous combination. More and more men and women are angry and ill. I work within a psychotherapy service in the British National Health Service. I became aware that there was a need to develop an anger management group as, increasingly, referrals from the Community Mental Health Teams were requesting an anger management group. The only anger management group in the locality was run by the Probation Service. It was designed for violent and abusive offenders with anger issues, and ran on a modular format for a year. It was not considered suitable for mentally ill patients who were coping with psychiatric problems on top of additional problems of usually covert anger manifesting as physical illness (Sarno, 1991).

I set up a group which met weekly, for one and a half hours, in the Community Mental Health Team premises. In a 10-week course there may be a certain tedium for the client going over the past story yet again. Does this process ingrain that angry behaviour more deeply into the person, even though information and homework offer alternative new behaviour?

Alternatively, if the clients were offered just a half-day workshop, the focus was solely on the group member's anger process – change agents and tools for change. If the leader's and the clients' expectations and impetus for success were paramount, it probably would work very well.

Working with Anger: A Constructivist Approach.
Edited by Peter Cummins. © 2006 John Wiley & Sons, Ltd.

What is it that makes the difference? What is the thing that, if changed, alters the person's construing and behaviour? What is the 'positive intention' of anger (O'Connor & Seymour, 1993), the core of anger (Bays, 1999), the positive learnings (James & Woodsmall, 1988), which, when identified, allows the anger to disappear? Is it *time*? Is it that people need to look at their behaviour and gradually reconstrue themselves, as assertively angry, or do they need the *tools* (the wherewithal) to just make the change?

What treatment modalities would most benefit clients if they were offered? A 10-week course for one and a half hours a week looking at all aspects of anger and what can be done to change, or a four-hour, half-day workshop concentrating on specific aspects and practical information and a process to follow? Which is most beneficial, in terms of a change agent, use of resources and cost effectiveness? The key to success is the 'eureka' factor, which, when realised, changes the situation without more ado. To reinforce the learning, it is important for the client to develop a 'well-formed outcome' combined with future pacing to establish this new construing (James, 1995; Bays, 1999) or, in PCP terms, to act out a mini-future fixed role sketch (Kelly, 1955). This process is visualised and practised in the client's daily life to ensure it becomes an established part of the person's construing.

When planning the anger management group, it was important to address the various issues. These range from practical considerations to theoretical ones, that reflected the philosophy and beliefs of the organisation, the leaders and the clients. The most obvious starting point was to define anger in the widest sense of the word. The definition we used was: Anger is *'a violent passion, excited by real or supposed injury; resentment'* (Patterson, 1977). I begin first with a look at the nature of anger.

THE NATURE OF ANGER

Purpose of Anger

Anger is a positive, powerful, quick constructive survival kit. It boosts energy, providing the wherewithal to the body and mind for getting out of difficult situations (Lindenfield, 1993). It is the 'fight' part of the fight or flight anxiety response that all animals have, to ensure their survival when threatened. It gives us courage to protect ourselves and our loved ones. It warns others not to use us or take advantage of us. It motivates us to improve the universe by inspiring justice and social action. It establishes our individuality, particularly when a child. Anger is designed to release pent-up tension and let off steam. The body should then return to normal, which is the calm state (Lindenfield, 1993).

Types of Anger

People experience different types of anger, and rationalise their response accordingly. This has a bearing on their perceived need for change. Justified or righteous rage is often construed as an excuse for the anger, and so it was deemed acceptable to 'punish the offender'. Blind rage, substance abuse rage, uncontrolled anger, or temper tantrums may be considered as outside one's control, therefore not possible to change. Kellyan hostility, the 'yes but' syndrome, tends to be happening when 'it was not my fault, it is the others'. The behaviour angry people exhibit basically fits into three main categories: aggressive, passive and assertive. Going back to the body's survival response, the fight or flight reaction happens immediately the reticular activating system, situated in the brain stem, becomes aware of danger. It instantly moves the body to respond to the threat. The behaviour is either aggressive (fight) or passive (flight or hide). The assertive behaviour is a secondary response, a learnt skill, generally more acceptable and successful in most situations.

Many patients, especially in the mental health field, have invested a lot of time and effort into staying with the anger. It is an important part of their having a dominant role – they are angry, have been angry, will be angry (Potter-Effron, 1994). Unless the person 'owns' the anger as his/hers and 'goes to cause' (James, 2001) anger will continue to smoulder inside, causing physical, emotional and spiritual damage, even death.

Negative Patterns of Anger

Repeated negative anger patterns gradually limit life experience and the person's world becomes more constricted and unhappy as relationships are spoilt and jobs are lost (Dryden, 1996). Excessive, unhealthy, negative anger is demonstrated by the following:

1. Constantly repeating similar anger actions and words in certain situations.
2. Frequent swearing, use of violent language and behaviour.
3. Brooding and fantasising about negative situations with people.
4. Using angry behaviour in most situations.
5. Using violence and being in trouble with the police.
6. Only feeling good about one's self when angry.
7. Not solving a problem, just getting angry about the situation.
8. Establishing a reputation as an angry person who is feared, appeased or teased about it.
9. Having strong prejudices about others because of race, creed, gender, age, etc.

Butler (2000) suggests numerous reasons for being stuck with negative anger. The following factors contribute to maintaining the angry behaviour:

- a symptom of some health condition, either physical, spiritual or psychological;
- habit – anger can become an automatic response;
- fear – being afraid is the fight part of the stress reaction;
- shame – the need to fight to preserve dignity and self-worth;

- loss – it is one of the emotions in grieving;
- non-assertiveness – an over-compensation for the need to be heard;
- tiredness – difficulty in keeping a realistic view on the situation when exhausted;
- low frustration level – unable to tolerate situations that others would take in their stride;
- stress – a fight response to anxiety;
- a post traumatic response – memories of past trauma may mean over-reaction to anything that seems threatening.

The pay-off to being angry is a 'buzz'. When you are angry, you feel in control, powerful, safe. These short-term benefits do not last and the long-term problems in all aspects of one's life obliterate any short-term gain.

Interestingly, there are better ways of getting the gains that are long-lasting and healthy. These include increasing self-confidence and self-esteem, doing regular exercise, positive thinking, and creative visualisation, to name just a few. At first, there may be some uncertainty and discomfort as the short-term gains disappear and the new behaviour is not quite established. The benefits of anger are: people listen to me; I feel good; it is exciting; I am not afraid; anger stops me being depressed; I feel I am someone; I know who I am.

Integrated Approaches to Anger Management

To run an effective anger management course it was necessary to do the following:

1. Pull together tools and techniques that would make 'a difference'.
2. Find ways of creating new experiences and behaviour from people who were already dealing with lots of challenges in their life.

Resources were taken from various theories that had already provided useful tools and approaches. The meta-theory of personal construct psychology (Kelly, 1955) provided the useful notion of 'man the scientist', focusing on testing the outcomes of behaviour. The exploration of individual constructs allows a precise examination of the person's psychological processes, showing limits and openings (Bannister & Fransella, 1982).

A contrasting approach to the whole person, incorporating mind, body and spirit, comes from the Vedic philosophy (Chopra, 1990a, 1990b), and focuses on well-being and balance in life. As well as tackling the psychology of health, this approach connects Western science to Eastern mysticism. To move towards healing, one must also pay attention to diet, breathing and spirit. It offers techniques of yoga, meditation, mantras and spiritual practice which are now finding support in modern psycho-immunology (Pert, 1997), quantum physics (Chopra, 1990a) and energy medicine (Oschman, 2000; Scott-Mumby, 2000).

To the above can be added the wide variety of techniques that come from Neuro Linguistic Programming (NLP) and related theories. NLP offers modelling excellence, and quick change techniques of trance (O'Connor & Seymour, 1993; Diltz, Hallbom & Smith, 1993; James, 1995), and modelling and change at the unconscious level. Using Time Line Therapy (TLT) it is possible to clear out past negative emotional events and move to a state of future pace (James & Woodsmall, 1988), through belief changes and metaphors (Gorden, 1978; Diltz et al., 1993; Fanning, 1994). The Solution Focused Therapy (de Shazer, 1985; O'Hanlon & Weiner-Davis, 1989) model offers a structured format, that firmly ensures the responsibility for change stays with the person, and focuses on the ability of the client, not the disability. It also offers a structure to the session, where unusually, the leaders/facilitators of the group leave the group about 15 minutes before the end of the session, to reflect on the group and to decide what feedback and homework are most relevant to the group members. Occupational therapy's (OT) model of occupation (Reed & Sanderson, 1983) is a powerful vehicle for positive change on all levels of occupational performance. Each model brings diverse yet complementary parts to the anger management programme, and we shall now discuss each of these models.

TECHNIQUES OF ANGER MANAGEMENT

Personal Construct Psychology

PCP is a comprehensive theory of personality, and gives a clear understanding of anger in psychological terms. Personal construct theory techniques used in the anger management groups include eliciting the bi-polar constructs, and pyramiding down from an abstract superordinate construct to a subordinate, concrete or a behavioural construct. This, combined with an occupational therapy theory, offers clear guidelines as to what homework or practical exercises are most beneficial to the client. Loaded and honest questions, the ABC technique (Tschudi, 1977), are used to establish implicative dilemmas, e.g. why a person chooses to stay where he/she is, 'being angry' rather than change to something they say they want, 'calm/confident'. The pay-off of being angry is that you are seen as 'tough, macho'. The cost of calm is being 'a wimp'. The aim is to find an orthogonal construct that can be developed to give a positive way forward to obtain the pay-off. The middle ground may be construed as 'confident and equal to anyone in a calm considered manner'.

Vedic Philosophy

Vedic philosophy and yoga (Chopra, 1990b; Simon, 1997) offer a holistic view of healthy diet, rest, exercise, meditation, mantras, and breathing techniques. Simple meditation techniques practised regularly (daily) give the person a feeling of calm, and well-being. Breathing techniques physiologically calm the body by taking in less oxygen as breathing is slower, and changing the acid/alkaline balance in the blood. Concentration while doing these exercises occupies the mind. Vocal mantras set up a vibration in the body that bring healthy well-being. The benefit of these are two fold, first, the deep breathing and breath control, and, second, a healing vibration is created in the body (Chopra, 1990b).

Neuro Linguistic Programming (NLP)

NLP was developed as a way of modelling excellence. It offers many powerful quick techniques of change. If the outcome is practised regularly, change is established and becomes part of the person's natural construing processes.

The Neuro Linguistic Programming Model of therapy starts with the present state and behaviour. The goal is to reach the desired state/behaviour. It sets out to do the following:

1. Explore the person's model of the world.
2. Loosen the person's model of world by using techniques and interventions that create change.
3. Ensure that the new model is ecologically satisfactory and the person is balanced.
4. Get the person to test if the old behaviour 'is gone' and move to 'future pace', the desired state in their future.

The process simply is moving from the old model of the world to the new model of the world (James, 1995).

The NLP techniques fit comfortably into personal construct philosophy, in fact, some techniques are virtually identical. Personal construct's laddering technique is the same as chunking up, and the pyramiding procedure is chunking down. A major difference is the importance Neuro Linguistic Programming puts on the unconscious - it is responsible for all behaviour, learning and change.

Submodalities

Neuro Linguistic Programming techniques used in the anger groups include changing negative visualisation to positive, using the submodality visual, auditory and kinaesthetic checklist. Submodalities are distinctions within our representational system; we use them to make sense of our world. They are the mental pictures, sounds and feelings that are the building blocks and qualities of our internal world. We build them from one or more of our five senses: visual, auditory, kinaesthetic, olfactory and gustatory. The fascinating thing about submodalities is to notice what happens when you change them. Some can be changed and nothing happens. Others are crucial to a particular memory, so changing them affects the whole way we view the memory, and impacts on that experience. It seems that the impact and meaning of a specific memory are not to do with the content, but more with a function of a few vital submodalities. We are unable to change an event that has already happened. In fact, we are responding to the memory of the event, not the event itself, and therefore the memory of that event can change (O'Connor & Seymour, 1993). By changing the crucial submodalities in therapy, the negative experience of the event may be reconstrued as positive learning. An example of this was a woman who was asked to describe a scenario when she was calm and happy. Her description was in full colour, in contrast to her angry situation that was in black and white. By asking her to put colour in the angry situation she became calm and relaxed and was able to reconstrue her ability to deal with the people involved.

Another useful NLP technique is asking detailed questions so the client can establish a positive outcome. This is known as creating an achievable outcome. The most interesting questions are:

> What will happen if you get what you want?
> What won't happen if you get what you want?
> What will happen if you don't get what you want?
> What won't happen if you don't get what you want?

Time Line Therapy

Time line therapy techniques are designed to enable the person to let go of negative memories and install positive resources. Briefly, this involves eliciting the time line and the root cause by asking the person to visualise their time line, then float above it, and go back into a past negative emotional experience. By changing the resources needed, the negative emotion is released, and the person can take the 'positive learning' from the experience (James & Woodsmall, 1988). To check if the learning is embedded and if the anger has gone, the person is asked to imagine the same situation happening in seven days time, then one month, then one year. This is a technique called future pace and allows the individual to imagine similar situations happening, not only without anger, but in a constructive way.

Occupational Therapy

The occupational therapy model enables the leaders to plan homework in a practical realistic fashion at the level of the client's ability. The tasks in the 10-week course were planned, yet flexible enough to cater for the particular needs of each group member.

All the sessions are run in a casual light-hearted humorous fashion (Mindless, 1971; Olson, 1976; Levine, 1977), when possible, as learning is easier when the person is more relaxed and receptive. This is reflected in the group name - Keep it Kool Group.

PROTOCOL FOR KEEP IT KOOL GROUP

The purpose of the group was to do the following:

1. To understand the process of anger and its effect on the mind/body/spirit aspects of a person.
2. To facilitate changing group members' habitual ways of coping with anger and trigger situations.
3. To learn, discuss and practise new and better ways of coping with anger without hostility.

The group is designed to find solutions for people who have negative issues regarding managing anger, self-esteem, confidence, and self-image. The aim is to create options for the person and not have them constantly resort to using anger as the only coping strategy.

The focus of the work is the following:

1. To identify and understand anger.
2. To understand how it affects ourselves and others.
3. To develop better coping skills to use in difficult situations.

Initially, the group was designed to run for 10 sessions, and later changed to a half-day workshop.

The short-term goals of the course were:

1. To provide a safe environment for a discussion of anger pertinent to the group members.
2. To understand and identify one's own and others' anger.
3. To inform and educate the members in relevant subjects.
4. To discover different solutions to anger-related problems.
5. To learn to anticipate the anger process and learn alternative ways to deal with stressful situations.
6. To learn target-setting exercises to enable the group members, through trial and error, to adopt new methods of coping with daily activities.
7. To identify goals for each person, that are reviewed/renewed every five weeks.

The long-term goals of the course were:

1. To enable group members to have greater choice in their ways of coping with anger-provoking situations.
2. To understand the implications of their change and be in control of their life in a healthier way.
3. To acknowledge and develop the inner self: self-worth, self-esteem and self-confidence.
4. To establish and embellish their strengths and abilities.

Working in the adult mental health service, as part of the psychological therapies team in the Community Mental Health setting presupposes certain criteria for referrals to the 'Keep Kool' Group. The person had to have a mental health problem as well as an anger problem. The client was referred by a member of the multidisciplinary team. Those excluded had florid symptoms of a psychiatric illness or were unable to tolerate a group setting.

Clients were included if they fulfilled the following conditions:

1. Acknowledged they had an anger problem.
2. Had angry behaviour affecting their life, e.g. verbal and physical violence.
3. Could commit to 10 sessions.
4. Could tolerate and control themselves in a group setting.

Process Criteria

The group had a minimum of four clients and a maximum of eight, with both facilitators present at all sessions. The group was cancelled if only one facilitator was able to be present. The following framework was set up:

1. *Media* – multimedia equipment, creative activities, discussion and role play.
2. *Format* – the group will meet weekly for 1.5 hours, and run for 10 sessions with a half-term break.
3. *Procedure* – Facilitators give a short introduction stating goals and focus of the workshop, check homework and review progress. They leave the group for 10 minutes just before the end to discuss group proceedings and select appropriate homework.

Role of Therapist/Facilitator

The following tasks were allocated to the therapist/facilitator:

• To allocate sufficient time for preparation prior to group starting and 'wash up' time at close of group.

- To organise regular supervision for group facilitators.
- To keep the boundaries, and specify the rules of group, e.g. confidentiality, no violence.
- To ensure the group members understand the goals and expectations and format of the group.
- To provide a safe environment.
- To provide an opportunity for every client to share his/her own experiences and opinions.
- To encourage group members to participate fully in the group.
- To ensure that each group member gets feedback at the end of each session and understands the task set for the following week.
- To encourage group members to complete any required documentation.

Outcome criteria were set so that clients would be able to demonstrate their knowledge of anger and related issues and how to apply this understanding and techniques in daily life. Clients completed the Clinical Outcomes in Routine Evaluation questionnaire for the assessment and outcome measure. (See Chapter 14, on assessment, by Pekkala et al.).

At the end of the course, each member writes an account of the group, of their progress and an outcome plan. A copy is kept by the client and a copy sent to the referrer who will then help the client to practise the new behaviour.

The Boundaries of the Group

The group keeps the confidentiality of any personal information shared in the session. Information regarding anger management techniques may be shared with all. Members agree to attend all 10 sessions. Time keeping is important, so they must come on time. If for any reason they are unable to attend, they must contact the facilitators prior to the session. No verbal or physical violence in the group. No carrying of offensive weapons. No intake of alcohol or social drugs prior to or during the group. Everyone's contribution is accepted and of equal value. Each member is treated in a respectful manner. Refreshments are provided at the start of the group.

CONCLUSION

Interestingly, the number of clients who attended the courses were about half the number of people invited to the course. This could be because they had to wait too long for the course (waiting time may be more than two months); or the person lost interest, or does not wish to change, or has moved on physically or emotionally, or was discharged by referrer, or because other people insisted the person attend the course and it was not their own choice. The drop-out rate, once the course had started, was nil. At the moment three 10-week groups and three half-day workshops have been run. The feedback from the clients has been positive, inasmuch that they are still practising their chosen task, including mantras, breathing, being assertive, etc. as long as referrers continue to support and facilitate the homework.

Theoretically, the course allows the individual to consider the consequences of their behaviour. It allows them space to practise their new behaviour, and consider what it means to them. There is a greater possibility to discuss the course content with their family and the professionals. Gradually the person and family can adjust to the new, hopefully calmer, person. However, sometimes procrastination and apathy creep in. There is ample opportunity for second and third thoughts to arise, and the boredom factor, 'We have talked all about that several times before.'

Possibly the person benefits most from the workshop because insight is not necessary for change (Kelly, 1955). It offers the difference that makes the difference (James & Woodsmall, 1988), is factual, light-hearted and non-judgmental. The focus is on the positive (de Shazer, 1985) and the techniques are easy to do, with instant results.

The leaders have decided to continue with the half-day workshop and drop the 10-week course. Although it is a very small sample, the evidence suggests that for effectiveness, efficiency and time restraints, the workshop seems to be the best way forward, enabling clients to understand, learn and practise good techniques for coping with negative emotions, e.g. anger, stress, etc. The outcomes of the course and workshop are not really different. The clients preferred the half-day workshop, as it was less disruptive to their life. I am sure the eureka factors is the difference that makes the difference.

There is never just one way to help a person reconstrue their problems or life and take the step to different, hopefully better, ways of being in the world. The exciting issue for the leaders of the Keep it Kool Group is continually to find new 'fast-track' ways of being the harbinger of the mind–body–spirit link to well-being.

APPENDIX: THE TEN-WEEK COURSE AND THE HALF-DAY WORKSHOP

The Ten-Week Course

Prior to the group, the leaders of the group meet to organise the session, ensuring that it is relevant to the members and their particular needs. Although the session is planned, the programme is flexible enough to be altered if required.

Format for the Keep it Kool Group

1. Group members are offered refreshments, prior to the group starting, so they can catch up with any outstanding homework, and settle more comfortably into the group session.
2. Warm-up is linked to the aims of the session, and is a gentle, often practical introduction to the group work.
3. Focus of the group session. The programme is designed so the least threatening topics, i.e. the physical and behavioural issues are discussed first. The emotional and spiritual beliefs of the group members, how anger affects self and others, are discussed in detail when trust has built within the group.
4. The discussion is related to the topic of that particular session.
5. The practical exercise is linked to the particular aims of that session.
6. Twenty minutes before the end of the session the leaders leave the group for approximately 10 minutes to reflect on the content of the group, and plan the homework based on the reflections.
7. The leaders share with the group members their collective thoughts and decisions about the session, and set homework with each group member for the week.
8. The group members depart, having agreed to do the homework.
9. In the 'wash-up' after the group, the leaders discuss the progress and outcome of the group.
10. The leaders complete the rating scale and document any relevant information. Any particular concerns about an individual group member is fed back to the care co-ordinator or referrer.
11. At the end of the ten sessions the progress of the group members is evaluated.

Selecting the appropriate course material was done by researching anger and the way to manage it more appropriately (Kelly, 1955; Lindenfield, 1993; Wykes, 1994; James, 1995). This research led us to identify the basic concepts required to ensure the clients would have an adequate knowledge and understanding of anger:

- how it affects all aspects of the person physically, emotionally and mentally;
- the short- and long-term effects of being angry;
- the types of anger, and how to identify them;
- benefits and implications of being angry;
- benefits and implication of change;
- to identify and understand the purpose of positive new skills;
- to practise doing, thinking and feeling the new skills;
- incorporating the new skills into the clients' habits;
- caring for self and having fun.

Overview of the Ten-Week Course

After introducing the subject and members of the group, people were asked to tell the story of why they were there, and how they liked to be handled when angry. Experiences of the anger and expectations of the group were discussed, and constructs were elicited.

Information was given on the physiology of anger and how it affects your thoughts and feelings. People focused on how they recognised anger, what made them angry, the process and consequences of an anger episode. Clarification was done by using the ABC model (Tschudi, 1977), and Time Line Therapy techniques were used to find positive learnings.

Topics discussed over the 10 weeks included: first anger event; childhood wounds; times when the problem did not exist; how other people's behaviour affects mood and spirit; what provokes anger in self and others; and acknowledging skills that already exist for coping effectively with anger. A video of *Fawlty Towers* was shown and the types of anger behaviour observed there were discussed, including perceived provocation, violence and chronic anger in others.

Recovery from the consequences of anger were important to work through, and a variety of techniques were introduced as appropriate. These included self-talk (internal dialogue), positive affirmations, mantras (repeating sounds to calm the energy level in the body), breathing exercises, healthy diet, taking regular exercise, assertiveness techniques, confidence building, reinforcing existing coping skills, and ways to disregard negative thoughts.

The Half-Day Workshop

After running three successful, but time-consuming, 10-week workshops, the possibility of refining the package to a half-day workshop was considered. Having a positive experience of regularly running a sucessful half-day stress management workshop, it was decided to try this format with the Keep Kool course. The key aspects of the anger management course were analysed, prioritised, and a half-day workshop was piloted.

The most important issues were how anger affected the person's mind/body and soul. The crucial focus was on how the group member construed anger and change. We then went on to offer new skills in a way they would be incorporated into the person's daily routine.

The topics included in the half-day workshop are shown in Figure 4.1.

Time	Aim to	Focus on
9.15	Register	Offer refreshments
		Complete registration
		Fill in assessment form
9.30	Introduce topic of anger	Discuss housekeeping – fire drill, etc.
		Discuss boundaries of group:
		Confidentiality, everyone equal
9.40	Understand what anger is	Figures 1 – Physiology of anger
	Understand how anger	Figure 2 – Affects of prolonged anger
	affects your mind,	
	body emotions and spirit	Figure 3 – Others/your perception of anger
10.20	**COFFEE**	Group is left alone to talk among themselves.
10.40	The implications of anger on	Figure 5 – The ABC of anger
	your self	
		Figure 6 – Brainstorm new possibilities
	Be able to manage anger in	Breathing techniques
	a better more	
	appropriate way	Diaphragmatic breathing
		Alternate nostril breathing
		Quick ways to cope and become calmer
		Stop technique
		Looking up
		Submodalities – change pattern
		Be assertive
11.45	**BREAK**	Group is left alone to talk among themselves.
12.00	Deal with other people's	Listen
	anger in a more	
	assertive manner	Pace, pace, lead.
		Assertive techniques
	Learn preventative	General calming strategies
	strategies that help alter	
	your general patterns of	Quick relaxation techniques
	behaviour	
		Breathing slowly, pushing down shoulders
		Smiling at people (produce endomorphs)
		Singing (improves breathing)
		Assertive techniques
	Improve self-esteem and	List your own good points
	confidence	
		List the everyday achievements
		Give self something daily because you're special
	Improve lifestyle, lifestyle	Rest and exercise
	changes	
		Healthy diet
		Pace self during day
		Practise new technique until it is a new habit.
		Have **FUN**
12.45	Select one task	Choose one skill learnt in workshop to
	Evaluation	practise until developed into a habit.
	Close	Complete an evaluation form.
		Give 'handouts' to group members
		Finish

Figure 4.1 Outline of half-day workshop

Evaluation of the Course and the Workshop

The clients at the end of the 10-week course and the half-day workshop were asked to fill in an evaluation form. The same form was given to both groups and the results were similar.

---

1. Enjoyable aspects of the workshop

The breathing techniques
Talking to someone who knows what they are talking about
I really enjoyed the whole session
I got the most out of the breathing/meditation
Understanding people's problems
The people
Knowing that I have been doing all the right things to control my anger
Being able to talk to people that have been through what I am going through
Speaking to other people with some of the same problems
Mantras
Sharing experiences with others
Surprising myself with my input and not being told to shut up.
Be able to open up and being listened to

2. Least enjoyable aspects of the workshop

Nothing
None
Attitude and bad language of a member of the group
Feeling my worst when talking about things
Getting here
Not relating to some of the theory

3. Most beneficial aspects of the workshop

People listening
Breathing/meditation
Talking to others
Hearing others
Lots more information given, to think and try out
Understanding my problem is real and curable
All – refresher
The breathing techniques

Visualisation mantras
Sharing
The exercises
Understanding that I am me!
I am not worthless and that sometimes anger can be a positive thing, and not just a thing that makes you want to self-destruct

The workshop could be improved by:

Talking to people who understood the problem
Can't think of any way
More open discussion
No other improvements needed
Sandwiches
Making into a series/course/revisiting
Nothing

Comments/suggestions

Thank you for listening
Thank you, I think this will help
As above
Great help thanks
Cost of stuck anger
Anger that is held inside the person for long periods
No!!!
Well done both of you
I really enjoyed it and knowing that other people have the same problem
Thank you

Background to Client's Needs

Clients were asked to fill in an assessment questionnaire to give the leaders more information. Below is a selection of the responses given by the clients of both the 10-week group and the half-day workshop.

Who decided you needed help with your situation?

Doctor   Community Psychiatric Nurse   Self
Therapist Social Worker

How did you feel about the idea?

Nervous   OK   Open-minded   Good idea   Fine
As long as it helps, feel good about it.

Have you had any therapy or help for a similar problem?

No   Yes [majority had therapy previously]

How did the problem start, how long ago and what started it?

1987 husband left   1997 new boss didn't like me
Bullied at school   When 6–7 years old
Always had bad temper, worse after loss of loved one
Depression 7 years ago   Redundancy Road traffic accident
Many years   Married late in life

What were you like before the problem started?

Don't know   OK   Cheerful but anxious   Controlled
Never knew true self Fine   Quiet   Passive
Normal   Happy   Very bad-tempered

How often do you see your GP/doctor regarding the problem?

Twice a week   Weekly   Monthly   Bi-monthly

How much does it affect your life?

Totally taken over my life   Life OK   Wrecked my life entirely

How would your life change if you did not have this problem?

Dramatically   You mean return to normal?   Have a life
Be depressed   Greatly – I would still have a family   Back to rat race
More stable   Affects all aspects of life   Enjoy life more

Everyone feels angry at times. Which situations make you feel particularly uncomfortable, e.g. home, work, social life, relationships?

Any relationship   Work   Feel out of control   Social life
Home

Do your problems make you do things that make you feel particularly uncomfortable?

Yes I cut myself   Ashamed

If so, what are you not able to do?

Make friends   Go out   Show affection   Stand up for myself
Not able to show true feeling

What happens to your body when you feel angry?

Shake	Sweat	Tears	Pleasure
Heartbeat increases	Get a buzz	Cannot breathe	
Severe tension	Pain in chest	Hot	Sick
Rage	Tense	Energy	Power

What goes through your mind when you are angry?

Hurt myself   See red   Self-loathing   Hate
Why can't I stand up for myself?   Suicidal feeling   Unfair

What other emotions do you feel when you are angry?

Hurt   Bitter sweet victory   Incompetence   Hatred
Sarcastic   Frustration   Upset   Don't know

What do you do at present to calm down?

Cut myself   Realisation that unacceptable behaviour has taken place
Go to bed   Get drunk   Deep breathing   Read
Take prozac   Smoke   Driving   Escape

What do you expect to get from attending the workshop?

Insight into my behaviour   Strategies to combat the stress of anger
Other way to control my anger rather than pain
Understanding of why I get angry   How to control it   Ways to deal
                                                                         with anger
New ideas to reduce stress   Open-minded   How to cope
Help to understand why I'm like this and prevent it happening again
More advice on how to stop myself getting angry again in the future
Don't know

What changes do you hope to make following participation in the half-day?

Not sure!   To express my point of view adequately
Make myself better   Let things go over the top of my head
To stay calm in difficult situations   Be safer
Turn negative feelings and emotions into positive ones
Be calm   Be happier
Open-minded.

REFERENCES

Bannister, D. & Fransella, F. (1982). *Inquiring Man: The Theory of Personal Constructs*. 2nd edn. Melbourne, Fl: Krieger Publishing.

Bays, B. (1999). The *Journey*. London: Thorsons.

Butler, C. (2000). http://www.ad.rhul.ac.uk/counselling/anger.ht

Carter, J. (1993). *Nasty Men: How to Stop Being Hurt by Them Without Stooping to their Level*. Chicago: Contemporary Press.

Chopra, D. (1990a). *Quantum Healing: Exploring the Frontiers of Mind/Body Medicine*. New York: Bantam Books.

Chopra, D. (1990b). *Perfect Health: The Complete Mind/Body Guide*. New York: Bantam Books.

De Shazer, S. (1985). *Keys to Solution in Brief Therapy*. New York: Norton.

Diltz, R., Hallbom, T. & Smith, S. (1993). *Beliefs Pathways to Health and Wellbeing*. Portland, OR: Metamorphous Press.

Dryden, W. (1996) *Overcoming Anger*. London: Sheldon Press.

Fanning, P. (1994) *Visualisation for Change*. Oakland, CA: New Harbinger Publications Inc.

Gorden, D. (1978) *Therapeutic Metaphors*. Capitola, CA: Meta Publications.

James, T. (1995). Time Line practitioner course manual. Unpublished.

James. T. (2001). Master practitioner Course manual. Unpublished.

James, T. & Woodsmall, W. (1988). *Time Line Therapy and the Basis of Personality*. Capitola, CA: Meta Publications.

Kelly, G. A. (1955) *The Psychology of Personal Constructs*. New York: Norton.

Kelly, G. (1977). The psychology of the unknown. In D. Bannister (ed.), *New Perspectives in Personal Construct Theory*. London: Academic Press.

Levine, J. (1977). Humour as a form of therapy. In A. J. Chapman & H. C. Foot (eds), *It's a Funny Thing, Humour*. Oxford: Pergamon.

Lindenfield, G. (1993). *Managing Anger*. London: Thorsons.

Mindless, H. (1971). *Laughter and Liberation*. Los Angeles: Nash.

O'Connor, J. & Seymour, J. (1993). *Introducing Neuro Linguistic Programming*. London: Thorsons.

O'Hanlon, W. & Weiner-Davis, M. (1989). *In Search of Solutions*. London: Norton & Company.

Olson, H. A. (1976). The use of humour in psychology. *Individual Psychology*, *13*, 34–37.

Oschman, J. L. (2000). *Energy Medicine: The Scientific Basis*. London: Churchill Livingstone.

Patterson, R. F. (ed.) (1977). *English Dictionary*. London: Tower Publishers.

Pert, C. (1997). *Molecules of Emotion*. Glasgow: Caledonian International.

Potter-Effron, R. (1994). *Angry All the Time*. London: New Harbinger.

Reed, K. L. & Sanderson, S. R. (1983). *Concepts of Occupational Therapy*. London: Williams & Wilkins.

Sarno, J. E. (1991). *Healing Backpain: The Mind–Body Connection*. New York: Warner Books.
Scott-Mumby, K. (2000). *Virtual Medicine*. London: Thorsons.
Simon, D. (1997). *The Wisdom of Healing*. London: Rider.
Tschudi, F. (1977). Loaded and honest questions: a construct theory view of symptoms and theory. In D. Bannister (ed.), *New Perspectives in Personal Construct Theory*. London: Academic Press.
Wykes, T. (1994). Violence and Health Care Professionals. London: Chapman & Hall.

5

EXPERIENTIAL PERSONAL CONSTRUCTIVISM AND ANGER

Larry M. Leitner and Jill C. Thomas

Joan had just announced her intention to divorce Kevin due to his long-term alcohol abuse. Kevin was enraged. Voices were raised, dishes broken, and furniture smashed. Eventually Kevin went to a local bar, leaving Joan with time to quickly pack some belongings and go to an apartment she had rented. However, for months afterwards, Kevin would break into her apartment and leave notes, threatening messages, and little signs that he still could reach her if he desired. Kevin and his mother also would belittle Joan to their children, eventually alienating her son and daughter from her.

Rachel had just announced her intention to divorce Dave due to her long-standing dissatisfaction with the marriage and the fact that she was in love with someone else. Devastated, Dave withdrew from the social world and eventually moved into an isolated cabin in the country. After a serious suicide attempt, he decided to try therapy. Dave did not want to be seen for an appointment later than 9:00 a.m. He felt that a later appointment increased the number of people he might come into physical contact with at the therapy office. He wanted to structure his life so that he saw as few people as possible.

Marsha had just announced her intention to divorce George due to increasing arguments over money and sex. George was devastated, voices were raised, and George decided to move into an apartment in the middle of the night so his friends and neighbors would not see. After months of pain, anger, and aloneness, George met someone

Working with Anger: A Constructivist Approach.
Edited by Peter Cummins. © 2006 John Wiley & Sons, Ltd.

else. As this new relationship developed, he was able to move beyond his anger at Marsha. Eventually, he and Marsha became casual social friends.

Obviously, Kevin, Dave, and George responded to their wives' announcements differently. Our desire for this chapter is to use their varied responses as a platform to talk about anger from an experiential personal construct psychological perspective. Through exploration of this conceptualization, it will become clear that while the *experience* of anger is neither positive nor negative, anger often points to both positive and negative aspects of our process of construing. We also can use anger either constructively or destructively. Finally, we will discuss issues around working with anger in experiential personal construct psychotherapy (EPCP).

EXPERIENTIAL PERSONAL CONSTRUCT PSYCHOLOGY (EPCP)

As previously suggested (Leitner, 1988) from the EPCP point of view, the central struggle in life is one between intimate connection with others, on the one hand, and protection from the terrors of role relationships, on the other. As such, Experiential Personal Construct Psychotherapy engages the person in this struggle. Leitner (1985) defined psychotherapy as an attempt to change pathological ways of organizing experience through the use of the deeply interpersonal relationship between client and therapist. In this way, psychotherapy deals directly with the terror of roles. Psychopathology in EPCP can be thought of as the problematic ways in which one chooses to deal with the core struggle between connection and protection in role relating, and symptoms can be seen as the way in which this struggle is communicated to others (Leitner & Faidley, 1995). Psychological health, on the other hand, or "optimal functioning," involves discrimination, flexibility, responsibility, openness, commitment, courage, forgiveness, and reverence in role relationships (for elaboration on these terms, see Leitner & Pfenninger, 1994).

An Experiential Personal Construct Conceptualization of Anger

Experiential personal constructivism assumes that all experiences can be seen as communications from us to us about us (Leitner, Faidley, & Celentana, 2000). Thus, anger, pain, sadness, hatred, and so on are not "negative" emotions. Rather, they communicate something powerful about our constructions of the world, particularly the frightening and exhilarating world of interpersonal connections.

EPCP holds that, as with all vital and powerful communications, we need to listen to the experience of anger and learn from it. From our perspective, anger can be seen as "A communication about a combination of felt injury and power." As we will see, this definition is slightly different from McCoy's (1977) famous definition in which she described anger as the awareness of invalidation leading to hostility.

Felt injury

Injury is something more than mere invalidation (which can be associated with surprise, irritation, anxiety, pain, etc.). Rather, injury, in addition to invalidation, refers to psychological damage (as opposed to pain, in which disconfirmation is experienced but may not be related to such damage). When injured I have the feeling that something fundamental to who I am as a person has been lost. Injury occurs, then, when my foundation has been invalidated, leading me to wonder if I will ever be stable in the world again. Hostility (trying to force the world to confirm meanings that have been disconfirmed) is a common response to such invalidation (Leitner, 1985).

Thus, as can be seen, our conceptualization of anger so far is consistent with McCoy's (1977) definition. In both views, injurious invalidation often does lead to hostility and anger. However, different from McCoy's view, it is our position also that people can be injured without necessarily experiencing either hostility or anger. Excruciating psychological distress, devastation, and anxiety also may be experienced when injured. (Note: we are not trying to imply that someone will feel only one of these emotions when injured. Often injuries evoke many of these emotions.) Further, anger is not the only emotion in which injury is linked with hostility. People experiencing anxiety, for example, might also very well be hostile in their attempts to hold onto meanings that have been called into question by the world. Rather, in our view, anger seems to involve a specific type of hostility – one associated with felt power.

Felt power

Within experiential personal constructivism, power can be defined as the ability to validate or invalidate the construing process of another (Leitner, Begley, & Faidley, 1996). When angry I am feeling injured by you. Power in anger communicates intolerance for and a rejection of the injury—it says, "I will not be hurt again." This communication, when heard by you, the injuring party, may not only change the way in which you construe yourself but also the way you construe me. At the same time, this communication, when heard by me (from me to me), may change the way I construe myself and the way I construe you.

This felt power experienced as part of anger distinguishes this response from other responses to traumatic events. One response to traumatic events (i.e., events that invalidate our very core) is a "freezing" of the construing process (Leitner, 1999). In these cases, the felt victimization from the event leads to an arrest in construction and an experienced loss of control and ability to continue to evolve and make sense of the world (often called the process of meaning making.) While anger clearly incorporates a feeling of victimization as part of the experience of injury, the sense of power in anger is at the same time a refusal to be a victim. Thus, rather than leading to an arrest in meaning making, the power in anger can lead one to act in ways to minimize the injury by using the experience to continue the process of meaning making and to restore or replace the parts of the core that were lost or damaged in the injury. On the other hand, the power in anger can also lead one to act in a way which does not lead to continued evolution and flexibility in meaning making, but rather results in a hostility that tries to conform the events of the world to fit into the meaning structure that already exists. This sense of power, this kind of refusal to be a victim, often results in injury to others.

From this, then, it can be seen that as the power in anger reflects a felt ability, indeed a right, to act, it also implies choice. With the ability *to* act, also comes the ability *not* to act. In addition, the felt ability to act that comes with power does not imply that there is one correct action to be taken. Rather, one is open to acting in many different ways. This choice, to act in a certain way and not others or to not act at all, contributes to the sense of control experienced in anger. If I have the choice of how to act or not to act, and I have the ability to do both, what I choose to do is up to me. In this sense, although what may have led to my anger was beyond my control, in anger I do have control. In this regard, consider the different choices Kevin and George made in our earlier examples. Each was enraged about his wife's decision to divorce. Kevin chose to "stalk" Joan while George engaged in a process of accepting Marsha's decision.

These examples illustrate not only the choice and control implicit in our definition of anger but also the responsibility that comes with anger. Responsibility as defined by Leitner and Pfenninger (1994) is the willingness to examine one's construct system and its implications for others. Part of the choice in anger is to use the felt sense of power to act in ways that ultimately could lead to an examination and change in one's construct system as well as a change in the constructions of those with whom one has intimate relations. When this choice is made, it acknowledges on some level that as partners in a relationship, we have actively created the meanings between us, we are responsible for this creation and thus for dealing with what we have created (Leitner & Pfenninger, 1994). The other choice in anger is not to act, or to act in such a manner as to impede any examination of one's constructs and how they impact others. This choice denies any responsibility for the creation of the relationship and for dealing with the relationship that has been created. This denial of responsibility ultimately leads to a limited ability to love and be loved as well as to engage the world in a meaningful way. George, for example, responsibly explored his relationship with Marsha as he came to terms with her. Kevin, on the other hand, refused to look at his contributions to the ending of the marriage.

Anger: Positive or Negative?

As should be clear by now, one implication of the EPCP position is that the *experience* of anger is, in and of itself, neither positive nor negative. Rather, it is what the anger communicates to us that can be seen as positive or negative. On the one hand, we can take the experience of anger and learn important things about our meaning making system. As we reflect on the experience, we might learn the ways that anger points to important and positive aspects of our process of meaning creation, those aspects that further our ability to richly engage the world. On the other hand, we might find that the experience of anger reveals aspects of our meaning making process that are most problematic in that they lead us to alienation, aloneness, and meaninglessness.

As stated above, anger, when it results in the ability to see parts of our construction process that allow us to engage the world in a meaningful way, can be viewed in a positive light. For example, to the extent that anger is experienced when constructions that allow us to lead a life filled with relational meaning are invalidated, we may choose to keep these constructions, despite their disconfirmation, and risk the potential for anger or other terrors in the future. Although positive, as the anger is pointing toward aspects of our construing that lead to meaning, this way of dealing with anger can also be seen as hostile in that, rather than changing constructions that have been invalidated, one instead tries to make the world conform to those constructions. However, like anger, there is a way in which hostility can also be viewed as positive or negative (Pfenninger & Klion, 1995).

Positive and negative hostility

George nicely illustrates this principle. Marsha's decision to divorce him led him to question central meanings about himself as a father and a relational partner. In therapy, George was invited to honor his experience of anger and explore its messages to him. He realized that part of loving and investing in another person is giving that other the power to affirm or disconfirm central aspects of your construction of self. In other words, George recognized that his anger was related to the inherent potential to be dislodged from core role constructs that comes with any intimate role relationship. Through this exploration he decided that his faith in his ability to connect with others was stronger than the doubts aroused by the disconfirmation. At this point, just as he was eventually able to risk opening his core to his therapist through the process of EPCP therapy, he also could cautiously and tentatively risk allowing another woman access to his most central personhood – a woman who, like Marsha, would have the ability to validate or invalidate these most central constructions.

In this example, George acted responsibly out of his anger, with a willingness to examine his meaning system and its impact on others, and with an openness to change.

After reflection, George decided that it was "better to fight than switch" (Pfenninger & Klion, 1995), and eventually he was able to risk invalidation of his core in another relationship. To the extent that this leads to meaning and richness in George's life, his hostility can be seen in a positive light.

The difference between hostility that is "good" and hostility that is "bad" is admittedly ambiguous. It takes responsibility, openness and reflection to determine when one's constructions are worth keeping despite previous disconfirmation. However, even these are not fail-safe methods of knowing what choice will lead to meaningfulness. Despite continued disconfirmation and continued reflection, one may decide over and over that certain core constructions are worth fighting for. This type of hostility can be seen as negative in that it is not responded to with validation and results in alienation, aloneness, and meaninglessness. But where is the line to be drawn? In other words, how is one to tell when to keep fighting or when to switch? As there is always the *possibility* for validation or invalidation with any construction, the difficulty comes in that one may never fully know when to hold on or when to give in.

The decision to change from anger rather than be hostile in anger is much clearer if we can recognize when certain constructions are inhibiting us from engaging the world meaningfully. To the extent that the experience of anger is tied to the invalidation of constructions that limit our ability to invest in others, we may need to find the courage to change our meanings. George, once again, illustrates this principle. In part, he was angry because Marsha was pointing out the ways that he could, at times, focus too much on matters like making money as opposed to experientially connecting with his partner. As he wrestled with this issue with his therapist, he had to struggle with constructions of a "good man" as a strong provider. These meanings, at a very low level of awareness, had been created when he was young and very dependent on his father for validation of what a man is. It took a great deal of work to risk fundamentally redefining himself as a "good man," even if he earned less money.

Positive and negative communications about power

As can be seen thus far, anger, though neither positive nor negative in and of itself, tells us both about the positive aspects of our construction process that further meaning making and engagement of the world, as well as the negative aspects that inhibit meaning making and lead to aloneness and meaninglessness. In other words, anger can be thought of as positive or negative in terms of what it communicates to me about myself. One such communication from anger is about power.

Anger and Power

As discussed earlier, one experiential component of anger is a sense of power or a sense of one's ability to validate or invalidate another's construing process. However, as we will develop further here, this sense of power is not only a felt experience, but when heard, can be a powerful communication. If I listen, anger may tell me something positive or negative about my experience of power in the world i.e. my ability to affect and be affected by others in my relationships.

George, for example, felt entitled to a belief that he could affect Marsha's meaning-making process. After all, she had allowed him to love her, giving him such power. In the same way, the injury experienced by George indicates that he had also allowed her to love him by exposing his very core and as such had also given her such power. Not believing that he had such power would have, in some ways, negated and belittled his history of loving her. However, George's experience of anger, including both felt injury and felt power, did not belittle his relationship with Marsha, and instead revealed the reciprocal nature of their role relationship.

On the other hand, Dave's experience with Rachel stands in contrast to George's. Dave's report of his experience contained no anger. A lack of anger can be viewed in two ways: it can imply either a felt sense of injury without the feeling of power, or the experience of neither injury nor power. Both represent serious limitations in the ability to enter into role relationships. Dave's lack of anger represents the first case. Dave's feelings of devastation communicate the injury he experienced at the invalidation of his core. However, his missing sense of power implies that he did not feel he had the right to affect Rachel's process of meaning creation. In other words, while Dave was able to attempt to enter into a role relationship by opening up his core for the possibility of confirmation or disconfirmation by another, at the same time he was not willing to say that a part of who he was could affect the other in the relationship. In this way Dave's lack of anger signalled a serious limitation in his ability to love and be loved by another.

As can be seen in the case above, not being angry sometimes can speak to a part of us that does not feel entitled to make a difference in the world. This part of us, by definition, cannot love another. More severely limiting, however, is the second case of lack of anger: no felt injury and no felt power. This absence of anger reveals a more severe limitation, as I not only do not believe I have the ability or right to affect change in another, but in addition I am not able to open the most central aspects of myself to another. For example, prior to his relationship with Rachel, Dave had been in a long-term relationship with Tina, which also ended with Tina leaving Dave for someone else. However, different from his break-up with Rachel, Dave had virtually no reaction to the split. During their relationship, Dave had not allowed himself to be vulnerable with Tina, thus not allowing her to affect him deeply in life-changing ways. As Dave did not allow Tina access to his core, she had virtually no power to validate or invalidate him, and was therefore unable to injure him in any way. Although Dave had successfully protected himself from injury by not opening up to Tina in meaningful ways, Dave also managed to spend years in an empty, superficial and unfulfilling relationship. As this example shows, by not risking invalidation I am not able to be hurt by another, but in addition, I am not able to love or be loved by another either. This inability to risk my core seriously limits my ability to make meaning in the world.

Far from the lack of power experienced by Dave or the healthy power experienced by George, Kevin's experience of anger points to another problem with power. Kevin's experience of power represents a sense of being so entitled to something that he cannot allow Joan to have her own experience of the world. Kevin's continual invasions and emotional assaults point to a construction of relationship in which his reality is the only one honored. He cannot simultaneously hold his experience as well as understand her separate experience from him. The ability to do so, the ability to blend connection and separation is a hallmark of a deeply intimate role relationship (Leitner, 1985, 2001; Leitner & Faidley, 1995). However, Kevin's tendency to so thoroughly objectify the other person, revealed to him through his anger, pointed to a fundamental struggle preventing him from ever achieving deeply rewarding, intimate, connections.

To this point, we have been speaking of anger in all-or-none terms. However, there are ways that such a discussion is limiting and distorting. For example, Kelly's ([1955] 1991) Fragmentation Corollary describes ways that we are not integrated into a single, coherent self. Rather, each person can be seen as a community of selves (Mair, 1977) relating to each other. For example, none of us, not even Dave, has had a life in which each and every experience shows that we have no effect on the world. Rather, at some level of awareness, he has had experiences that have led to constructions of self as entitled to make a difference (Leitner, 1999). Those constructions would lead to an experience of anger at Rachel. In other words, even as much of Dave's construing of self in the world led to his feeling no anger toward Rachel, other meanings, at a lower level of awareness, held the potential for anger.

One of the tasks for Dave in therapy would be to access the parts of him that do feel able to have an effect on the world, that do experience a sense of power in relationships, and determine whether they can further his ability to engage the world more than the ones he more consciously lives life through. Not doing this leaves him unable to love someone in yet another way: I cannot share who I am with another if I do not allow myself to honestly know me. In other words, ignoring the part of him that is angry dishonors him and leaves him limited. In the therapy relationship, Dave was able to acknowledge the depths of his feelings of love for Rachel. In so doing, Dave and his therapist could explore what it means to love, exploring many of the issues we are discussing here. Honoring his experience of love meant that he had to recognize that Rachel once had loved him. As he realized this, he began to acknowledge that, as a part of her loving him, he had been capable of impacting her. This aspect of his construction of his relationship with her led to his experience of anger at the ending of the marriage.

DEGREES OF ANGER

Dave's experience clearly illustrates that anger is not all-or-none in that parts of me may not have the experience of anger at the same time that other parts of me may feel angry. Anger is also not an all-or-none experience in another way. In the discussion thus far we have talked about anger as present or not present, but this does not fully capture the experiential nature of anger, as often it is not that we are just angry or we are not angry, but instead we experience different degrees of anger.

Anger and Injury

Based on our definition of anger as felt injury and felt power, varied degrees of anger can be understood in terms of varied degrees of injury. In other words, the severity of the injury or the degree to which the injury reaches my very core impacts the extent of the damage that is done and affects the intensity of the anger I feel. As my core represents my most fundamental meanings upon which my entire meaning-making structure is built, the closer to my core the injury, the greater the impact on my system as a whole, and the greater the felt injury. (Note: Many construct therapists may use laddering procedures to clarify these meanings, as those meanings that are closer to one's core may be the more superordinate meanings reached using this technique.) Although still damaging, injury that strikes an aspect of my meaning-making system further from my core may not be able to reach my most fundamental meanings and thus may not have the same power to damage me in such an extensive way. As such, the anger experienced with this type of injury may not be as intense.

Constructive and Destructive Anger

So far, we have focused on defining anger within EPCP as well as looking at the ways anger can point to more positive or more negative aspects of our meaning-making system. However, there also is the question of what do we *do* with anger. Do we use our anger to further the rich fabric of connections we have with others in our world? Or do we use our anger to shred this fabric, leaving us more alone, empty, and embittered? To the extent that anger is used to further connections, we can call the anger *constructive anger*; to the extent our anger is used to isolate us and leave us empty, we can call the anger *destructive anger*.

A beginning overview

The distinction between anger pointing to positive or negative aspects of our construction process versus the constructive or destructive use of anger in our actions is somewhat arbitrary and forced. It seems obvious that if our actions are based upon our constructions, actions that are destructive to relational connections can be seen as tied to constructions that are more problematic. However, the relationship between constructions and action is not quite so simple. To elaborate on this complexity, we will use the distinction, despite its arbitrariness, for three reasons. First, all constructions divide the flow of experiential reality into somewhat arbitrary chunks. Thus, the issue is not whether we have arbitrarily separated experience by using this construction. Rather, the issue is whether this construction can point to useful ways of understanding anger.

Second, the distinction can be used to point to differing aspects of our meaning-making system. Looking at constructive versus destructive uses of anger focuses us more on constructions around *actions* based upon our emotions. As we shall see, I may have more problematic construings of self-in-the-world that I use in more constructive ways or I could have more positive construings that I use more destructively.

Finally, by making this distinction between feelings and actions, focusing on constructive versus destructive *uses* of anger also allows us to keep the entire issue of choice and responsibility more clearly in mind. In this regard, there are many people who have such literalistic constructions of the linkage between feelings and actions that they feel they have no choice but to respond in impulsive and destructive ways (Anderson & Leitner, 1996; Landfield, 1980; Leitner, 1981a, 1981b, 1982). Helping such clients distinguish between the feeling and the action can be a vital aspect of therapy. For example, Kevin would instantly have to break into Joan's apartment when he felt angry. Kevin *had* to instantly and aggressively act on his anger. Part of Kevin's therapy involved him accessing his anger. His therapist then would have Kevin just sit with the anger and do nothing other than pay attention to it. After he had focused on it for several minutes, Kevin and his therapist could elaborate on choices he had over his anger. He could, for example, continue to break into Joan's apartment and express his anger while dishonoring other values he had. Alternatively, Kevin eventually was able to decide to use his anger to elaborate his ways of understanding self and others that allowed for his happiness despite Joan's decision to leave him.

On the other hand, there are clients whose linkages between affect and action are so fragmented that they cannot use their feelings interpersonally in any way. They can feel enraged, for example, without any behavioral expression of that anger. This stance clouds, if not denies the issues of choice and responsibility inherent in anger. Aspects of Dave's experience illustrate this fragmenting of anger and action. Feelings of anger would come and go, with Dave unable to express them in any overt way. Helpless and powerless to do anything with his anger, Dave eventually tried to end his life. Dave's therapy involved extensive exploration of why he could never act upon his anger when he was able to act on other emotions. This led to Dave's experiences of overwhelming terror (Leitner, 1987, 1988) at his father's violent outbursts and the ways he had literally and psychologically "frozen" in response to these attacks (Leitner, Faidley, & Celentana, 2000).

Constructive Uses of Anger

As mentioned earlier, anger that is used to increase one's sense of relational connection can be seen as constructive. For example, Suzanna, Kevin's daughter, was angry at her father for drinking too much at a family gathering. She confronted her father by saying that, as she had reflected on what he did, she had become aware that she was angry because, when he acted like that, others did not see his finer qualities. This confrontation allowed Kevin to simultaneously see the pain and disappointment his drinking caused his daughter as well as that she was so hurt because she cared for him. Kevin responded to Suzanna's distress by agreeing that he drank too much, apologizing for the pain it caused her, and committing himself to controlling his drinking at social events when his children were present.

Anger tied to more negative, problematic, constructions also can be used constructively. For example, Kevin eventually was able to look at the ways his anger at Joan was linked to constructions of her as an object without her own subjective experience of the world. As he saw the ways these meanings limited his ability to connect with others, he was able to find the courage to elaborate ways of understanding self and others that allowed for more richness and mutual respect. Interestingly, when he applied these newer meanings to his former relationship with Joan, Kevin, now acting out of his current core role structure, felt extremely guilty. Importantly, Kevin now recognized that he had a choice, early on, to learn from his anger and change his more problematic constructions. In other words, he did not have to do the terrible things he did to Joan just because the anger was based upon more problematic constructions. In this way, Kevin was able to learn from what his anger communicated to him about the negative aspects of his construing and about the choice inherent in anger, leading to his newfound ability to enter into more meaningful relationships.

Destructive Use of Anger

Anger, whether based on more positive or more negative aspects of meaning making, also can be used destructively. Kevin used his anger at Joan quite destructively when he was breaking into her apartment and alienating their kids from her. His choice to use his anger in that way injured both Joan and their children. Because Kevin has been so interconnected with these people, damaging them also damages him.

Dave also used anger in a destructive way. His withdrawal and fear of trusting others were tied to a blanket assumption that others can arbitrarily betray and destroy you. Further, as discussed earlier, his focus on being devastated and withdrawing from others dishonors the part of him that is angry. His refusal to openly acknowledge the part of him that is angry prevents him from exploring the ways he might be using the anger in destructive as opposed to constructive ways. Until he could find the courage to access his angry side and explore what it is saying to him, Dave continued to lead a life filled with fear and aloneness. In other words, his refusal to explore his anger is a destructive use of anger.

As we discussed earlier, George's anger was linked to important constructions that facilitated role relationships. However, George also used this more positively-based anger destructively at times. For example, his decision to move out of the house in the middle of the night furthered his sense of alienation and isolation. This decision was based on constructions that, if his friends knew what was happening, they would not accept him. He would be blamed and rejected, and they would take Marsha's side. In other words, while his anger at Marsha was based upon more positive relational constructions being injured, the anger, once experienced, linked to constructions that had more problematic implications for role relationships.

SUMMARY

To this point, we have suggested that, within experiential personal construct psychology, anger is a combination of both felt injury and power that serves as a powerful communication about many aspects of one's lived experience. Anger and its communications can be an indication of the invalidation of important constructs linking us to the rich world of interpersonal connections, important constructions preventing us from living in the world as richly as we could, or, more likely, both. In addition, once we experience anger, we can use it either to facilitate or destroy interpersonal connections. We turn now to using this understanding in therapy.

ANGER AND THERAPY

Experiential personal construct psychotherapy engages the client in the dilemma of fundamentally connecting with others (leading to a life of richness and meaningfulness yet filled with potential terror) and retreating from such intimacy (leading to a life that is safe yet empty). In so doing, the EPCP therapist rarely sets specific time restrictions. Dave, for example, was seen several times per week for several years. Kevin and George were seen weekly for less than a year. While all client experiences can be useful in exploring the client's relational struggles, those that are particularly intense often point to the most profound issues. Anger, being an intense emotion, is of particular interest to the psychotherapist.

Therapist Comfort with Anger

Therapists who are not comfortable with intense affect, including anger, will not be of much help to their clients within experiential personal construct therapy. If I am too frightened, my own fears are more salient than your experience, leading to a therapeutic relationship in which I am not optimally distant (Leitner, 1995). If I cannot experience your anger intensely while recognizing that it is your anger, not mine, you will not be able to fundamentally grow in the area of life the anger is pointing you toward. After all, a role relationship, so central to life and growth, involves both connection and the separation. If I am too caught up in my own issues with anger, I may experience the rage so intensely that it is my emotion more than my therapeutically experiencing yours. On the other hand, if I am too conflicted about anger, I may be so distant and intellectual that there can be little connection in the therapy relationship. I may opt for problem-solving, rational thinking lectures, and other techniques to help you avoid the intense passion your anger is pointing you toward. Therefore, a fundamental requirement for a good experiential personal construct psychotherapist is that he or she be comfortable with intense, often angry, emotions.

This requirement is particularly important with more severe disturbances. Anger is tied to felt injury, as described earlier, and people who receive more severe diagnosis have been subjected to more extensive injuries than those of us less severely diagnosed (Bannister, 1962; Leitner & Celentana, 1997). Obviously, then, people who are seriously disturbed will have experiences of much greater anger. A therapist who is not able to tolerate and connect with intense anger might as well refer the severely disturbed client for chemicals, shocks, or other brain-damaging "treatments."

Student therapists' inability to tolerate intense emotion is the major reasons I (LML) recommend they seek therapy themselves in terms of their growth as therapists. Once the therapist can embrace intense affects, he or she can utilize the client's anger as a creative opportunity in therapy. We only will describe a couple of techniques for doing this as we believe therapists must use their own subjectivity to spontaneously create a connection within the rage, rather than relying on "techniques."

Becoming friends with anger

This is a useful approach for clients who are scared to touch their anger because of the threatening implications it has for them. The therapist, in the safety of the therapy room, helps the client listen to the anger in ways not possible in the real world. Clients who are visual may see the anger as a particular type of object. They can use that object in the therapy room and engage it in a dialogue. The therapist can listen to the dialogue and point out the ways that the anger is informing them of something, not trying to totally define them as a human being. For example, Dave initially had great difficulty accessing the parts of him that were angry because, for him, the angry emotion and the destructive actions his father committed in anger were virtually inseparable. It was intolerable for Dave to view himself as angry, as that meant for him that he would inevitably be violent like his father. To help Dave begin to see the emotion as both separate from the action and as a part but not the whole of himself, the therapist suggested that Dave imagine his anger as a figure or character of some sort. Out of a collection of sand tray objects in the room, Dave chose a large blue monster with a red head with horns to represent his anger. The therapist invited Dave to dialogue with the monster, and he began to ask questions of it in an effort to understand the purpose and meaning of his anger. As he continued to do this over the course of therapy, he began to own some of his angry feelings without feeling defined by them or doomed to violent action.

Other clients may experience the anger more somatically and can let their bodily feelings lead them to issues associated with injury. Dave again illustrates this point. As he came to allow his angry feelings to be a more integral part of his lived experience, Dave began to notice the various bodily sensations that served as signals of his anger. He explained to his therapist that he felt "weird" at these times but could not describe the sensation. To help him access this experience in the room, the therapist invited Dave to demonstrate with his body the feeling that he gets when he is angry. In response to this, Dave slumped his shoulders and hung his head. The therapist then mirrored Dave's posture. There was a palpable sadness in the room, as the therapist sat with this posture. After sitting in this position for a few moments, the therapist asked Dave what he was experiencing while in the position. Dave was able to speak to the intense sadness and loneliness he was feeling along with memories of past abandonments. This opened the door to much fruitful exploration of the connection between anger and abandonment for Dave and ultimately to his fundamental lack of self-worth.

Destructive/constructive anger

Like Dave, often clients who literally equate anger with poisonous and destructive acts need to work on separating the experience of anger from what they do with that experience. Alert therapists can seize opportunities to help this separation. For example, when Kevin, a history buff, equated anger with Nazi atrocities, his therapist invited him to reflect on who was angrier: Hitler who used his rage to almost destroy the world, or Roosevelt and Churchill who used their rage to save a world. George, on the other hand, had come of age in the 1960s. When his equating of anger with evil came up, his therapist invited him to sort out whether Charles Manson, whose rage led to horrible murders, was angrier than Martin Luther King, whose rage touched the conscience of a nation. While these were useful, the best way to experience the difference between constructive and destructive anger is in the actual live relationship in the therapy room. For example, Kevin's therapist became angry when Kevin "forgot" a session. The therapist shared the experience with Kevin, who became quite terrified. Extensive work on this issue allowed Kevin to experience his therapist's anger as constructive as it was tied, in part, to the therapist's caring for Kevin's personal well-being.

Anger and choice

Focusing on the issue of choice often is helpful for those who tend to "act out" their anger. For example, Kevin's therapist would ask him why he chose to do the things he did to Joan. Kevin would talk about being so enraged that he could not help himself. This led to explorations about what it said about him that he could not choose to express his anger in any other way. Eventually, Kevin could see that his violent expressions were tied to very deep wounds and vulnerabilities – wounds he could not let himself clearly see as they contradicted core constructions of a man being strong and unafraid. This led the discussion into the ways he was trying to hurt Joan because he was afraid. Eventually, as he became more comfortable with pain and fear, he was able to stop behaving so destructively to her. He started to use the experience of anger as a communication to him that he was frightened and hurting.

Forgiveness

Forgiveness, the reconstruing of self and other such that past injuries do not prevent you from future intimacies (Leitner & Pfenninger, 1994), is a central part of dealing with anger. Forgiveness is the ability to construe the less honorable things we have done or have been done to us such that we can let ourselves and others off the hook for being scared, vulnerable, and human. However, forgiveness cannot be rushed. Prior to forgiveness, we must thoroughly and experientially grasp all the ways we have injured/been injured by the other. Only at that point do we even know what we are forgiving.

Forgiveness often arises spontaneously as we heal from the injuries our anger points us toward. Therapists are wise to wait for it to come up from the client in the therapy session. This can be a powerful communication that the client is ready to be done with this past injury. At this point, with a visual client, for example, one can help the client visualize either self or other and saying, "I forgive you." Or, have the client take the anger and bitterness, place it in a sack, and put it in a drawer. They then can leave it but are free to retrieve it if necessary. With less visual and concrete clients, the therapist may have to help the client arrange situations where she or he can act on forgiveness. For example, Kevin asked Joan to come into a therapy session with him so that he could tell her what he had learned and ask for her forgiveness.

SOME FINAL THOUGHTS

In summary, we hope that it is clear how from the experiential personal construct point of view the experience of anger can be seen as a combination of both felt injury and felt power and as a communication to me, from me, about me. We hope that it is also now clear how anger is in and of itself neither positive nor negative, neither constructive nor destructive. However, anger as we have shown, can *point* to positive and negative aspects of our meaning making and can be *used* in both constructive and destructive ways. In other words, anger can lead to both a deepening of role relationships and meaninglessness and aloneness depending on what the anger reveals and how its message is used. In this, as with all of our most deeply human experiences, all of us must courageously and openly wrestle with using our experience to learn more about the personal truths we have staked our lives on.

REFERENCES

Anderson, T. & Leitner, L. M. (1996). Symptomatology and the use of affect constructs to influence value and behaviour constructs. *Journal of Counseling Psychology, 43*, 77–83.

Bannister, D. (1962). The nature and measurement of schizophrenic thought disorder. *Journal of Mental Science, 108*, 825–842.

Kelly, G. A. ([1955] 1991). *The Psychology of Personal Constructs* (vols 1 and 2). London: Routledge.

Landfield, A. W. (1980). The person as perspectivist, literalist, and chaotic fragmentalist. In A. W. Landfield & L. M. Leitner (eds), *Personal Construct Psychology: Psychotherapy and Personality*. New York: Wiley Interscience, pp. 289–320.

Leitner, L. M. (1981a). Construct validity of a repertory grid measure of personality styles. *Journal of Personality Assessment, 45*, 539–544.

Leitner, L. M. (1981b). Psychopathology and the differentiation of values, emotions, and behaviors: a repertory grid study. *British Journal of Psychiatry, 138*, 147–153.

Leitner, L. M. (1982). Literalism, perspectivism, chaotic fragmentalism, and psychotherapy techniques. *British Journal of Medical Psychology, 55*, 307–317.

Leitner, L. M. (1985). The terrors of cognition: on the experiential validity of personal construct theory. In D. Bannister (ed.), *Issues and Approaches in Personal Construct Theory*. London: Academic Press, pp. 83–103.

Leitner, L. M. (1987). Crisis of the self: the terror of personal evolution. In G. Neimeyer & R. Neimeyer (eds), *Personal Construct Therapy Casebook*. New York: Springer, pp. 39–56.

Leitner, L. M. (1988). Terror, risk, and reverence: experiential personal construct psychotherapy. *International Journal of Personal Construct Psychology, 1*, 261–272.

Leitner, L. M. (1995). Optimal therapeutic distance: a therapist's experience of personal construct psychotherapy. In R. Neimeyer & M. Mahoney (eds), *Constructivism in Psychotherapy*. Washington, DC: American Psychological Association, pp. 357–370.

Leitner, L. M. (1999). Levels of awareness in experiential personal construct psychotherapy. *Journal of Constructivist Psychology, 12*, 239–252.

Leitner, L. M. (2001). The role of awe in experiential personal construct psychology. *The Psychotherapy Patient, 11*, (3,4), 149–162.

Leitner, L. M., Begley, E. A., & Faidley, A. J. (1996). Sociality, commonality, individuality, and mutuality: a personal construct approach to non-dominant groups. In D. Kalekin-Fishman & B. Walker (eds), *The Construction of Group Realities: Culture, Society and Personal Construct Theory*. Melbourne, FL: Krieger, pp. 323–340.

Leitner, L. M. & Celentana, M. A. (1997). Constructivist therapy with serious disturbances. *The Humanistic Psychologist, 25*, 271–285.

Leitner, L. M. & Faidley, A. J. (1995). The awful, aweful nature of ROLE relationships. In G. Neimeyer & R. Neimeyer (eds), *Advances in Personal Construct Psychology: vol. 3*. Greenwich, CT: JAI, pp. 291–314.

Leitner, L. M., Faidley, A. J. & Celentana, M. A. (2000). Diagnosing human meaning making: an experiential constructivist approach. In R. Neimeyer & J. Raskin (eds), *Construction of Disorders: Meaning Making Frameworks for Psychotherapy*. Washington, DC: American Psychological Association, pp. 175–203.

Leitner, L. M. & Pfenninger, D. T. (1994). Sociality and optimal functioning. *Journal of Constructivist Psychology*, 7, 119–135.

Mair, J. M. M. (1977). The community of self. In D. Bannister (ed.), *New Perspectives in Personal Construct Theory*. London: Academic Press, pp. 125–149.

McCoy, M. (1977). A reconstruction of emotion. In D. Bannister (ed.), *New Perspectives in Personal Construct Theory*. London: Academic Press, pp. 93–124.

Pfenninger, D. T. & Klion, R. E. (1995). Re-thinking hostility: Is it ever better to fight than switch? In R. Neimeyer & G. Neimeyer (eds), *Advances in Personal Construct Psychology: vol. 3*. Greenwich, CT: JAI, pp. 271–289.

6

WORKING WITH ANGRY CHILDREN

Heather Moran

INTRODUCTION

Recent years have seen an increased awareness of the need for services for children and adolescents with emotional and behavioural difficulties, and an emphasis upon the need for statutory and voluntary agencies to work together, to address the problems of their communities (Wallace, Crown, Berger & Cox, 1997). A particular concern has been those children who fail to control their aggressive behaviour, a pattern observed more often in boys than girls (Buntaine & Costenbader, 1997; Hubbard, 2001). These children are vulnerable to exclusion from school and family life and then are more likely to become involved with anti-social behaviour and crime (Denham, Blair, Schmidt & DeMulder, 2002). Problems with anger can be part of a mood disorder in those children who are also vulnerable to anxiety and perfectionism (Hewitt, Caelian, Flett, Collins & Flynn, 2002). It has also been noted that children with anger problems are four times more likely to experience a depressive episode in young adulthood (Mason et al., 2004). There is clearly a need to find treatments, which reduce the intensity and frequency of angry aggressive outbursts in childhood, and thus avoid these poor social and emotional outcomes.

Services involved with children are developing strategies to encourage greater self-management of angry feelings by children and research confirms that this can be successful (Valliant, Jensen & Raven-Brook, 1995; Flay et al., 2004). This chapter will consider some issues which are particularly relevant for working with children who show very angry behaviour. It will also present the case of a 12-year-old with

Working with Anger: A Constructivist Approach.
Edited by Peter Cummins. © 2006 John Wiley & Sons, Ltd.

an extreme anger problem and describe a Personal Construct Psychology technique, which was used to understand his view of the problem.

ISSUES FOR WORKING WITH CHILDREN WITH ANGER PROBLEMS

Definition of the Problem

The first issue is the definition of the problem. In the case of children, parents and teachers generally make this definition of the 'anger problem'. Adults determine the point at which help is requested and, in almost all cases, children are referred to services using those adults' description of the problem. The decision to make a referral implies that the anger problem cannot be addressed by other people changing or by manipulating the environment, and suggests that the problem is likely to respond to some sort of treatment.

Consent to Referral

Children may be asked if they agree to the referral but they may not be in a position to give true consent. They are unlikely to be aware that their agreement implies *they* will be required to engage with treatment, rather than their parents or teachers. Children are unlikely to realise that the requested treatment will be an attempt to change something about them, rather than to address their circumstances.

In a clinic setting, it is tempting to take the referral at face value, accepting the parent's and/or teacher's reports of angry behaviour and setting up 'anger management' for the child. This means that children may well be offered treatments, which they do not engage with because they do not share the definition or view of the problem. My own experience of children attending anger management groups within a children's mental health service is that children attend sessions because their parents bring them to appointments, but they rarely change their behaviour in the longer term. One of the features of group and individual work has been that children have often reported factors outside their control, which contributed significantly to their anger. They could also be angry and difficult in group sessions, displaying the very behaviour they were referred for. It was for these reasons (problem definition, consent and engagement) that 'anger management' was abandoned within the service. We therefore decided to try a different approach.

GROUP WORK WITH CHILDREN'S ANGER PROBLEMS USING A PERSONAL CONSTRUCT APPROACH

I have been involved in an experimental group, which tried to address these issues of problem definition and consent, for children aged 11–16 years. The emphasis was changed from treatment to assessment: we would provide two group sessions within which we would aim to provide an understanding of the child's problems within the context of his/her family relationships and try to determine the most appropriate therapy for that family. The group was called 'Anger in Relationships', and involved parents attending two group sessions at the same time as their child's group sessions. The protocol was that the decision to refer to the group was discussed with the child and the family; and the children were only referred if there was parental agreement to engage in the groups alongside their child. Immediately, this reduced the number of referrals (even though this was the only specifically anger-related treatment on offer at that time) and the group was made up of five families. Two families had single parents.

The sessions with parents looked at the temperaments of all family members and the way they interacted. It obtained a detailed picture of the nature of the child's anger problems, the way the individuals in the family managed their angry feelings, and the way parents managed their child's angry behaviour. It explored theories the parents had developed which accounted for their child's problems. Parents completed the Parenting Stress Index (Abidin, 1995), which is made up of two main subscales: one focusing on within-child factors (e.g. being difficult to relate to) and one focusing on parental factors (e.g. money worries, marital problems). The parental group sessions indicated that the 'problem' child was often viewed as being very different from their siblings and was also seen as the cause of problems within family and marital relationships. Attachment to the child was often reported as a problem, both as a within-child factor (with the child not attaching well to parents) and as a parental factor (parents feeling that they had not attached well to their child). Parents reported that they had generally tried a wide range of strategies yet the problems had persisted and worsened as the child grew up.

The children's group looked at descriptions of family and relationships and issues around self and their relationship with their 'anger problem'. The aim was to ascertain the child's view of their problem, and whether they would be likely to respond to treatment for an anger problem. Interestingly, some youngsters drew attention to their feeling that they needed their anger and would be very unlikely to change their behaviour. Others pointed out that their parents had similar problems with anger. Some children expressed feelings of siblings being favoured over them, which contributed to them feeling angry.

The staff running the two groups met to compare views and to consider the best options for treatment for each family, in the light of the assessment. It became clear that there was a need for family-based treatments in most cases. These options were discussed with the family at a feedback appointment and if both parties were willing to try this, recommendations were made to refer to the family therapy service. There was the option of a further treatment group for the children, but the two children who wanted to opt in were not supported by their parents (who wanted them to have individual therapy).

The issues of Guilt and Threat were very apparent in parents in the group. They struggled with the idea that they could have produced such a different and difficult child and often felt completely invalidated in their role as parent. Hostility (in the Kellyan sense) was evident in the parents' request for treatment for their child, but refusal to support their children's attendance at a group. In other cases, there was a realisation that what they had been looking for (treatment for their child) and what they needed (treatment for their family) were different.

It is interesting that internal referrals for anger management have reduced massively as a result of the group and the feedback to referrers. The reaction of referrers has generally been positive, with the information being seen as enlightening or as confirming their view that the child should not be treated separately from the family. Where feedback has been less positive, it was in cases where many other treatments had already been offered and had failed. This seems to suggest that the referring professional's sense of effectiveness was being invalidated by not being able to find a treatment which worked.

WORKING FROM A CHILD'S PERSONAL VIEWPOINT

Working with children using a Personal Construct approach is not necessarily easy: children are generally taught to agree with adults in authority, whatever their own feelings and personal views. Part of adjustment to a school environment requires acceptance that the teacher's views are somehow 'more right', or for the child to develop the ability to pretend they agree with the teacher without feeling too threatened. Children who express opposing views in words are quickly in trouble in school. Those who, because they lack the words, tend to 'act it out', are likely to be excluded.

The credulous Personal Construct approach can seem very strange to many children and one can almost feel their surprise at being asked for their theories about their circumstances. It is important that professionals working with children use techniques which facilitate their expression. Children may find that they can 'say' more when talking is supported by drawing and clay work, using objects or acting. The following case study used an approach called Drawing the Ideal Self (Moran, 2001), which is a structured drawing and writing task to elicit and elaborate constructs (see Appendix). This technique can be used to evaluate self-esteem and is suitable for use with any age of client (although its development was for work with children). It promotes the idea of partnership with the child through a joint task, and helps the child to express ambitions for his/her future development.

Matt was a 12-year-old boy who has Autistic Spectrum Disorder (ASD). He had always struggled with social relationships and had never had any lasting friendships. Although his autism would be described as mild in the sense that he had few very unusual behaviours, Matt had always had extreme difficulty seeing things from any other view point than his own, and adapting his behaviour according to social situations.

Under pressure, Matt lacked proficiency with words but showed his construing fairly clearly through his behaviour. When he was calm and away from anxiety-provoking situations, he was able to express his views clearly enough using appropriate vocabulary and very fluent speech.

When he had moved to secondary school, Matt failed very quickly, resulting in a referral back to the child and adolescent mental health service in his first term, with the suggestion that he could not manage a mainstream school situation. One of the school's concerns was that he did not seem to be like other children with ASD because he seemed to deliberately annoy teachers. The concerns at school were focused on his angry outbursts, which could become violent, destroying school property and kicking staff. He would flare with anger in lessons at the slightest provocation and sometimes with what seemed to be no provocation at all. He would run away from anyone who tried to reprimand him, whatever his or her status in the school. Matt would shout, scream and swear at anyone who corrected his behaviour, and sometimes at teachers who merely tried to help him with his work. He was sent out of lessons very frequently, to the 'on call' manager who would talk calmly to him about what had happened. Matt had been excluded from school and was under threat of further exclusions if things did not change quickly. His family were distressed by his problems but felt powerless to change things because, perhaps surprisingly, there were no similar problems at home. A meeting was arranged in school for the end of term, with the aim of all agencies involved to produce a co-ordinated plan to support Matt. The meeting was to involve his parents, the educational psychologist, the autism support service specialist teacher, the learning support co-ordinator, the behaviour support service specialist teacher, his year head and myself. In the meantime, an assessment was begun into exactly what Matt thought his problems were.

Matt presented as a very polite and smart youngster. He was small but wore his school uniform with some style and had a very fashionable appearance. One would not have suspected that he had ASD from his physical presentation and this certainly made him vulnerable because people at school would be unlikely to make allowances for him immediately and would be liable to easily forget that he had a disability. The most obvious feature of his social communication problem was his very poor eye contact. Matt told me that when teachers told him to look at them, he would say, 'I don't do eye contact', which usually resulted in a reprimand for cheekiness and this would prompt an explosion of anger on his part. He did not explain that eye contact made him feel uncomfortable and distracted him from listening to them. He was very definite that he wanted help and that he was willing to try to change things. He was worried about his future at school if things did not improve.

Matt and I worked together to produce two pictures using a variation on the Drawing the Ideal Self technique. The instructions for this technique may be found in the Appendix. This involves a step-by-step production of a coherent picture of 'The kind of person I would not like to be like'. The picture emerges gradually, with the child providing the drawings, and the therapist writing the child's descriptions. This is important: it is a joint enterprise and keeps the child's attention focused. It also avoids literacy problems interfering with the process and encourages the child to say more (rather than only writing words he/she can spell easily).

In Matt's case, we produced a drawing of 'the kind of person who always gets angry' (Figure 6.1), and then of 'the kind of person who never gets angry' (Figure 6.2). In Matt's picture, 'the kind of person who always gets angry' is seen as someone who is 'just an angry person' who 'never calms down'. He fails in his schoolwork, shouts at his teachers, hits other children and shouts at his parents. His greatest fear is of being threatened by someone bigger and angrier. This person became angry 'because of the teachers – they picked on him'. His future looked dismal: 'he ain't going to get a job, living on the streets'.

In contrast, (Figure 6.2) 'the kind of person who never gets angry' is 'happy', gets 'good grades' and is the 'brightest boy in the class'. This boy is very successful in his schoolwork and he gets on well with teachers: 'doesn't get picked on', is 'friends with them' and 'likes school'. He also gets on well with his family: he will 'hug them because they are exactly alike and he looks like them'. His greatest fear is snakes. He does have a problem with other children though, because he 'gets picked on by popular people'. This boy has a history of academic success because he 'got good grades since nursery and then got even better'. His future is rosy: he will 'get a good job and get paid a lot of money' and 'have three children and get married'.

Looking at Matt's pictures it was interesting that he did notice facial expressions, even though he had poor eye contact. As we discussed the pictures and moved on to complete his rating scale, it became clear that his physical size was very relevant to his problems. Matt was highly aware of his small size and thought he was the smallest person in his school. Looking closely at his pictures, the angry boy is bigger in relation to other children. Importantly, Matt thinks he risks being bullied if he stops being so angry. Realistically, being small with very few friends in school would make him more vulnerable to bullying than most children.

A rating scale was useful as a means of measuring perceived progress, with Matt rating himself along the construct between the two elaborated poles of 'always gets angry' to 'never gets angry'. The same scale was used to re-rate at further appointments. Matt's rating scale is shown in Figure 6.3 with Matt's initial rating and later ratings on the same page. The initial ratings indicated that Matt saw himself as being very different from his ideal self. He was also something of a perfectionist and would not settle for less than his ideal. At a glance, one can see that there is a huge gap between the way Matt saw himself and the way he wanted to be. His assessment of himself was very consistent with the reports of his teachers (see first rating on 17 February 2004).

However, Matt's teachers seemed to be unaware of his positive ambitions, of the degree of difficulty he had making relationships and of the fact that he felt pretty

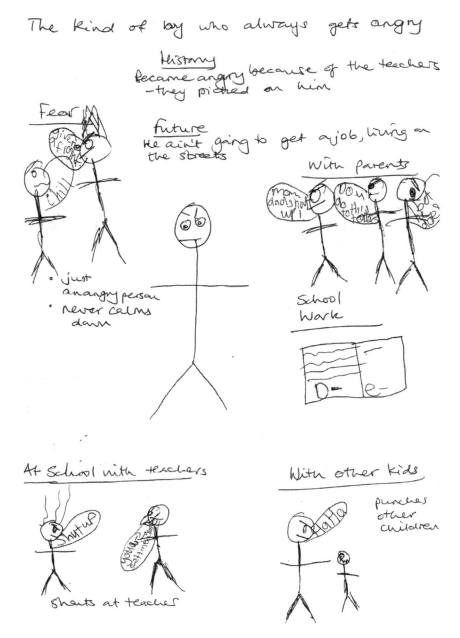

Figure 6.1 The kind of boy who always gets angry

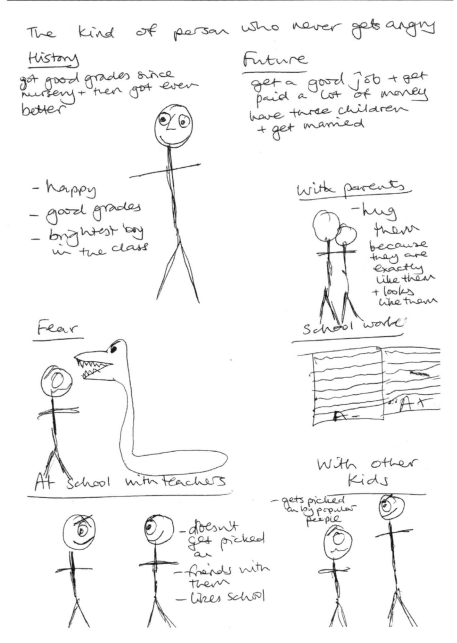

The kind of person who never gets angry

History
got good grades since nursery + then got even better

Future
get a good job + get paid a lot of money
have three children + get married

- happy
- good grades
- brightest boy in the class

With parents
- hug them because they are exactly like them + looks like them

Fear

School work

At School with teachers

With other kids
- gets picked on by popular people

- doesn't get picked on
- friends with them
- likes school

Figure 6.2   The kind of person who never gets angry

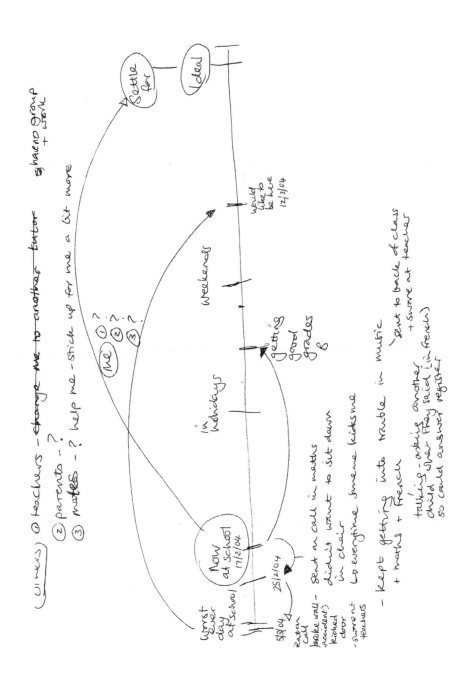

Figure 6.3 Matt's rating scale

helpless to change things. Matt was unable to think of anything at all which he could do to help him move towards being the kind of boy who did not get angry. He also struggled to think of what teachers could do to help him. He eventually suggested that teachers should allow him to move out of his tutor group, initially suggesting that he moved to another group, then changing his mind to having no tutor group at all and registering and working in the learning support room. Matt could not think of any way his parents could help him. He thought his friends might help him by sticking up for him more.

Matt was invited to explore his refusal to stay in a lesson once he had been in trouble with the teacher. His ladder (Figure 6.4) explains that his extreme behaviour is an attempt to stick up for himself and be more like other children. Matt preferred to leave

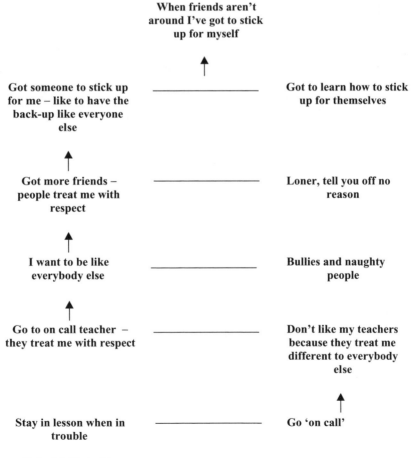

Figure 6.4 Matt's ladder

the room and go to the 'on call' teacher because they 'treat me with respect' (rather than 'treat me different to everybody else'). Matt preferred this because he wanted 'to be like everybody else' (rather than being like 'bullies and naughty people'). He thought that being like other people would mean he would get 'more friends – people treat me with respect' (rather than being a 'loner' and having others 'tell you off for no reason'. Matt wanted more friends so that he had 'got someone to stick up for me – like to have the back-up like everyone else does' (rather than being like people who had to 'learn to stick up for themselves'). Matt could not decide which he preferred of these two options (to stick up for himself vs. someone to stick up for him) and was determined that he needed to take a middle position because 'when friends aren't around, I've got to stick up for myself'.

It was clear that Matt felt threatened in school and that he had recognised that the difference between him and other children related to his friendship skills. Matt explained that he felt that his size was the root of the problem: he was small and therefore at risk. He knew his brother was sociable and had friends and felt that this was because he was much bigger than Matt (he was two years older). At home, Matt did not feel so threatened by the fact that he was small because he had a smaller (and younger) sister. He said he felt as if he were shrinking as he left home to go to school. This began once he met up with other children. Matt drew pictures of the actual size he thought he was, and the size he felt compared with other children, teachers and friends (Figure 6.5). These pictures clearly illustrate how very small he felt compared with other children and teachers. He also underestimated his actual height. Matt felt closer in height to his friends, suggesting that how tall he felt was related to feeling comfortable with people. He talked about strategies he used to 'act tall' when he walked near other

Figure 6.5 Matt's feelings about his height

children: 'stick head up', 'walk past them', 'walk with heels up' (on tiptoes) and 'walk quickly'. In a secondary school of approximately 1,000 pupils and with almost no friends, maintaining this must have been difficult.

After this point, our work was discussed with Matt and his mother with a view to providing a report for the school and other professionals to consider before our meeting. At the meeting, considerable surprise was expressed at the difference between what the teachers had thought Matt was doing (being deliberately disruptive to upset teachers) and his construing of the situation and of the causes of his problems. His behaviour had deteriorated further and he was in grave danger of exclusion or a recommendation being made for special schooling. A plan was drawn up to provide for Matt's poor friendship skills, his lack of construing of degrees of anger (e.g. irritated, annoyed, furious), his desire to limit his contact with other people, his complete helplessness in addressing the problems himself and the nature of feedback from school to home. He was allowed to register in the learning support room and this was to be his bolthole if he needed to be out of a lesson or to avoid playtimes and lunch breaks. There were other vulnerable children registering in this way and their day began peacefully in a small unstructured group situation. This reduced the number of people he needed to relate to and gave better chance of success because it was closely supervised. A very simple behaviour recording system was set up with a reward of a chocolate bar for good reports (teachers recorded praise and acceptable behaviour). His year head (one of the regular on-call teachers) was to see Matt to reward or praise him but not to be involved in any criticism or sanctions and would write positive reports home on an intermittent basis. My own involvement was to work with Matt on his construing of anger, trying to increase his constructs to include lesser degrees of anger, and to help him to recognise them in others. This was through a combination of using computer software with video clips, audio clips and example causes of various anger-related emotions. These were then related to real-life situations, with Matt describing events, which could make him feel these various degrees of anger.

My next appointment with Matt was a few weeks into the new term. He was much happier and felt that he had made progress. Matt rated his progress according to how tall he felt (using Figure 6.5). This showed that he felt taller compared with teachers and his friends than at the earlier rating. Progress was being made: he felt bigger even though he had had very few outbursts of anger in school. Matt's ratings made a lot of sense in terms of the plans for him to have more limited contact with other children: he had been protected from them by the separation but not helped to develop relationships with them. Matt rated himself again on the rating scale in Figure 6.3, and reported a very significant change. For the first time ever he had managed to return to two lessons after he had been sent out. This was a remarkable contrast from the violent reactions of a couple of months earlier.

Matt's story will continue with a series of reviews and modifications of strategies. It was interesting to hear staff at the review at the end of the term saying that there had really been no significant problems since that term began with the new strategies. They spoke of him with warmth and empathy compared with the threat, which was very evident in my earliest contact with school. There seemed to be a shift towards construing Matt as a very frightened little boy who lacked the skills to understand other people. The work with Matt had enlightened them and enabled staff to see ways forward for their work with him. There has been no further talk of exclusion or removal from the school. Without the examination of his view of the problematic situation, the likelihood is that he would have continued to pose the same problems because he could not generate any other solutions. The Personal Construct approach allowed discovery of the problem underlying his behaviour, rather than seeing his behaviour as the cause of the problem (Ravenette, 1997).

SUMMARY

Working with children with anger problems is a necessary part of most child psychologists' and child therapists' roles. A Personal Construct approach can be closely tailored to the child's own view of the problem and, therefore, it has good potential to succeed. Working with children and their parents using a Personal Construct approach can be exciting: the therapist does not have a clear idea which direction the therapy will take until the assessment phase is nearing completion. However, it does require the conviction that the child's view is of paramount importance and that true *therapy* will be unable to proceed without it.

APPENDIX: DRAWING THE IDEAL SELF

Equipment

Plain paper (A4 is a good size) and black pen.

Instructions

Part 1: Drawing the Kind of Person You Would Not Like to Be Like

The Person

Think about the kind of person you would not like to be like. This is not a real person. Make a quick sketch of this person in the middle of the page.

How would you describe this person? What kind of a person are they? Tell me three things about what he/she is like. Write the labels for the client.

The Bag

This person goes out each day and takes his/her bag. What kind of a bag would that be and what would be inside it? Sketch and label the items.

The Birthday Present

What would this person like for his/her birthday? Sketch and label the present.

With Family

How would this person be with his/her family? Sketch and give three descriptions.

With Friends

How would this person be with his/her friends? Sketch and give three descriptions.

What Would Be This Person's Greatest Fear in Life?

Everyone is afraid of something. What would this person be afraid of? Sketch and label.

History

How did this person come to be like this? What is his/her history? Was he/she always like this from birth or did he/she become like this? What happened to him/her?

Future

What will this person's future be like? What will become of him/her?

Part 2: Drawing the Kind of Person You Would Like to Be Like

Using the same instructions as above, make a further labelled drawing.

Part 3: Mapping Development and Movement Towards the Person He/She Wants to Be Like

Place the two drawings on the table, with the first on the left. Place a piece of paper in a landscape position on the table in between the drawings and draw a horizontal line the length of the page. Mark the mid-point on the line.

Map where the client would rate him/herself and label each point. The most essential points are where he/she would say he/she is now and where he/she would like to be (ideal self). It may be helpful to check the point they would settle for (is ideal the only option?).

How did you get there?

Look at differences between points (e.g. between now and an earlier point). Ask the client for the reasons for these changes. How come you moved from here to here? What was happening to help you move up/what made you move down? This is especially useful for exploring any large changes.

How could you move towards your ideal?

Ask for three things others can do to help the client move from where they are now to their ideal rating point. Ask for three things the client could do to help them get to their ideal point.

Other Mapping Options

Mapping development over time.

Map where the client would rate him/herself at different points in time. (e.g. Where were you as a child of 5? What about when you started secondary school?) Label each point.

Ask about the differences between points in time.

Mapping Different Views of the Client

Where would other people say you were along this line? Why would they say that? (e.g. Where would your mum say you were? What about your sister? Where would your friend say you were?)

Ask about the differences in views. What effects do the various views have on the client?

REFERENCES

Abidin, R. R. (1995). *The Parenting Stress Index.* Oxford: The Psychological Corporation.

Buntaine, R. L. & Costenbader, V. K. (1997). Self-reported differences in the experience and expression of anger between girls and boys. *Sex Roles, 36*(9), 625–637.

Denham, S. A., Blair, K., Schmidt, M. & DeMulder, E. (2002). Compromised emotional competence: seeds of violence sown early? *American Journal of Orthopsychiatry, 72*(1), 70–82.

Flay, B. R, Graumlich, S., Segawa, E., Burns, J. L., Holliday, M. Y. & Aban Aya Investigators (2004). Effects of 2 prevention programs on high-risk behaviours among African American youth: a randomized trial. *Archives of Pediatrics and Adolescent Medicine, 158*(4), 377–84.

Hewitt, P. L., Caelian, C., Flett, G. L., Collins, L. & Flynn, C. (2002). Perfectionism in children and adolescents: associations with depression, anxiety, and anger. *Personality and Individual Differences, 32*(6), 1049–1061.

Hubbard, J.A. (2001). Emotion expression processes in children's peer interaction: the role of peer rejection, aggression, and gender. *Child Development, 72*(5), 1426–1438.

Mason, W. A., Kosterman, R., Hawkins, J. D., Herrenkohl, T. I., Lengua, L. J., McCauley, E. (2004). Predicting depression, social phobia, and violence in early adulthood from childhood behaviour problems. *Journal of the American Academy of Child and Adolescent Psychiatry, 43*(3), 307–315.

Moran, H. (2001). Who do you think you are? Drawing the Ideal Self: a technique to explore a child's sense of self. *Clinical Child Psychology and Psychiatry, 6,* 599–604.

Ravenette, A. T. (1997). *Tom Ravenette: Selected Papers. Personal Construct Psychology and the Practice of an Educational Psychologist.* Farnborough: EPCA.

Valliant, P. M., Jensen, B. & Raven-Brook, L. (1995). Brief cognitive behavioural therapy with male adolescent offenders in open custody or on probation: an evaluation of management of anger. *Psychological Reports, 76*(3), 1056–1058.

Wallace, S. A., Crown, J. M., Berger, M. and Cox, A. D. (1997). Child and adolescent mental health. In A. Stevens and J. Raftery (eds), *Health Care Needs Assessment.* 2nd series. Oxford: Radcliffe.

7

THE ANGRY ADOLESCENT AND CONSTRUCTIVIST REBT

Robert W. Adelman

The present chapter reviews an attempt to identify psychosocial deficits typical of an adolescent substance abuse population at Sundown Ranch in Canton, Texas, and to match these deficits to adjunctive treatment methods aimed at improving clinical outcomes. The project was conceived in response to an initiative by the Joint Commission on Accreditation of Hospital Organizations calling for utilization of objective markers of clinical performance. The performance improvement project that emerged came to be recognized as a 2004 Codman Award recipient by the Joint Commission. The award is given in honor of Ernest A. Codman, the man regarded as the founder of performance outcomes measurement in healthcare.

The mission of Sundown Ranch for 17 years has been to provide effective substance abuse treatment to young people, aged 12–24 years, and their families. These are individuals who have become developmentally delayed in relation to their peers, due to a growing chemical abuse habit. In many cases, they have had excessive absences from school or have completely dropped out. In almost every case, their grades have at least notably declined, yet they continued to maintain the belief that their substance abuse was not a problem. In some cases, they reported the belief that their abuse of substances was an acceptable or necessary way of life.

The effects of adolescent substance abuse prior to treatment may be noted by parents in relation to mood or personality changes, increased defiance or opposition toward parents and other authority figures, changes in sleeping or eating habits, or decreased motivation toward activities that were previously viewed as pleasurable. Often parents

Working with Anger: A Constructivist Approach.
Edited by Peter Cummins. © 2006 John Wiley & Sons, Ltd.

report the fear that they are losing the child that they knew and that they fear for the physical safety of their child, due to the propensity of high-risk behaviors. The latter may include selling drugs, stealing for drugs, use of intravenous substances, promiscuous sexual behavior, etc. The decision to come to treatment is often a last ditch effort to restore the young person to a more normative path of development. The absence of treatment or the failure of treatment could, in some cases, lead to a progressive downward spiral that ends finally in an untimely death.

In recent years there has been an increased emphasis on establishing evidence for the benefits of treatment services delivered within the substance abuse field, as well as an interest in establishing which treatment methods are most advantageous. Rates of abstinence following treatment are one type of outcome measure that has been widespread in the addictions field. Unfortunately, these measures have also appeared to have questionable reliability, i.e., "Were the ex-clients reporting their post-treatment drug use accurately?" and validity, i.e., "What is to be judged an acceptable rate of post-treatment recovery?". Thus, it is conjectured here that the use of abstinence data has changed few people's minds about the effectiveness of treatment. The same people, who advocated treatment before the studies, probably continue to advocate it after the studies. The same people, who doubted the value of treatment before the studies, probably continue to question it after the studies.

In addition to these statistical issues, and perhaps more decisive from a clinical performance improvement point of view, the abstinence data were not found to be an "actionable" form of data. In simple terms, the abstinence data offered no insight about the specific treatment changes occurring during the course of treatment that made abstinence possible, nothing about the factors that might facilitate the process of change, and therefore, offered no strategic targets for performance improvement.

THE PERFORMANCE IMPROVEMENT MODEL

It stands to reason that in order to most effectively treat a clinical population, it would be beneficial to know the specific psychological characteristics of that population. A research problem for practitioners has been that each individual case provides only an N of 1, and that the outpatient population is too diverse to consider as a single population. In contrast, the clinical activity of a specialized treatment center, combined with the convenience of brief, computerized assessment instruments, provides new opportunities to demonstrate clinical performance improvement. The goal of clinical performance improvement, here, is to provide more effective interventions for each individual client, as well as to establish the best practice approach toward the clinical population as a whole.

In 1999 the Joint Commission of Accredited Hospital Organizations (JCAHO) mandated that all accredited facilities must engage in performance improvement activities on an ongoing basis. The performance improvement model parallels the scientific method in the stages of: (1) identification of a measurable clinical process for study; (2) hypothesis generation; (3) the following of defined procedures; and (4) the collection and analysis of data. Within the performance improvement model the data results are also used to plan program changes, with the goal of improving clinical performance.

Initially, the project committee chose six measures from the scales of the Treatment Outcome Package (TOP), an assessment instrument developed by Access Measurement Systems, as targets for clinical improvement. The selected scales were depression, anxiety, psychosis, temper/anger, impulsivity, and social problems. The decision was made for every client to receive the assessment at both admission and discharge. The admission TOP was used as a baseline measure of general functioning to assist with the treatment planning process. The discharge TOP was used to evaluate problem resolution and readiness for discharge.

The admission and discharge TOP tests were also used on an aggregate basis. The average of the scale scores from the admission tests were used as a baseline of the presenting psycho-social problems of the clinical population as a whole. The average of the scale scores from the discharge tests were used as a profile of the psycho-social problems of the clinical population at the conclusion of treatment. A comparison of the admission to discharge results revealed the changes in the clinical population that had occurred as a result of treatment. These profiles continued to be aggregated by computer over time, forming an ongoing view of treatment population characteristics and treatment effects.

For the performance improvement project, the clinical process for study was the resolution of client anger problems during the course of treatment. This selection was made in light of the clinical elevations observed on the aggregate TOP profiles at admission and discharge, collected over an 18-month period. These data are summarized in Figure 7.1. Note that the left-hand column of each test scale applies to the admission scale scores and the right-hand column represents the discharge scale scores. It was noted that the TOP temper scale was one of the two highest scales at admission and the highest scale at discharge. Thus, anger issues appeared to be highly typical of the clinical population of adolescent substance abusers and was the area of psychosocial functioning least affected by the treatment received. These findings for anger were counter-intuitive to the predictions of the project committee. The group consensus had been that anxiety or depression would be the most prevalent psycho-social problem for the substance abuse population.

The project committee viewed the degree of anger resolution in the clinical population as unsatisfactory. It was hypothesized that the direct care staff lacked the specialized training and skills to deal with this type of client emotional disturbance effectively. It was further noted that client anger often interfered with the recovery process.

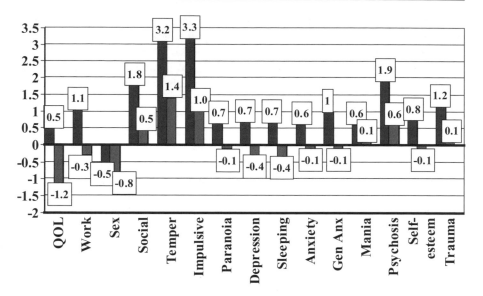

Figure 7.1 Adult TOP outcome graph: clients with initial and follow-up data

Note: Y axis represents Z score comparison to general population; lower scores are healthier: Mean days between intake and follow-up: 82.09091. Follow-up rate = 49.20% (154 Follow-ups from an initial population of 313). Report includes data from 1 July 1999 to 31 January 2001.

The program at this time was mainly focused on the Twelve Step Model. Key to this model is the acceptance by the client of a higher power that they can trust and believe in, as "their own best thinking" had led to their addiction and the denial or minimization of the negative consequences of their addiction. The Twelve Step Model also includes achieving recognition of the unmanageability of one's life as a consequence of the use of chemical substances, the taking of a rigorous moral inventory regarding one's past, and making amends to others for the harmful effects of one's actions. Clients are encouraged to work through the Twelve Step Model through their affiliation with more experienced recovering persons within the program.

As the data results strongly suggested limited effectiveness of the Twelve Step Model with the functioning of the clients in regard to anger, the committee began to discuss types of interventions that might improve staff handling of client anger issues, as well as improve the eventual outcome of treatment. The following considerations comprised the committee's rationale for selecting Rational Emotive Behavior Therapy (REBT) as a performance improvement activity to be directed at the reduction of client anger problems:

1. Some of the primary counseling staff already used some of the elements of REBT to varying degrees.
2. There was an almost 50-year history of practice and research with REBT with applications to a wide range of clinical problems.

3. There was evidence to suggest that adolescents do not do well with a confrontational style of therapy (US Department of Health & Human Services, 1999). The REBT method, in contrast, promotes a collaborative working relationship between counselor and client, which was regarded as potentially more efficacious.
4. REBT focuses on the client's present functioning rather than their past. It works actively and vigorously (though not confrontationally) toward the cognitive core of the client's dysfunction.
5. REBT promotes self-responsibility and the goal of taking increased control of one's life.
6. The REBT emphasis on reducing unhealthy, negative emotions seemed useful toward the goal of diminishing client's propensity toward anger and acting out behaviors.

RATIONAL EMOTIVE BEHAVIOR THERAPY AND CONSTRUCTIVISM

Rational Emotive Behavior Therapy was developed by Dr Albert Ellis in 1955. It is considered today to be the first model of cognitive-behavioral therapy, and its most fundamental tenet, i.e., that distorted thinking habits drive emotional and behavioral dysfunction, has been adopted by virtually all the succeeding forms of cognitive-behavioral approaches. In addition, there is a constructivist aspect to REBT (Ellis, 1998) that makes it highly suitable to working with young "personal scientists" (Kelly, 1955), i.e., adolescents.

In Ellis' system, "A" stands for the activating event and "C" for the emotional and/or behavioral consequences that flow from the interaction of "A" with the core irrational beliefs, "B". Thus, the client's experience of "A" is created depending on how the "A" is evaluated by the client's belief system. At step "D" the evidence for the belief is examined on empirical logical and practical grounds, and arguments for overthrowing the belief are presented. At step "E", the therapist helps the client to constructively elaborate new beliefs that have more promise toward producing favorable life results.

Due to the path of development and their limited fund of experience, adolescents have not had the opportunity to elaborate much of a construct system for interpreting the world they live in. As a result, they tend to form conclusions about themselves, the world, and others on the basis of just a few experiences, and are prone to cognitive distortions. According to REBT, there are four main classes of cognitive distortions which are described as "negative, irrational core beliefs". These distortions are *negative* because holding these beliefs is self-limiting and block further personal development. They are *irrational* because they are not based on sufficient evidence to become hard fast rules for effective living. They are *core* in that they operate at a super-ordinate level of the individual's cognitive structures and thus have a pervasive influence on a large portion of the person's thinking, feeling, and behaving.

The techniques of REBT, however, can be used as a fast track teaching program for adolescents in learning how they consistently distort their experience in a rigid, automatic fashion, to the detriment of their personal wishes and goals. Through REBT, they can also learn a process of reconstruction in which they challenge their old, irrational beliefs, and generate new, potentially more adaptive beliefs. As more adaptive beliefs become established, the emotional reactivity of adolescent clients becomes less, and they are more able to become effective problem solvers, rather than simply reactors to environmental stimuli.

The constructivist approach avoids buying into the victimhood of the client (Kelly, 1955). In the case of the adolescent client, this is especially important, as it is easy for the therapist to fall prey to the adolescent's vengeful anger or their demands of the world and others. A constructivist REBT approach holds that depression and anger do not exist as fixed traits or entities within the person, but instead are actively constructed by the client in relation to events. It is the therapist's job to show the client how he "does himself in" through maintaining negative, irrational core beliefs that color his emotional response to events in the world. The approach thus gets adolescent clients to look at the underlying premises behind their feelings, beliefs, and actions.

Through the REBT model the therapist strives to reduce the adolescents' focus on "A", i.e. what happens to them, and teach them they don't have to be a victim of their circumstances, and help them to construct alternatives (new narratives), which become pathways to healthier beliefs, attitudes, and behaviors.

In the context of substance abuse, it is essential to educate the client on the self-constructive aspect of their disturbance. Thus, adolescent clients can learn how they are "depressing" themselves, and how they are "angering" themselves in relation to the activating events in their lives. They can then begin to face up to the source of their emotional disturbance and learn adaptive coping mechanisms based on their new beliefs, rather than continue to avoid or self-medicate their emotions with chemical substances.

Many constructivist therapists view REBT therapists as imposing their view of what is rational and irrational upon the client (Neimeyer & Raskin, 2001). While REBT is more active-directive and more didactic than other constructivist methods (Winter & Watson, 1999), this emphasis may be necessary in reaching a severely at-risk adolescent population. When the consequences of personal constructions are so limiting, and potentially destructive, it may be ethically necessary to more forcefully talk young people out of their toxic, irrational core beliefs.

On the other hand, REBT may be more constructivist in nature than has been credited by constructivist therapists. Videotapes of Albert Ellis' therapeutic work show him rigorously demonstrating to clients, in a theatrical manner, a series of contrasting scenarios of the logical consequences of their current belief system, as opposed to the likely consequences of alternative beliefs. Thus, the approach is an educative one and the final choice is left up to the client.

METHOD

In May 2001, formal training in Rational Emotive Behavior Therapy, across all levels of direct care staff was begun, with the goal of improving clinical outcomes in the resolution of client anger problems. By logical extension, the positive impact of reduced client anger was hypothesized to increase positive adjustment and to reduce client relapse potential.

- *Subjects.* The subjects were 541 consecutive admissions to an adolescent substance abuse facility from July 1, 1999 to December 31, 2002. Most of the subjects had a primary diagnosis of chemical dependency. Most had co-occurring diagnoses as well. The subjects ranged in age from 12 to 24 years.
- *Materials.* The Treatment Outcome Package (TOP) is a 107-item, 15-scale questionnaire written at a sixth grade level. The instrument is published by Behavioral Health Laboratories (formerly Access Measurements). Behavioral Health Laboratories is one of the accredited measurement systems operating under the JCAHO, and thus, serves a number of facilities and treatment providers as an objective third party, scoring and compiling the data from all test administrations.
- *Procedure.* Each subject completed an objective, self-report questionnaire at admission and a second administration of the test within the last week prior to discharge. No subjects refused to complete the test. There were a small number of subjects who were discharged unexpectedly before they were able to complete the second test. These subjects were dropped from the database.

PERFORMANCE IMPROVEMENT ACTIVITIES

Phase I

In Phase I initial staff training began in May 2001. The training included all direct care staff, including counselors, assistant counselors, nursing staff, and school teachers. The training topics included an introduction to cognitive-behavioral methods, a discussion of anger as a psycho physiological construct, and an introduction to the A, B, Cs of REBT. The first quarter year of training culminated in a telephone consultation with Dr Ellis by members of the clinical team, regarding the implementation of REBT with the clinical population of the treatment center.

Phase I Results

Figure 7.2 shows a comparison of the baseline TOP test scores (1 July 1999–1 February 2001) and the first quarter of data (1 May 2001–31 August 2001). The scores were

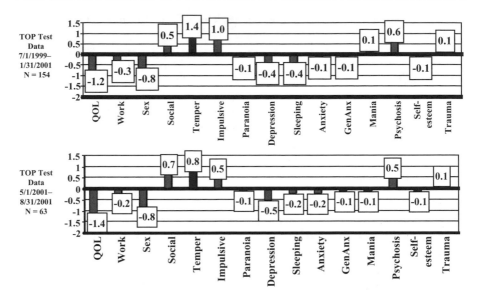

Figure 7.2 The effects of treatment on the psychosocial functioning of adolescent drug users in residential treatment: comparison of TOP test data 7/1/1999–1/31/2001 and 5/1/2001–8/31/2001

taken from tests administered at the time of discharge, and thus exhibit a comparison of treatment effects before and after the beginning of performance improvement activities. The results showed a decline in elevation of the temper scale of .6 standard deviations. There was also a decline in elevation of the impulsivity scale of .5 standard deviations.

Phase II

In Phase II the second quarter year of training focused on integration of REBT into the clients' treatment program. Specialized therapy groups were substituted for some of the more traditional process groups. The clients rotated in and out of groups devoted to basic REBT principles and anger management training.

Phase II Results

During the next stage of the study; Behavioral Health Laboratories re-factored the scales of the TOP. The temper and impulsivity scales were combined into one scale and relabeled "violence." The social scale was relabeled the interpersonal problems scale. Hence, at this point the project committee began to track the violence and interpersonal scale, instead of the temper and social scale.

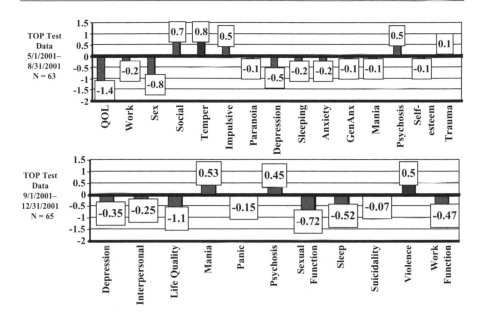

Figure 7.3 The effects of treatment on the psychosocial functioning of adolescent drug users in residential treatment: comparison of TOP test data 5/1/2001–8/31/2001 and 9/1/2001–12/31/2001

At the end of the second quarter of the study, the performance measures were reviewed in relation to the original baseline and first quarter data. Figure 7.3 shows a comparison of the discharge data between the first two quarters of data. A decline in elevation from .8 to .5 standard deviations was noted. Thus, in the eight months since the study began, the temper and violence scales had declined a total of .9 standard deviations, from a high of 1.4 standard deviations.

Phase III

The results of the first two stages of the study were very convincing to the project committee. It was the consensus of the committee that the changes in the performance measures reflected significant improvement of anger resolution. It was further noted that the Figure 7.1 profile; which reflected elevated temper, impulsivity, and social scales, had been highly stable throughout the 18 months prior to the introduction of Rational Emotive Behavior Therapy. The performance improvement was attributed to the steps taken toward training and implementation of Rational Emotive Behavior Therapy from 1 May 2001 onward.

A committee decision was made to seek more advanced training in Rational Emotive Behavior Therapy. Five staff members subsequently attended training at the Albert

Ellis Institute in February 2002. Two of them were enrolled in and completed the primary certificate training in REBT. After the Institute, the group continued to meet onsite at the treatment facility to practice and discuss REBT principles. This core group then prepared a three-part training for the rest of the direct care staff that took place over the summer of 2002.

Phase III Results

The results were viewed for another 12 months. Comparisons were made on a quarterly basis. Figure 7.4 showed a further decline in the scale elevation for temper to .175 standard deviations. Figure 7.5 showed a rise in temper scale scores for the first time, to .85 standard deviations. This figure was still significantly below the baseline of 1.4 standard deviations; however. Figure 7.6 again showed a decline in the scale elevation for temper, to −.15 standard deviations. It was also noted that the interpersonal scale did not show any significant elevations through these three data quarters.

Figure 7.7 is a control chart that tracks the process of anger resolution on a month-by-month basis for the duration of the study. The descending curve maps the lessening

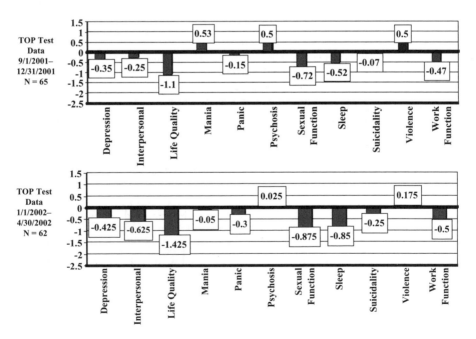

Figure 7.4   The effects of treatment on the psychosocial functioning of adolescent drug users in residential treatment: comparison of TOP test data 9/1/2001–12/31/2001 and 1/1/2002–4/30/2002

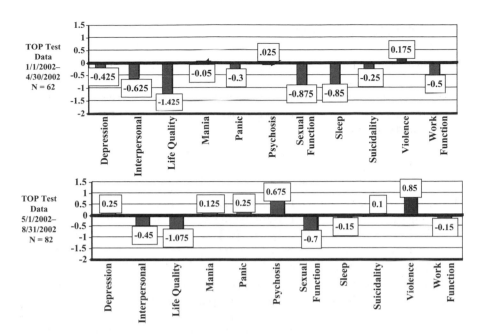

Figure 7.5 The effects of treatment on the psychosocial functioning of adolescent drug users in residential treatment: comparison of TOP test data 1/1/2002–4/30/2002 and 5/1/2002–8/31/2002

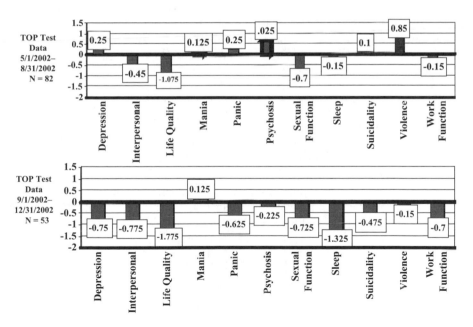

Figure 7.6 The effects of treatment on the psychosocial functioning of adolescent drug users in residential treatment: comparison of TOP test data 5/1/2002–8/31/2002 and 9/1/2002–12/31/2002

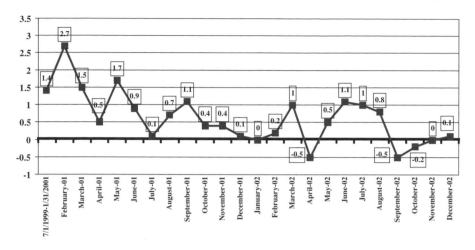

Figure 7.7 Violence/temper scale July 1999–December 2002

Source: © Joint Commission Resources (2005). Reducing adolescent clients' anger in a residential substance abuse treatment facility. *Joint Commission Journal on Quality and Patient Safety, 31*(6), 325–327. Reprinted with permission.

of anger problems in the treatment population by the end of treatment, following the multi-pronged introduction of REBT into the program. As cited above, REBT was introduced in a gradual progression through staff onsite training, peer supervision, primary certificate training of clinical supervisors, and psycho-educational client therapy groups.

CONCLUSION

The present study produced noteworthy results in a number of ways. First, the client population of the treatment center was shown to be characterized by issues with anger, as opposed to the more traditional co-morbidities of depression, anxiety, or psychosis. Thus, without the input of this baseline population data, treatment additions targeted at the latter problems would have been unlikely to improve the overall benefits of treatment. Second, anger issues were insufficiently attenuated by the existing treatment prior to May 1, 2001, likely leaving the clients vulnerable to relapse in the face of environmental triggers for their anger. Third, the training and program changes did produce reductions in temper scale scores and interpersonal problem scale scores that increased and were maintained over a period of 20 months. These reductions were also reflected in reduced numbers of anger incidents as documented by staff reports during the course of treatment, and are hypothesized to provide a link to better psychological functioning in recovery, increased abstinence rates, and greater harm reduction.

Several observations are offered about the process of integrating REBT into the life of a chemical dependency treatment center. These are addressed below as barriers to integration, and paradigm shifts following the incorporation of REBT into the treatment program.

The principles of REBT were slowly and methodically introduced to staff, which allowed staff to make the needed conceptual transitions. REBT was integrated as an adjunct to the already existing Twelve Step Model, rather than as a replacement to earlier treatment orientations. Initial resistance changed to an attitude of curiosity, and finally, acceptance and enthusiasm. Training, demonstration, role-play, supervised practice, and the specific application of REBT-style interventions to common behavioral management issues with clients, all helped staff to realize the value of REBT. If there was a problem with incorporating the self-control philosophy of REBT with the high power concept of the Twelve Steps Model, it was addressed as "let's help your higher power to not have to work so hard." Finally, the data results from the study convinced many that the REBT methods were helping and generated a desire to learn more about REBT.

Everything did not go completely smoothly, however. One staff member felt slighted that REBT seemed to be given all the credit for the positive aspects of treatment taking place. Also several of the counselors with a Twelve Step orientation were slow to accept the model. One of these counselors had a dramatic shift in attitude after attending an Albert Ellis workshop. The onsite training appeared to have the most impact on the assistant counselors (analogous to mental health techs) who did not have a background of professional training. The REBT model seemed to provide them with a foundation for interacting and working with clients, that had previously been lacking or limited.

Several paradigm shifts were noted in the course of training. First, there was a shift from an autocratic, "my way or the highway," approach to recovery to a more collaborative model of helping relationship. Essential to this shift appeared to be a new understanding from staff that client behaviors were not about them, but about the client. Staff began to ask themselves, "what irrational statements might the clients be telling themselves, to have produced the observed high level of emotional/behavioral arousal?" Second, there was a shift from a view of anger as an irritant to the treatment process, to a view of anger as an issue of psychological functioning worthy of intervention in its own right. The prior position on anger had led to harsh and dismissive counselor judgments of the client, e.g. "You don't want recovery!!" Also the clinical team began to view the low frustration tolerance of the client population as a potential common denominator, between their emotional reactivity and their propensity to abuse substances, in the face of frustrating, triggering events.

A third shift seemed to occur in the willingness of staff to explore other means of intervening with clients besides the sometimes heavily confrontational methods that often accompanies those adhering to the Twelve Step approach. Staff became more comfortable with practicing a more detached, yet collaborative, form of therapeutic alliance in which they assisted clients in exploring the results and implications of their beliefs, attitudes, and behaviors. This new stance was based on the "D" step of disputation within the REBT model. The step may also be understood as a stage of deconstruction or overturning of old, maladaptive beliefs that is a prerequisite to the formation of adaptive new beliefs "Step E." The combined action of these two steps appears to be consistent with constructive alternativism (Kelly, 1955) and the constructivist philosophy of change.

These paradigm shifts appear to have enabled staff to be their "best selves" more of the time with the clients and with less effort and emotional strain exerted in the process. While not every staff member has become equally comfortable or adept with using all the steps of the model, most can at least rely on the first three steps as an assessment tool to better understand client behavior. In this respect, it is believed that the REBT model has provided a more accessible and pragmatic model of client dysfunction. Evidence for this shift in staff attitude and their conceptualization of client problems is shown in the following comments gathered during REBT training:

Gained new insight into client's behaviors and how to change.

Helps me to talk to clients better when they are angry.

Helps to intervene more effectively with clients.

Helps to emotionally de-escalate clients.

Has helped me to reflect upon myself and be more cognizant of client needs and problems.

Has increased insight into client thought patterns and related irrational beliefs.

Helps to get at the emotions behind the behaviors and not just harp on the behaviors.

In conclusion, the results of the performance improvement project appear to attest to a significant enhancement of treatment effects in the area of anger resolution, after the formal inclusion of REBT as an additional therapy modality in the treatment of substance-abusing adolescents. REBT increased the ability of the clinical staff to work collaboratively with angry and difficult clients. The success of the project also suggests that parallels and complements may be found between REBT and the Twelve Step philosophy that promote therapeutic engagement with adolescent substance abuse clients.

In addition, the constructivist aspects of REBT appear to be particularly relevant in dealing with the special problems of treating this population. These points were summarized as follows:

1. Adolescents are particularly prone to cognitive distortion and emotional over-reaction to frustrating life events.
2. Adolescent core philosophies, or personal constructions, both influence and maintain these dysfunctional feelings and behavior.
3. Maladaptive actions tend to stem from disturbed emotions, e.g., the use of chemical substances by adolescents for emotional coping.
4. The REBT model can provide a concrete model for how people participate in the active construction of their emotional disturbance, e.g., anger.
5. The REBT model can demonstrate to the adolescent client how they actively construe their experience of events, and can teach them how to replace their maladaptive core beliefs with more adaptive beliefs.

ACKNOWLEDGEMENTS

The author would like to express his gratitude to Sundown Ranch, Inc., for its ongoing support of the research.

REFERENCES

Ellis, A. (1998). How rational emotive behavior therapy belongs in the constructivist camp. In M. F. Hoyt (ed.), *The Handbook of Constructivist Therapies*. San Francisco: Jossey-Bass, pp. 83–99.

Kelly, G. A. (1955). *The Psychology of Personal Constructs*. New York: Norton.

Neimeyer, R. & Raskin, J. (2001). Varieties of constructivism in psychothcrapy. In K. Dobson (ed.), *Handbook of Cognitve Behavioral Therapies*. New York: Guilford Press, pp. 393–423.

US Department of Health and Human Services (1999). *Treatment of Adolescents with Substance Use Disorders*. Rockville, MD: Center for Substance Abuse Treatment.

Winter, D. A. & Watson, S. (1999). Personal construct theory and the cognitive therapies. *Journal of Constructivist Psychology*, *12*, 1–22.

8

MR ANGRY

Graeme Sutherland

The italics in this chapter are the PCP therapist's observations and thoughts which you may find compromise the flow of Mr Angry's writing. You may wish to ignore them or return to them on a second reading of the chapter.

I

I was driving happily when I noticed the twig on my dashboard. It was a short, fine twig shaped rather like a large matchstick and it had been sitting there above my glove compartment for nearly a week. I noticed it with a shock of recognition at first and then pride. The fact that it was there at all meant I was getting better.

A week before, I had not been a happy driver. We were late for an appointment. I entered the car park with the determination of the hunter – there was no way I was going to wait in line for a space! I spotted a driver preparing to leave, fiddling with her shopping and kids in tow. It would take a couple of minutes, but I would be ahead of the long line of cars in front of me. I waited. Eventually, the space was empty and I started towards it. Suddenly, and to my horror, another car appeared in front of me filling MY space. The driver at the head of the queue had come all the way round and found an empty space behind my one. She had then driven through into mine! I was appalled.

However, I tried to keep calm. I had my wife and baby daughter with me. I had months of psychotherapy under my belt. I was doing everything I could to turn over a new leaf. But this situation would try the patience of a saint. I made eye contact, I smiled.

I pointed to myself and then at the space. She ignored me. I beeped my horn, nicely, helpfully, only once. She mouthed the word 'What?' She made a face. What was I supposed to do?

I undid my seatbelt and immediately felt my wife's restraining grip on my arm.

'No', she said, 'Let her have the space . . . '

'It's all right'. I reassured her. 'I'm just going to ask'.

Breaking free and opening the door, I heard her long, long sigh behind me. I approached the offending vehicle. The driver was fiddling with her handbag, oblivious to me. Oblivious to the world, I thought. I tapped on the window and the head jerked round. She looked anxious but I smiled and raised my eyebrows. 'Could you move back, please?'

She wound down the window.

'Could you reverse, please? I was about to park here . . . ' I indicated the still vacant space behind her. She shook her head. She frowned.

'Why should I?'

Yes, indeed, why should she? Why should she be a nice person, do the friendly thing, respect me as an individual – my right to park as close to the entrance as possible?

'You could have parked there . . . ' I said politely. I didn't feel polite. The blood was singing in my ears, my heart beating audibly in my chest. I was beginning to sweat. I could feel my mouth drying up, the words getting difficult to speak. '*You* park there then!' She spat and the discussion was over. She rewound the window and turned away. I was left bewildered and mortified. I just didn't know what to do. I felt like smashing her window in, grabbing her by the hair and forcing her to see reason. Yes, that might work.

In the next instant, my wife was calling me. She had spotted another nearby space, just vacated. If I didn't hurry up, I'd lose that one too! My humiliation was complete – one space stolen by a woman, another found for me by another woman. Parking is man's work. I had failed.

As I went to buy the parking ticket, I had to pass my nemesis returning with hers. I was very good. I had been warned. As she passed, I muttered a vile obscenity or two. Only two and I only muttered them. A few months earlier and we would have had a stand-up fight! I paid for my ticket and returned to my family.

'Good boy'. My wife told me. I seethed.

I went to put the ticket inside the windscreen and as I did I spotted the twig. I grabbed it surreptitiously and looked about me. My wife was busy with the baby. I trimmed off the excess bits of dead bark and regarded the twig with anticipation. Yes, I said to myself, that will do the bitch's tyres perfectly! I placed my secret weapon on the dashboard and closed the door. Inside I was smiling, I had a plan. We went off to our appointment, my blood pressure returning gradually to normal as I contemplated my sweet revenge.

And a week later – the twig was still there! I congratulated myself; I hadn't needed to actually let down that woman's tyres. I hadn't potentially endangered her and other people's lives for the sake of a parking space. I could be proud; I had come a very long way. I had wanted to, of course, for that moment. I would have happily taken a sledgehammer to her and her four-wheel drive suburban jeep! But I didn't.

Things haven't always been this good, this controlled. There have been incidents.

Once in a supermarket café, they wouldn't serve me a hot beef sandwich. I was queuing up and I hate queues. Inside I see the people in front of me as my enemies. What are they doing in front of me? Well, I had my eyes on the beef in gravy. It was Sunday lunchtime and beef was the roast of the day.

The others in the queue were taking their time as usual, but eventually my turn came. I asked for a hot beef sandwich. No, I couldn't have one – it wasn't on the menu. I felt the heat creeping across my face. 'You have beef, don't you? And you have bread. Just put one between the other and there we are ... ' 'Sorry. You can only have beef with the Sunday Roast. Do you want the Sunday Roast?'

No, I did not want the Sunday Roast. I remonstrated with her at length. I pointed out the ridiculousness of her stance. I pleaded for a more relaxed attitude to her catering manifesto. But she remained adamant: I could have the roast or I could have a sandwich from the menu, and never the twain will twixt.

'To hell with it then!'

The phrase was mild by my standards, but I did leave my tray, which was piled with drinks and a salad for my wife. I left the tray dramatically standing on the counter, in the way of everybody queuing behind me. I stomped off majestically.

Of course my wife wanted to know where her salad was. I tried to explain how cruelly I had been treated, but she seemed to be on their side. She was more interested in whether I had made a show of myself, of whether we'd ever be able to shop in our favourite supermarket again.

That was when the shopping trolley nudged me. I suppose I may have nudged the trolley but, in the mood I was in, I definitely detected a malign intent within it. I turned on it and grabbed it, whirling it round until I found the perfect target. A nearby table had been piled messily with dirty plates. The staff in here, I thought, can't even be bothered to collect up the crockery! I'd save them the bother.

Crash, crash, crash went the trolley! Not once or twice but three times. The plates broke on the floor, just held together in places by congealed gravy. My wife was up and ready to go. She expected me to follow, but I wanted a reaction. No staff came running with dustpan and brush. No security man to escort me off the premises. Frankly, I was disgusted.

'You are going to clear that up, aren't you?' I looked around and saw a middle-aged woman staring up at me with the word 'appalled' written across her face. She was only a customer, eating her Sunday roast, but she would do. 'No', I told her casually, 'that's what they keep slaves in here for . . . '

'Really! What if everybody thought like that?'

She really shouldn't have asked. 'Then it would get very messy, I suppose . . . '

I began to leave, turning my back on her harrumphing.

'You mean you're really not going to clear this up?'

I turned on her, savagely. 'That's right. *You* do it!'

I pointed at her. She was outraged. She exploded, ran about, complained and demanded justice. But by then, Mr Angry had left the building.

Having made what he thought was a reasonable request, to create a non-menu sand-wich, the refusal was heard by him as AN invalidation, which he struggled to find a way of absorbing or resolving. This sense of invalidation was far stronger than any rational concern about his wife's salad or her concern about the social shame of the outburst.

Then there was the time I was crossing the road outside another supermarket. There were lots of cars leaving the car park. They seemed to think they had right of way. They didn't seem to understand that I wanted to cross. I stood and looked hopeful. I expected someone to wave me across. I would have done – if I'd not been in too much of a hurry. Then the woman came driving along. She could see me waiting, but she had no intention of stopping for me. Behind her was a space in the traffic; all I had to do was wait. But this woman was driving so slowly . . .

I walked out. She'd have to stop. Yes, she'd have to stop and indeed she did, but a little too late for my liking. It was as if she expected me to run the rest of the way or something, so as not to unduly delay her progress. How dare she presume, how dare she try to hurry me up?

This is a very good example of the set of constructs (constellatory constructs) that can, via a hierarchy, (see Chapter 1) lead to anger.

So, I slowed down. I came to an almost halt in the middle of the road, walking in slow motion. A few cars joined the queue behind her. She wound down her window and stuck her head out.

'Excuse me'.

I did not move.

'Excuse me, I'm in a hurry'.

I did not move, again.

Then she did it, she beeped her horn. She waved her hand angrily. She shouted something with the word 'stupid' in it.

I raged at her in pure Anglo-Saxon. I paraded grotesquely and flicked Vs at her with both hands. The cars behind were tooting their annoyance. The woman was frantic, but still trying to feign superiority. She folded her arms as if waiting patiently for my tirade to end. I knew I had won.

I crossed to the other side to let her pass, but as she shifted gear her car stalled. Red-faced she stared at me. She called me a bastard and some other things that were lost in the angry beeping of the cars behind her. Smiling, I walked away.

I felt elated, vindicated. I sang as I drove home.

Validation is a valuable reward in itself.

However, it was when driving that Mr Angry was at his worst, his most dangerous. In the car I felt a need for total control and total respect from other road users. If I was delayed unduly, then that was a lack of respect. The old woman who didn't put her foot down for an amber light was just taking liberties with me. And, of course, the car makes an excellent weapon of revenge.

One time, I was trying to merge onto the city ring road, a notoriously tricky manoeuvre. The traffic was light, however, and I shouldn't have had any difficulty. Except that, as I came down the slip road, I could see another car in my side-view mirror. This car was in the inside lane of the ring road and despite my indication was refusing to pull over into the outside lane.

There was nothing to stop him pulling over.

So he was getting at ME.

There were no other vehicles in sight and now we were side by side as I rapidly approached the junction. I stared at the driver as he came alongside. He was oblivious to my presence, staring ahead as happy as his beard was long. I tooted and he shot me a rapid glance. The effort of looking had him almost losing control of his vehicle, he fought to get it straight again but he did not pull over.

I had to slam on my brakes. In the slip road to a dual carriageway, at about 50 miles an hour, I had to do an emergency stop. The other driver just continued on his way. I put my foot down. Now I was behind him, flashing my lights and sounding the horn. He waved me past – how ironic! I came alongside, caught his eye again. I waved my fist and mouthed angrily. I swung my car at his side like I'd seen on TV. It was the chariot race from *Ben Hur*.

The terrified driver suddenly indicated and swerved off the upcoming exit. I wasn't about to let him go. I pulled across both lanes to follow him. I pursued him for a couple of miles, never letting him forget I was there.

Then the fog lifted. Where the hell was I going? I was supposed to meet my wife and now I was going in the opposite direction.

I let the little man go with a flash of my lights and turned the car. I felt foolish and drained. The exhilaration of revenge had turned into a sort of post-coital awkwardness and indifference. But at least I had won, even though I was late meeting my wife.

So things come to a head.

Picture the scene. I am waiting to pick up my wife from work, a daily gauntlet of potential frustrations and humiliations. Somebody always boxes me in. A delivery van always wants me to move. My wife always takes much longer than she said. *Bloody* traffic wardens!

And so the list of situations that provoke lengthens. By laddering each of these, almost without exception the issue of respect and validation will emerge.

This time everything goes relatively smoothly. My wife gets in, we kiss hello. I pull out into the traffic and indicate into a nearby road-mouth to turn round. A gap appears in the approaching traffic and I swing across, only to find another car parked, *parked* in the entrance to the junction! I am caught in mid-turn half-way across the road. There are cars coming both ways. I sound the horn, but the driver of the offending vehicle isn't even in the driver's seat! She is fiddling around putting shopping in the boot.

I am on hard lock; I can't steer out of the situation. I am being harassed by drivers behind, so I can't reverse. I am stuck until this twit decides to shift herself, I am totally at her mercy and she is taking her own sweet time.

My stomach is tickling with the thousand wriggly things I get when something's going terribly wrong. I am in an ecstasy of rage. I am performing Wagner's Ring Cycle on my hooter. Just then my wife pipes up:

'Oh my God! I know that person . . . '

I don't pay any attention because just then a gap opens up behind me and I can reverse a little. I do so, waving apologies to the drivers surprised to find someone reversing up the wrong way into a major road. I finally get to pull up alongside the parked car.

'Leave it, please leave it. It's someone I know, just drive, will you . . . '

I wheel down the window. I tell this woman what I think of her, *in gynaecological detail*. The woman stares at me, amazed. My wife has shrunk down in her seat trying not to be seen. The woman comes to and starts returning the insults, swearing like a particularly crude trooper. I speed away.

'What is it?' I ask my wife, 'What's wrong with you?'

Here we can see the lack of sociality being acted out. As described in Chapter 1, sociality involves understanding how the other person sees the world. Mr Angry clearly does not understand his wife's perspective.

'That was Judy from work'. She says this as if that would explain it.

'Well, in that case, Judy from work is a . . . XXXX'. QED.

My wife does not see the logic of my defence. This woman was in the wrong and deserved what she got.

'But I've got to face her tomorrow!' She starts crying real tears and I know I'm in for a hard time.

Just then Judy drives past in the other lane and makes an obscene gesture. Apparently, as far as my wife is concerned, it is all right for Judy to do this but not for me to reply.

'Did you have to do that?' She wails.

'Yes'. I tell her. The honour of her man was at stake. Couldn't she see that?

Well, er, no.

I didn't hear the end of the Judy episode. My wife threatened divorce, telling my mother, taking my car keys away. Taking my car keys away! It couldn't be that bad, could it? Apparently it was.

Judy kept up the pressure by coming to see my wife at work and publicly complaining about my bullying behaviour. It didn't really matter who was right or wrong about the incident – the fall-out was now affecting the innocent. That was one thing.

The other thing was that my wife was six months pregnant. I was bringing a child into the world, this world where daddy rages and screams at strangers, smashes up plates in public, risks life and limb taking petty revenge on thoughtless motorists.

It had to stop.

This is a very common point reached by many of the people, whom we work well with or who gain most from the group. This realisation, that their children's experience of family life is going to be a repeat of their own childhood, is a powerful reason for change, particularly as they then 'see' their children sitting where they are in the group, in years to come.

II

But where did it start, this anger? It comes from within, I know that now. I used to think it really was the fault of those people or things that had upset or frustrated me. I realise now that my reactions are out of proportion with the offences, be they real or imagined.

Did I have a whole lot of anger inside that could only come out in situations like these? And when it did, it erupted like Vesuvius all over the Pompey branch of a supermarket. If so, where did this anger come from, what was I really angry about?

This is the key question. The initial response is to be puzzled about the fact that the things that make him angry do not justify the level of anger. See discussion re. 'silly things' in chapter one. Why does he get so angry in the supermarket? It is not enough to manage it, only when its origins are understood can there be revalidation.

I was the only child. Until my Grandma turned up that is. I was reasonably happy before that except for the screaming matches my parents had. Apart from my Dad almost never being there, and my Mum drinking. Reasonably happy.

Materially, I had everything I could hope for. I just couldn't stand living in the 1970s' *Play for Today* world that was my home life. Sordid scenes of domestic tragedy were played out nightly for my entertainment. I only had one escape. At the weekends, I went to stay with my grandparents and experienced the idyllic world told of in children's books and Sunday afternoon serials. I could play, safe from the fear of invading rows, of adult business impinging on my happiness. My grandparents seemed very happy together, they doted on me. I was the centre of their world during those weekends, not the forgotten witness to my parents' melodrama.

That was my only escape then, apart from the booze. I started stealing drink from my Mum when I was about 8 or 9. It helped with the run up to the evening's main event. As she got more blotto, so did I. She didn't notice or care. In fact she could always be relied upon to provide me with some drink 'legitimately'. When I was just 11 it all got much worse. My Granddad, the most beloved person in my life, was killed in a car crash. My Grandma came to live with us, permanently. Although barely in her sixties, my grandmother became a pathetically dependent character. She soon joined my Mum in the bottle and refused to come out.

As described in Chapter 2, many of our clients report such significant experiences at this age. See Chapter 11 by Mascolo et al. which explores the developmental tasks of this age.

So the three of us became a drinks club. As soon as I got home from school I started knocking back the Martini. We would shore ourselves up in alcohol against the ogre, my Dad, and his disapproving looks. My Dad was violently opposed to alcohol abuse, although he drank moderately himself. He had grown up with drinkers. So did I, Dad – why didn't you do something?

I despaired of getting out alive! My school work suffered, AND my friendships and relationships. I didn't have the typical middle-class suburban home life that I saw on TV. What a family sit-com we would have made!

I have told my wife all the stories, in lurid detail. They came flooding out. I told her that I was so ashamed, as if the way my family were was my fault – I felt that keenly. She always said how surprised she was that I wasn't angry with them – I was sad, ashamed, disgusted, but not angry. She found this inexplicable.

Perhaps it was all too close to me then. I felt I had to try and maintain the veneer of normality. I wasn't going to be the one to add the straw that broke the camel's back. The only thing that mattered to me then was keeping my parents together. I didn't matter. I never mattered.

This is the heart of the invalidation; not mattering to anyone and therefore with no right to be validated.

Maybe I have got cause to be angry after all, but I NOW KNOW these causes are not in the checkout queue at the supermarket!

III

It is important to point out that I am not usually angry at all. I am a binge rager. Normally I am a very laid-back sort of person, stoic even. Throughout my life I have been described as quiet or withdrawn and have been praised for keeping my own counsel. These outbursts have only been occurring for the past ten years or so, gradually increasing in intensity – ever since I went into teaching!

I really wanted to be a teacher. I loved working with the children, imparting knowledge and engendering enthusiasm in my subject. I'd graduated from teacher training with distinction. I was determined to be a success.

I was a disaster.

My veneer of self-confidence was too thin to endure the ravages of life in an inner city comprehensive. The difficult minority of pupils intent on trouble found me easy game in their war against authority.

'Sir, are you a virgin?'

'Sir, are you gay?'

'How old are you, Sir, are you eighteen yet?'

'Do you shave?'

'Have you ever had a girlfriend?'

''Course he hasn't. He's a poof!'

'He's a baby!'

'He's wearing make-up!'

And they sat there blinking. Blinking. Twenty-eight pairs of eyes ruthlessly mimicking 'Sir's' stress-related facial tick.

And I'm thinking: *'How do they know? How did they find out? Is it so obvious? My effeminacy, my weakness, my immaturity? How were they able to aim so well, to hit their targets with such deadly accuracy?'*

These thoughts would have perplexed my wife or my friends from university or anyone else who really knew me. It shouldn't have bothered me. It should have been water off a proverbial duck. I was married, wasn't I? I had a hell-raising social life, didn't I? But somehow they hit home; those adolescent taunts connected with a softer, more vulnerable me than the world at large ever saw. They uncovered the person I feared I was, to devastating effect. I crumpled.

And began to experience extreme invalidation.

Funnily enough, it was then that my temper began to surface. At first, against inanimate objects that might get in my way. I maltreated a standard lamp to my wife's astonishment. There never seemed to be a rational explanation for these incidents, but deep down I knew that I was desperately close to cracking up.

I began shouting at my pupils, sometimes even at the ones who had actually 'deserved' it. Any little thing would set me off. I felt as if everybody hated me, belittled me, treated me with disdain. Maybe they did. I certainly became very easy to dislike. I got a reputation for being a humourless, bad-tempered bastard, and I was.

The crunch came one day when I had a boy by the throat. I had been walking along the corridor, minding my own business. Suddenly a pair of hands connected with my back and sent me sprawling. I was quick, very quick. I spun myself round and grabbed at the presumed culprit – a squat lad quite literally dedicated to ruining my life. I'm not exaggerating!

I pulled him up by the lapels of his non-regulation, quilted jacket and pinned him against the wall.

'Why?' I shouted at him. 'Why did you do that, just tell me why!'

The boy did not answer, he swivelled his big eyes around in his big pink face and refused to co-operate. I shook him and tightened my grasp.

'Look! You won't even get into trouble. I just have to know WHY!' I couldn't see it, of course, but I just knew my face was as bright red as his was getting.

He tried to answer, or at the very least cry for help. I couldn't understand why the child, usually a notorious motor-mouth, was so reluctant to speak. Then I realised. I had him by the throat and was choking the breath out of him. I went into a kind of shock and dropped him immediately. He gasped for breath and started screaming in a high-pitched voice.

'You're mad, you are! I'm goin' tell the head on youse! You've lost it, you have ...'

A perfect diagnosis.

Anger is an emotional expression of invalidation.

IV

So I gave up teaching. Eventually things returned to normal; I could drive past a school again without feeling nauseous, I could pass a group of teenagers without grinding my teeth together so hard it hurt. I stopped blinking incessantly, except when very tired. Yes, life went back to normal. Except for the anger.

The anger stayed near the surface. I wasn't going to be humiliated again, put upon by vicious little people who want to put me down just for the sake of it. I would fight back at every injustice, real or perceived. If I was kept waiting too long in a queue in the Post Office, if someone tried to cut me up at a junction, if an old lady took too much time getting out of my way . . . So perish all enemies of me!

I am not going to put up with invalidation, anger validates me.

This new insistence on my rights as a person and my recently acquired sense of self-worth would be a very positive thing, were it not for the fact that I would allow myself to fly into paroxysms of rage entirely out of proportion to the scale of the provocation. Sometimes there didn't even have to be a provocation.

Around the same time, I finally gave up drinking. The bottle had been my most faithful and supportive friend for so many years. It had seen me through the dark days at home with my family. It had gone off to university with me and had a marvellous time! It had been there to anaesthetise my nights after a tormenting day in the classroom. Now it had to stop, it had turned on me.

My alcohol abuse had always been an issue between my wife and myself. Either right there in my face or just bubbling under the surface. I defended my right to drink as fiercely as later I would defend my right to rage.

'I have it under control; I like to drink, what was wrong with that? Don't be such a kill joy'. All the arguments my Mum used on me, I reflected back on my wife. I hated myself for it, for the weakness, for the way I had become just like my Mum and Grandma.

But still, I defended my friend loyally – until it turned on me. Twice I was arrested for being drunk and disorderly. Two nights spent in the cells, up in court, a fine, humiliation. Then I was knocked down by a car, I can't even remember it, and I woke up as they were carrying me into the ambulance. My friend was trying to kill me. Deep down I knew it always would, but slowly or so I supposed. This was too much, my wife threatened to leave. She'd done that before, of course, to no avail. But now, and with the intervention of a good solid father-figure alcohol counsellor, I kicked the habit.

If the drink had been my escape before, now it was my anger. I began looking forward to shopping trips, because they now always meant a run-in with somebody. Driving became especially bad. Everybody: motorists, cyclists, pedestrians – all were potential enemies, possible objects of my scorn. The curses flew, the bile flowed, AND revenge triumphed.

Throughout this, my wife suffered valiantly and at first in silence. She was so glad I'd stopped drinking; she didn't want to say anything to upset me. I had noticed how, although she passed her test with flying colours, she was very unwilling to drive. This I put down to lack of courage, and in a way I was right. She *was* scared – scared of ever coming up against another driver like me!

Eventually we were blessed with a successful pregnancy. I began to worry about whether my behaviour would affect a future child. Did I want to screw up my son or daughter in the way that I'd been screwed up by my parents? I thought of Philip Larkin's much quoted observation about how parents 'fuck you up' unintentionally.

So off to the doctors I go, and into therapy.

V

Of course I had been in therapy before; for depression, dealing with my breakdown, the aftermath of my childhood. But now I had a real incentive – I did not want my child to have to live with any of the instability that I lived with. I did not want her to see me as an irrational and even dangerous presence in her life. I needed to get to the bottom of my anger and do something about it.

So I recounted my experiences to my psychotherapist. It wasn't easy and I was guarding against his disapproval. I presented myself as the wounded party: I was right to get angry, wasn't I? Everybody was being unreasonable around me, weren't they?

Well, to a certain extent: yes. My therapist showed me that often my initial annoyance in these types of situations was indeed perfectly understandable. What was not, however, was the degree of my reaction to them. Where most people would respond with a sigh or an inward curse, I turned into The Incredible Hulk!

A disturbing pattern began to emerge: Why was it that I usually lost my temper with women and not men? All the worst incidents seemed to involve middle-aged ladies!

I began to fear that I was a raving misogynist, and as the father of a baby daughter this worried me even more.

But again, this seemed to be understandable – taken in conjunction with my early family history at least. My mother and my Grandma were both middle-aged ladies, weren't they? Could it be that they, in the past, had more to do with my anger than the complete strangers I kept raging at in the present day?

This is why we put such emphasis on family trees. Anger as a social construct clearly has major 'family of origin' implications.

Highly logical, perhaps utterly obvious. I hadn't considered it before, but now it seemed to make perfect sense:

When that café assistant in the supermarket refused to give me what I wanted – that was my mother refusing to give up drinking. That old woman telling me off about breaking the plates, was my Grandma making unreasonable demands.

Likewise the woman in the car wanting me to hurry out of her way and showing me no consideration, or the cyclists breaking rules that I was expected to obey. They were shadows of the past. They were treading on the toes of previous wrongs against me. Wrongs that I had never challenged, wrongs that I had buried deep for 25 years or more!

My psychotherapist explained. He told me about 'invalidation', said that whereas in most situations we have a gradation of response – A goes on to B goes on to C, etc. – sometimes, given a particular trigger, we might go straight to Z.

A nice description of REGNANCY (see section on hierarchy in Chapter 1).

I had in-built sensitivities to certain types of experience, those which triggered off memories of my past, and in those situations I found it very difficult to respond in moderation. I didn't use my judgement or my maturity – I went straight into being the frightened, outraged child. In other words: I'd lose it!

This made sense to me in abstract. I could buy the premise but I couldn't be sure. Was it just an excuse for my bad behaviour? I needed to open my heart to the idea as well as my brain. My psychotherapist asked me to go back to a recent incident in my mind. Then he asked me a very simple question: 'How do you feel?'

There I am in that car park again. That arrogant woman with her four-wheeled battering ram at my ego. I'm holding the twig in my hand and contemplating revenge.

'How do you feel?'

'Angry!'

'Just angry?'

'Bloody furious!'

'Why?'

Ah, that's more difficult. I can't answer straight away.

'Because she took my space . . . '

'You found another one, you weren't late in the end'.

'No. But . . . '

'What did you feel when she took your space?'

'I felt: How dare you! How dare you do that to me! What about me!'

Strangely, I began to feel very sad. I could feel tears stinging under my eyelids. I fought them, manfully.

'What about you?'

'Yes. She didn't care about me, my feelings, my rights! She didn't even see me! It was like I didn't exist'.

I cried.

Invalidation. Taking away my right to exist. And who was this 'she' that didn't care about my feelings and rights? Well, it wasn't some stranger in a car park. Suddenly, I knew that was true. I felt it was true.

Construing is not just verbal, this is an emotional truth.

All the years of keeping it in. Keeping up the pretence of a happy family – for their sake more than for mine. The quite righteous anger at the way my child-hood self had been robbed of his innocence and security was bubbling to the surface. No, not bubbling – escaping like jets of pressurised steam from a geyser! Watch out!

Understanding where it is coming from is only part of the battle. However, it is that victory that takes the dread out of the war. I was scared that I was becoming some kind of a monster and now I know that all along I was really a tormented little boy.

The next battle will be the one for control. Understanding the root cause does not help me avoid upsetting people in public. It is no comfort for them. I have to try to take things from A to B to C, rather than allowing minor frustrations to trigger off the full pendulum swing to Z and the crazy-man who lives there.

But knowing makes it easier. I am not a monster.

VI

So now I'd like to say I'm not Mr Angry any more, that I've turned the corner and become a Mr Placid or a Mr Nice-To-Strangers. However, only two days ago I tore a strip off an assistant in a bookshop, just because she was trying to tell me that:

'Customers are not allowed to use the cash registers, sir'.

'I will do as I like!'

'Not in this shop, sir, you can't'.

'I will do as I like! I am always right! Zip it! Zip it! I wanted to know how much this book is and you weren't there! I AM JUSTIFIED!'

'I'll call the manager'.

'Yes, please do, I'll take him on as well!'

And I would have done too, but then I saw my wife's face through the crowd; confusion and fear mingling there, our daughter in her arms. I left it. The blood was still pounding, my neck tight and the muscles of my face still pulled into a grimace. But I left it and walked away.

Ho hum . . .

So for now, just call me Mr Still-Working-At-It. And pray you don't stall at the lights while I'm sitting behind you.

9

MAKING ME ANGRY
THE CONSTRUCTIONS OF ANGER

Harry Procter and Rudi Dallos

INTRODUCTION

This chapter is about anger, and the role that families play in shaping each other's experience of anger. In addition to a long-standing interest in the applications of Personal Construct Psychology (PCP) to clinical psychology, we are also both committed to a systemic perspective. This is mirrored by our personal perspectives too, in that they have given us insights into the role of family dynamics in shaping beliefs, actions and problems in our lives. More specifically, we have both attempted to weave together an analysis of individual worlds and family dynamics by integrating construct theory with systemic approaches (Dallos, 1991; Procter, 1981, 1985, 1996). One of us (HP), proposed two further corollaries – the family and group corollaries – as part of this attempt at integrating systemic approaches and PCP (Procter, 1981, 2001). We want to offer in this chapter an example of this integration as applied to the ubiquitous topic of anger.

At first glance it might appear that the two traditions occupy contrasting epistemological positions. Systemic family therapy is concerned with analyses of dynamics in families and PCP with internal individual worlds. Yet the PCP definition of hostility (Kelly, [1955] 1991, p. 391) already suggests an interpersonal analysis. A significant part of our lives, and especially our development, occurs in families, as does a great proportion of anger, especially very serious anger, such as assault, rape and murder. The victims of these typically are other family members.

Working with Anger: A Constructivist Approach.
Edited by Peter Cummins. © 2006 John Wiley & Sons, Ltd.

ACCOUNTS OF ANGER

Before we continue, we will turn to some personal accounts to give us some windows into how people view anger:

> I think like a lot of women, I am afraid of both witnessing and feeling anger, and will go to elaborate lengths to avoid provoking it. I learnt avoidance at a very early age from my mother and paternal grandmother, who both had to cope with aggressive, moody and volatile husbands. Their way of dealing with it was to meekly accept whatever was hurled at them, they were submissive, penitent and never answered back.
>
> I don't think I ever knew, as a child, why my father and grandfather got angry. There were no obvious causes, so I was often confused by its manifestations as well as frightened.
>
> I think that the ways in which my parents dealt with anger had a lot to do with my rejection of them both as role models. I did not want to be moody and aggressive like my Dad, nor weak and submissive like my Mum. This dichotomy has perhaps led to my own responses to anger being either inappropriate or delayed, e.g. I can get instantly angry about small, unimportant things, but will often not be able to react to big emotional crises until the day after they happen. I have only experienced incandescent anger once in my life, it was a very scary experience and one that I do not want to repeat.
>
> Anger can be a very positive emotion when it fuels the passion to fight injustice and bring about change. It can look beautiful on the faces of people who believe what they are fighting for – Martin Luther King, Bernadette Devlin, Bob Geldof spring to mind. But on a purely personal level I have never been able to harness the constructive side of anger. I do not like the aggressive person I become when I am unable to suppress it in myself or the meek person I try to diffuse it in others.
>
> (Rachel, aged 42)
>
> I suppose that as a man I am ambivalent about anger. Much of the time I think about it as a negative emotion and as an abusive way of being in the world. However, I frequently flip back to experiences at school where to be 'hard', to be able to 'stand up for yourself' was an admired quality. Basically you were a 'bit of a wanker' if you couldn't show that you were hard enough to stand up and fight back if necessary. People might talk about aggression being bad and ugly but somehow you knew, maybe in people's looks and the imagined admiration of girls that you might be understood as being a pacifist but you would not really gain respect unless you could also show that you could fight back. I suppose that story repeats itself a million times over, especially in Hollywood movies.
>
> But, of course, there is more to it than that. I know that standing up for yourself doesn't have to mean being overly aggressive or physically violent. Maybe my difficulty has been that in my family feelings were often uncontained – arguments would boil over out of control and sometimes there would be actual physical violence. My mother was very angry and frustrated a lot of the time and would spit venom at her men. As a young boy seeing this going on and the man's eventual threatening response was frightening. It left me both hating anger and violence, but also being familiar with it. Maybe worse, it left me a bit frozen about expressing anger because I worry that it may escalate out of control. Certainly some of my fantasies about what I would like to do when someone has really upset me is to be pretty physically violent. There again, the images that come

to mind may, at least in part, be inspired by the proliferation of violent images that we see endlessly in the media; TV, movies, magazines and of course, computer games. In fact much of what I describe about my own family seems to be displayed on TV soaps like, *EastEnders* and *Brookside* – maybe that's why I can't bear to watch them.

(Rick, aged 53)

Kiran (aged 10) in conversation with Harry:

K: I felt like it was, cos I had been waiting to do it for quite a long time, but so had my brother, for the bubble thing. Um ... I felt ashamed, sort of ... well, I sort of, went on a bit ... [I called him a] 'Plonker!' (*Laughing*)

H: Why were you angry?

K: I got angry because my brother was ... he was getting his way and I wanted to do my thing. [When you get angry] you sort of feel ... you sort of feel like you want to go and hit someone.

H: When do you think it is all right to get angry and when is it not all right to get angry?

K: Well, it's not all right to get angry with, like ... if you're with your friends or something. It's rude and they would not invite you around or anything. People get angry when someone is bullying you or being nasty to you. You feel angry then and you might feel angry when you're jealous or something ... like, I wanted a Playstation but it was too much and I was not allowed one.

What are your impressions of these accounts? Some of the issues that stand out for us are:

- Nature of the experience – maybe the first and most obvious aspect of the accounts is that anger is a powerful experience and one that is at the core of people's experience. The words used to describe it include:
  - Rachel's account – afraid, avoid, moody, volatile, meekly accepting, confusing, frightening, incandescent, suppressing, diffuse it in others, positive, constructive, bringing about change, weak, submissive, scary, standing up for yourself.
  - Rick's account – frightening, admiration, ugly, bad respect, boiling over, escalate out of control, frustrated, uncontained, hating, frozen, upset, hating (anger), hardness, violent fantasies.
  - Kiran's account - I went on a bit, feel like you want to go and hit someone, ashamed, rude, jealous.
- Meanings and implications for action – as Kelly ([1955] 1991) argued, inherent in the construction of actions is both the meaning (denotative) aspects but also the implications for actions (implicative). The meanings we ascribe to events contain within them implications for our choices of action:
  - Rachel – the implication, or solutions in her family were to engage in 'meek acceptance', to be penitent and never answer back to male violence, to delay responding to violence, to express it (sublimate it?) by over-reacting to minutiae.

- Rick – the implications appear to be more ambivalent to both avoid violence but also to admire it and to have internal fantasies, to be frozen about expressing it, to avoid exposure to depictions of familiar violence (as in TV soaps, etc.)
- Kiran – anger when one feels *entitled* to something. However, it is *rude* and he feels *ashamed*. A response to attack.

- Gender differences – the accounts suggest that men and women, boys and girls assimilate a set of culturally shared discourses or super-ordinate constructs about the place of anger in their lives. In fact, we can see that anger is an integral part of a male vs. female identity. Rick describes how for a boy to be 'hard' and capable of showing your anger, through violence if necessary was experienced as essential to being accepted by his peers. Quite the reverse can be seen in Rachel's account: what is taught for women is the value of passivity, a denial of their anger along with an acceptance of the legitimacy of men's anger.

- In talking to children of 9 or 10 years of age, such as Kiran, it was notable that they tended to define the reason for their anger in terms of situational triggers, although at the end, Kiran moves to *internal* experience when he speculates about jealousy. Kiran invokes the word 'ashamed' on being asked 'what anger feels like'. Research looking at this in children no doubt exists but we are not aware of it. It is certainly our clinical experience that it is hard to get children to *take responsibility* for their angry actions. It is often hard generally to persuade people who are angry that it is an aspect of their *construction* of *events*, rather than a response to events. In the children, there was also an emphasis on *getting into trouble* for being angry, as Kiran implies, in saying that he was ashamed. This can be seen within developmental lens of concrete thinking – that anger is bad because you get punished for it (Piaget, 1955).

- However, a sense of shame also implies that Kiran has moved to a position where he has internalised such consequences to offer a contrast between a good or ideal as opposed to a bad self. The good self feels ashamed of the bad self who has angry thoughts and calls his brother a 'plonker'.

- The importance of ethical discourse in Kiran's account is perhaps already implicit – that there *should be* fairness and justice in how the two brothers take turns on the computer. Anger then becomes an expression that a perceived ethical principle is being flouted as well as a means for doing something about this.

- It is possible to see from these accounts, that the *family* is the context where much of the learning about anger takes place. In experiencing the interactions between parents and others in the family, people learn what meanings to ascribe to actions and the implications for actions: what actions mean and what we should do about them.

- At the same time it is possible to see in these accounts that anger has the potential to separate and isolate. For example, Rachel did not, and perhaps still does not, know why her father and grandfather got angry. Nor was Rick able to find out what was making his mother and stepfather so angry. They can guess but anger generates fear of asking, it can shut down discourse. Though as Rachel suggests, 'positive' anger can also inspire and unite.

THEORETICAL APPROACHES TO ANGER

Anger as Something Inside Us

In his book, *The Songlines*, Bruce Chatwin, takes the ethologist, Konrad Lorenz, to task for assuming that human beings evolved fundamentally as an aggressive species. Lorenz compared the behaviour of soldiers marching to battle as 'fixed action patterns' similar to the mating rituals of mallard ducks and frogs (Chatwin, 1987). His idea of anger as being a 'drive' analogous to the accumulation of a hydraulic fluid that needs 'discharging', has entered the popular culture. Similar ideas are to be found in psychoanalytic thinking, most notably the 'death instinct'. However, even in Freud, anger and aggression are already linked to interpersonal scenarios such as the oedipal triangle.

Of course, being angry is likely to be linked to corresponding physiological changes, such as raised levels of adrenalin and nor-adrenalin (Schildkraut & Kety, 1967). (It is interesting, incidentally, that general psychiatry has not pathologised anger in the same way as it has certain other negative emotions and moods such as depression, claiming that it is 'caused by' changes in amines, etc, possibly because there is no drug that efficiently controls anger.) The seminal research of Schachter and Singer (1962) showed that the effects of adrenalin were totally transformed by the different interpretations by the subjects of the situations that they were in.

The idea that anger is something inside the person can be encountered in daily practice in working with families. One of us (HP) remembers vividly the expression of fear and horror on the face of a mother as she stared at her 5-year-old boy, while I was hearing about examples of his tantrums and aggressive behaviour. Her construing of him was truly that he was possessed by an evil influence. I was sure that in his turn, the boy was frequently angry because he felt the rejection that his mother's construing engendered for him. Enabling her to see what *he was getting angry about* in specific situations soon altered the pattern of escalation between them.

Anger as Something Between Us

Anger is a crucial *regulator of human interaction* according to the *cybernetic* view of human interaction (e.g. Watzlawick et al., 1967). Bateson (1972), the first theorist in this tradition, looked at animals as well as people in interaction and described the now well-known patterns of symmetrical escalation and complementary rigidity. Clearly anger is a common component of both these scenarios. Two brothers fight over the computer, one saying, 'It's my turn now' or saying to his mother, 'He's been on there for half-an-hour, tell him to let me have a go!' The other may respond with symmetrical protest, or give in. The pattern changes to the complementary mode.

Likewise, the complementary situations (e.g. a normally passive partner who goes along with the other's demands) suddenly 'flips' when the one in the 'down position' suddenly says angrily: 'I've had enough of this, go and do it yourself!'

Bateson argued that communication always occurs at two levels in which a message about the relationship is sent or shared as well the content. I may send you an angry expression but it may be qualified by another sign, which says, 'this is play' (Bateson, 1955). The two aspects of the message may fit together coherently or they may contradict one another as in the famous *double bind* scenario (Bateson, Jackson, Haley & Weakland, 1956). A 'thank you' is accompanied by an angry expression, which says, 'I'm annoyed with you!' In families who have a long history of intimate association, these signals may become so telegraphic that they barely need to be sent, because shared memories of previous communications are evoked anew. One reaction to receiving a double bind is to attack the person or to internalise the contradiction and seethe within.

Light is also thrown on anger in the structural family therapy perspective, which emphasises the nature of family organisations in constructing experiences. Key concepts include the ideas of boundary, hierarchy and sub-systems in families. For example, a child in a sibling hierarchy may be furious because his younger brother has sat down next to his father. A son feels a sense of intrusion into his personal space when his mother comes to tidy his bedroom. A child is angry at over-familiarity where she is treated as if she is in an earlier stage of the family life cycle. A father becomes angry because his son does not offer him the respect that he feels he is due.

Structural approaches have highlighted the importance of *triads* as the basis of family functioning. In his notion of triangulation, Minuchin (1974) suggests that anger between a dyad in a family may be *detoured* through a third person. For example, that escalating anger between the parents may be halted through the expression of distress in a child. In turn, recognition of the distress in their child may prompt experiences of guilt. However, this may lead to subsequent accusations and blame of each other, which re-evokes the anger in their interaction. Haley has described the *perverse triangle* as one where there is a coalition across hierarchical levels, for instance, a parent has a favourite among her children, in whom she confides her negative feelings about one of the siblings. A daughter may object that her mother speaks too openly about her father, this lack of a boundary around the couple subsystem resulting in the daughter feeling a conflict of loyalties. Such situations may be commonly found in organisations with consequent unhappiness, time spent on back-biting and enormous frustration and rage in the person disadvantaged.

The family therapists, Goldner et al. (1990) made an important contribution in their discussion of *gendered violence*. In their work with couples they emphasised the common finding that violence is far more frequently perpetrated by men on women than vice versa. They suggested that this is intimately tied up with a man feeling that he is privileged and entitled to treat the woman's body as *his* possession, which he is *free to attack*. Instead, they proposed that the male must take responsibility for his violence and the woman should take responsibility for protecting herself. They used a technique called *deconstructing the violent moment*, in which the man, who commonly denies that his violent actions were intended, is helped to recognise that he had agency over them. Similar points are made in the area of child sexual abuse (Essex et al., 1996) and violence perpetrated by adolescents (Downey, 1997).

Originally, these interpersonal analyses were contrasted to 'intrapsychic approaches' such as psychoanalytic or cognitive approaches (Haley, 1963). The latter were seen as inadequate because they focused on the individual and missed the patterning at a multipersonal level. Analogous to the behavioural revolution in the 1920s, Haley explicitly declared his lack of interest in subjective realities or internal worlds. While the systemic tradition was an enormously important development with huge implications for effective therapy, it could be criticised in its turn for leaving the *person* out of the equation (Procter, 1981).

Anger as Familial

To take an example mentioned under structural family therapy above, a boy is furious because his younger brother has taken his seat next to their father in a restaurant. The structural approach emphasises the pecking order being violated as explaining the anger and potential conflict. But actually, such patterns of behaviour are observable in most animal species including the proverbial chickens and even small fish! (Procter, D.A., 1996). From a constructivist perspective, we want to know what construings underlie these forms of organisations. In this example it may be that the child's fury results from an implicit construing that there is a legitimate hierarchy among siblings according to age and his younger brother has violated this belief. We will not have an adequate picture of this anger until we have established *which construct is being used* and the semantic context of this construct in both the *personal construct system* and the *family construct system*.

The deepest anger may occur when one of these shared constructs is invalidated. There is a feeling of betrayal because the other has seen the world in a different way to that which we agreed. There will be certain constructs, which we call *family constructs*, which define the family group as opposed to people outside the group (e.g. We are

Christian, unlike those bad people down the road) or distinguish between subsystems in the family (e.g. Parents in this family have authority over the children). Such constructs are more or less successfully negotiated by the members, using expectations from the tradition in which they were brought up. Members may hold family constructs, not because they have been particularly validated in their own experience, but because they have internalised them simply through loyalty to their family tradition. No doubt much construing associated prejudice against class or ethnic groups is of this type.

Anger as Choice

Likewise, we make a choice to construe something that involves being angry as opposed to the opposite pole (e.g. he's my friend and he's basically alright, even though I don't like the way he's talking). However, we tend to accumulate evidence and if the person goes too far or has gone on too long, we may suddenly 'flip' into construing it in the angry way. In effect, this contains a very common clinical observation that anger is seen as a response to some external trigger/s. Often this is stated as a sense of being provoked in a way that caused the anger. However, often what may look like a 'trigger' is mobilised by an internal anger, which has a longer duration in time. A construct governs the 'flip' (e.g. he's my friend vs he's a bastard) but more superordinate construing will be ethically judging the situation (I tolerated that vs this has gone too far). This construing is not necessarily easily amenable to conscious exploration. A considerable amount of therapeutic conversation is often required for a person to recognise the events in his or her recent and past life, which may have contributed to the flare-up into anger. Kelly ([1955] 1991) clearly pointed out that to understand a person, we need to be able to understand their actions not just in terms of specific constructs but in terms of how these are located within their broader personal construct system or life story.

In describing their experience of anger, people typically describe that their anger is a response to other's actions, 'he was winding me up', 'taking the piss', 'putting me down', 'laughing at me', 'giving me a look', and so on. At times the triggers may be even more direct, such as an actual threat or attack.

In the construction inherent in the above statements it is apparent that people are construing actions in particular ways, i.e. there is a choice. In fact, some of the descriptions are quite vague or ambiguous. For example, how is 'being given a look' defined? 'Prolonged eye contact accompanied by a sneer'. Each of us has a set of constructions about how we interpret certain actions or events. Furthermore, our construct system is likely to predispose us to selectively attend to certain events, actions or cues more than others. For example, if our construction is that the world is a hostile place and no one can be trusted, we may be continually on the alert for signs or confirmation of our constructions. Hence, although to perceive people as angry or threatening towards us is in part negative and anxiety-provoking, it may at the same time be fundamentally validating such a construct system.

Anger as Validation or Invalidation

This offers an additional analysis to McCoy's (1977) idea that anger involves *invalidation*. In a construct system, which is primed to perceive threat and anger, it is possible that anger then occurs through *validation*. Possibly this suggestion that anger can occur through validation as well as invalidation connects our PCP analysis more with a CBT approach. However, the difference in our position is that we do not necessarily see the person as engaged in dysfunctional thinking but in thinking that makes sense that 'fits' and has evolved in a particular developmental context. The therapeutic implications are that we need to explore how these beliefs have evolved and the super-ordinate constructs, especially about the self and ideal self, to which they are connected.

Anger as Reconstruction

Kelly emphasised that our beliefs were linked into a construct system, which is hierarchically organised. At the top of this system are constructs about the self – who and what we are. But not just any self will do. We all have a preferred or ideal self – what we aspire to be like. We are told in our families what it is to be a good vs bad boy or girl and in turn our families are informed by what is acceptable in society. Some suggest that we are increasingly charged with installing socially acceptable values and norms – conducting normalising processes (Gergen & Davis, 1985; White & Epston, 1990). However, Kelly also gave the option of *contrast reconstruction*. We can choose to reject large amounts of construing presented to us in our families and wider culture and frequently will, in adolescence particularly, reject the way our parents choose to construe things. Rachel gives us a beautiful example of this 'I did not want to be moody and aggressive like my Dad nor weak and submissive like my Mum'. It is notable though, especially in a child-abuse context, how hard it can be to carry this contra-identification to the full – parents often say how much they hated the abuse meted out to them, but then find themselves punishing their children in very similar ways. They have elaborated quite large subsystems of constructs from their parents and in the heat of the moment, revert back to these, despite their best intentions.

Anger as Internal/External

It is also common to distinguish *internally* vs *externally* directed anger. One of us (RD) works in two contexts: the first is with young people who exhibit eating disorders and self-harm and the second, young people who engage in various criminal activities, especially violence. It may be no surprise that 90 per cent of the first group are females and the latter nearly all males. Returning again to our accounts, we can see indications that this might happen. For Rick, a male discourse can be seen to prevail which not only encourages, but also locates his ideal self as within a construing of *to be strong* equals to *show your anger*. In contrast, for Rachel, her response can be seen to be shaped by the contrast pole of this discourse, which is that to be *female*, is to be *passive* and *be able to placate or nurture men, to ease their anger*. Within this construing it may also imply that she is to blame if she is unsuccessful in achieving this. This blaming of the self can become converted to anger towards the self, for one's inadequacies for falling short of the ideal-self.

Anger as Interpersonal

Perhaps one of the most significant contributions that Kelly offered was his concept of *sociality*. This preceded the concepts of *theory of mind*, (Baron-Cohen, 1997), *reflective functioning* and *meta-cognition* (Main et al., 1985, Fonagy et al., 1994) or *inter-subjectivity* (Shotter, 1987; Trevarthen, 1992). By sociality, Kelly meant that our relating to others is centrally based on our inferences about their construing. For example, I may try to assess whether someone deliberately or accidentally spilt my drink, or whether he or she realised that they had done so as part of my decision about how to react. Our initial actions may in fact be largely attempts to try to ascertain the nature of the other's construing before we respond. So, we might wait for an apology or invite some explanation by commenting, 'There's not much room here is there!'. Alternatively, some of the young offenders we work with appear to assume very rapidly that the action was deliberate or that it might be fun to use this as an excuse to start a fight. In turn, the latter is typically based on a construing about the other, such as whether they likewise have an aggressive view of the world and are likely to retaliate or have a 'wimpish' attitude, which will mean they will back off or be less of a real threat.

Anger will commonly involve *failures of sociality* too. We may get furious because someone misunderstands us, especially if our expectation is that they should bloody understand! If someone imputes a motive to us that we deny, we will likely be cross. Of course, a person may be angry because of the accuracy of the other's sociality. A young woman is cross because her father has correctly identified that she is sad because her boyfriend has not telephoned and 'It is *none of his business!*' Perhaps her construal of herself as grown up and independent now has been transgressed.

Anger as Hierarchical

A baby is already well able to express anger in the first few weeks of life, perhaps when too hot, hungry or in pain. A hierarchical construct system will gradually be elaborated, subsuming these subordinate constructs perhaps as unhappy or uncomfortable (but not yet verbalised). Over the second year of life, the toddler is learning to distinguish *me* from *you* and learning to alter another's state through teasing, offering comfort, showing concern and offering help (Dunn, 1993; Stern, 1998). This is likely to be the point where the *ethical* comes into play. Once the child recognises another's intention, it will be possible to be angry because you should let me have it, not just because I'm angry because I haven't got it.

The child with autism has difficulty in developing a hierarchical construct system (Procter, 2001). Screaming in infancy in autism is common and probably already evidence of a very young child responding to confusion and an inability to predict. Later on, the young child is more likely to be angry because something in the world is out of place or happening at the wrong time. They may be angry at the other because their expression is wrong, not being able to understand the signs of the other's feelings. The child with autism has difficulty with sociality and subsuming another's view and will respond at a more subordinate level, for example to disruption of routines and change. Anger may suddenly come out of the bluc because the poor super-ordinate structure precludes making a social prediction (Miles & Southwick, 2000). An example of this is a man with autism who gets in a rage at the mention of a particular topic although calms down immediately if distracted to something else.

Anger as Physiological

The James–Lange theory of emotion considers the nature of emotions in terms of whether the physiological state has precedence over the interpretative process – I must be angry because I *feel* anger. There is a dilemma in this view in that in order for the physiological response to occur, a process of interpretation, albeit perhaps at an unconscious level has already taken place. An idea which connects with this can also be seen within the narrative perspective in the notion of being 'out of discourse' – a sense of not knowing why I feel angry. From a Kellyan perspective, of course, we suggest that this is an unhelpful separation in that emotions, such as anger, are part and parcel of forming, or attempting to form, distinctions. The construct 'he's a fucking bastard' (said passionately) *is* the construct – it contains cognitive, emotional and relational content all in one package. Only psychological theory comes along and interprets such a statement as emphasising only one of these at the expense of the others!

The James–Lange approach, though, does alert us to the importance of considering the role of the interpretation of internal states in anger. One of the central roles of the family is the fundamental part it plays in giving meanings, or constructing the meanings of emotional states. For the young child the understanding of his or her internal experiences is shaped by the actions and utterances of family members. For example, a mother might say 'Jo, you shouldn't be getting angry, Dianne was only trying to help you'. In this statement she is both defining Jo's internal state as anger but also calling into doubt the legitimacy of this feeling and inviting a different emotion of gratitude.

Anger and Religion

Of course, we have not space here to do justice to the rich discourses themselves that underlie family construing of anger in different cultural and religious groups. There is a strong tradition of righteous anger in Judaism (for example, God's anger at Job) which continued into Christianity, for example, Christ's overturning the moneylenders' tables (Woodcock, personal communication, 2002). Anger and swearing in Christianity, even if only to have angry thoughts will often, however, be seen as evil. In Buddhism, anger is often seen as evidence of attachment to a delusory idea and denial of reality being fundamentally impermanent. These kind of beliefs will be embedded in family construing but possibly in quite an unaware way. Powerful images, such as Christ and the moneylenders, are likely to be influential validators of beliefs that people will often evoke in justification of their actions.

SOCIAL CONSTRUCTIONISM AND LANGUAGE

In the accounts of anger with which we started the chapter and in subsequent examples we can hear not only uniqueness in the ways in which people describe 'anger' in idiosyncratic ways, but also some commonalities in the language that is used. Social constructionist orientations (Foucault, 1975; Gergen & Davis, 1985) emphasise the centrality of language in constructing experiences. Most importantly, they emphasise how language connects each person to the heritage of ideas that construct our social world. They refer to constellations of ideas, which map out areas of experience as *discourses*. In many ways this connects with PCP ideas of commonality and shared construing, at the societal rather than the inter-personal level (Procter, 1996). In order to participate in our cultural context, we need to be aware of these shared assumptions even if we choose to contest them. This view is similar to Harré and Secord's (1972) notion of knowledge of cultural rules or episodes.

Social constructionism sees language as being much more central than PCP does. For the latter, constructs are distinctions or choices that are not primarily linguistic (e.g. they may be pre-verbal, for example, kinaesthetic or visual). A verbal label is attached to a construct pole as a symbol (Kelly, [1955] 1991). For social constructionists language is primary, with a doubt about the existence or importance of personal construing. We would wish to synthesise these positions into one model where societal and personal construing are both given weight and importance.

The Language of Anger

In Box 9.1 is a list of 24 words used in English. This is, of course, not a complete list by any means. It would be boosted tremendously if we were to consider the many words and phrases used in specific families, localities or cultural groups. 'Ballistic' is currently a popular word which crops up in our work with families in our area, the county of Somerset in the UK. We do not know how widespread its use is, but its origin is clearly recent and presumably reflects the preoccupations of the Cold War era.

Box 9.1 Words in English used in the area of anger

Anger	Crossness	Indignance	Tantrums
Aggravation	Crotchety	Irritability	Temper
Aggression	Fighting	Peevishness	Violence
Arguments	Fury	Rage	Venom
Ballistic	Hate	Resentment	Vexation
Conflict	Hostility	Stroppiness	Wrath

The following observations on these words can be made, which are relevant to how language unconsciously structures the way we might think about the topic.

- Most of the words are nouns or adjectives implying that the anger is something that people *are* or *have*. As psychologists working in our tradition, we might have preferred an emphasis on *verbs* (arguing, fighting) which would reflect anger as a doing or an action.
- Some words, for example, *aggression*, *violence* and *hostility*, imply the involvement of another person or persons, as opposed to *anger*, *rage* or *fury* which refer to emotions, not necessarily directed to an object or person.
- Even where the word does connote a process between the angry person and another (e.g. *hostility*), the implication is still that it is a quality or action belonging to an *individual* directed at another. '*Conflict*' is one of the few words above that genuinely refers to a *relationship* as opposed to an individual actor. This is in line with Haley's observation (1963) about the number of words in the language that there are for individual pathology as opposed to disturbed relationships. This may reflect many centuries of construing in this area of a more individualistic kind. The interactional approaches, only developed in the twentieth century, may be genuinely new ways of construing human behaviour and experience.
- PCP emphasises the importance of a *contrast pole* in understanding the meaning of any construct. Unlike many words in English, strangely, there seem to be few natural contrasts to the examples listed in Box 9.1. What are the opposites of these words? – calm?, tolerant?, forgiveness?, reconciliation? These hardly seem satisfactory. One cannot even attach the prefix 'un-' to any of the words above. This is highly relevant to therapy, which emphasises *solutions* and *goals* as opposed to *problems*.

For social constructionism, language carries assumptions about how we 'should' act, notions of legitimate as opposed to an illegitimate self. Discourses map out for us possible and permissible selves and locate us in terms of gender, age, and religion. For example, in our internal conversations we may berate ourselves for being too 'childish', or for being not manly enough in our responses. They appear to map out different domains of possibilities for men and women and may lead to perpetuating discrimination and disqualification of particular groups.

SOME INTEGRATIONS

Many theoretical approaches to anger reflect commonly held Western discourses regarding anger, which often tend to favour construing anger as an intra-personal phenomenon in contrast to a more subjugated view of anger as inter-personal. A good example of this is Livingstone's (2001) study which showed that staff looking after older adults during intimate care procedures tended to construe their anger and aggression as being *uncontrollable* (e.g. due to dementia) and *internal* (as opposed to an aspect of the caring relationship).

Gergen (1997), in the social constructionist tradition, describes sequences of anger and other emotions, grounding their handling in the social conventions and narratives of the society in which they occur. In the tradition of constructive alternativism (Kelly, [1955] 1991), Goldner and her colleagues (1990) suggest that we think about anger in terms of *multiple lenses*: individual emotional development, systemic patterns and escalations and finally in terms of the culturally shared discourses that guide our actions. Goldner suggests that anger and violence in couples is to be seen as an example *in extremis* of the typical gendered ideas dominant in Western and other cultures about the role of men and women. She describes how strong and stereotypical notions of masculinity and femininity influenced many of the men she worked with. They felt it was their role to be the breadwinners, to be tough and dominant. In fact, at the moment of violence many of the men admitted that they felt weak and vulnerable, that they felt they were losing control of their partners and terrified that they might be abandoned. Furthermore, these feelings of vulnerability were a direct threat to their ideas of their ideal self – strong, invulnerable, tough, unemotional, and so on. More broadly, we are suggesting that the widely used concept of the 'ideal self' in PCT can potentially be linked to a cultural level of analysis. The ideal self can be seen as the reservoir of 'shoulds': how I should act, feel, and think as a man or woman. In contrast to the male position, Goldner also wrote that many of the women were in a similar way strongly influenced by traditional ideas of femininity, especially that they should be nurturing, loving and caring and put themselves second. In part, she argued that many of the women were caught in this discourse, which led them to a view that they were failures as women if their love and care could not heal their men.

THERAPEUTIC CONSIDERATIONS

There are many approaches which are useful in working with children and young people around anger including PCP approaches (Butler & Green, 1998; Ravenette,

1999) and the use of *qualitative grids* (Procter, 2002). Ravenette's technique, 'a drawing and its opposite' is particularly useful in getting to a child's constructs about anger, with less emphasis on verbal communication in the session. There are practical books with useful ideas for parents and children (see, for example, Eastman & Rozen, 1994; Oram, 1982). It is useful to use words like 'cross' or 'stroppy' in therapy with children and young people as they have a whimsical quality about them that reduces the risk of unwittingly evoking the angry feelings in the session, which can result in the child ceasing to cooperate.

Working with family members together has an enormous contribution to make to the resolution of problems although the work needs to be handled with great skill and sensitivity. The family therapist can facilitate a conversation about the most difficult issues through to some constructive negotiation and reflection, where otherwise the members would have escalated into a conflict or go storming out of the room. The therapist's empathy, politeness and humour are crucial here. Kellyan acceptance and respect for all family members' positions (including absent ones) are fundamental. The art here is to do this simultaneously but the philosophy of *constructive alternativism* helps with this. If the therapist's ability to *subsume* the members' positions is lost, she needs to seek supervision to reclaim her sense of impartiality. We agree with Herr and Weakland (1979) that one should avoid getting into an argument oneself with clients in therapy. Is it ever right to be angry for a therapeutic purpose? Milton Erickson describes a case in which he deliberately provokes a proud man of German origin who has suffered a debilitating stroke. He does this in order to motivate him to engage in the super-human struggle which is required in his rehabilitation.

Particular types of question are helpful. Asking about the specific examples of difficulty and going through the 'facts' of who said what in a blow-by-blow account is very helpful. Asking who gets the angriest in the family. Who tends to calm down the quickest? How did you eventually resolve it? These are helpful questions. The therapist must remain calm, be unfazed by the expression of anger and be willing to actively slow down the pace of the conversation. If an argument erupts, the therapist may politely say how useful it is to experience this as it helps her to understand much more clearly what each party wants to say. This often calms things down. She may ask whether this is a typical example of an argument, or if it goes differently to how it happens in other settings. However, If potential violence in or after the session is likely, then conjoint work may be contra-indicated (Goldner, 1985).

CONCLUSION

Of course clients will bring their rage and fury to the session but the systemic construct practitioner will steer the session towards reflecting on angry episodes, exploring the implications of what they mean and encouraging creative discussion and thinking about them. If an argument arises in the session, the therapist will want to intervene to regulate the pace and ensure that the process remains therapeutic and not allow damaging reprisal and point scoring.

This therapeutic stance has the potential to encourage some new processes around anger in families, for example, that critical feelings can be voiced and considered without an escalation into destructive patterns. Many families describe the helpful aspects of family therapy just in these terms. Mrs Taylor said to RD: 'I've been impressed how my family . . . we've all talked together, talked about things much easier than at home, possibly because you're the adjudicator and perhaps triggered off questions that would have been difficult to get round to in a sensible way in a more claustrophobic atmosphere when we are getting wound up about talking about things' (Dallos & Draper, 2001, p. 2).

REFERENCES

Baron-Cohen, S. (1997). *Mindblindness: An Essay on Autism and Theory of Mind*. Cambridge, MA: MIT Press.

Bateson, G. (1955). A theory of play and fantasy. *Psychiatric Research Reports*, 2, 39–51.

Bateson, G. (1972). *Steps to an Ecology of Mind*. New York: Ballantyne.

Bateson, G., Jackson, D., Haley, J. and Weakland, J. (1956) Toward a theory of schizophrenia. *Behavioural Science*, 1, 251–264.

Beck, A. T. (1967). *Depression: Clinical, Experiential and Theoretical Aspects*. New York: Harper & Row.

Brazelton, T. B. (1974). *Monographs of the Society for Research into Child Development*. Chicago: University of Chicago Press.

Brazelton, T. B. and Cramer, B. G. (1991). *The Earliest Relationship: Parents, Infants and the Drama of Early Attachment*. London: Karnac Books.

Butler, R. & Green, D. (1998). *The Child Within: The Exploration of Personal Construct Psychology with Young People*. Oxford: Butterworth-Heinemann.

Chatwin, B. (1987). *The Songlines*. London: Jonathan Cape.

Dallos, R. (1991). *Family Belief Systems, Therapy and Change: A Constructional Approach*. Milton Keynes: Open University Press.

Dallos, R. D. & Draper, R. (2002). *Introduction to Family Therapy*. Milton Keynes: Open University Press.

Downey, L. (1997). Adolescent violence: a systemic and feminist perspective. *A.N.Z. Journal of Family Therapy*, 18(2), 70–79.

Dunn, J. (1993). *Young Children's Close Relationships: Beyond Attachment*. London: Sage.

Eastman, M. & Rozen, R. C. (1994). *Taming the Dragon in Your Child: Solutions for Breaking the Cycle of Family Anger*. Chichester: John Wiley & Sons.

Ellis, A. (1977). *Anger: How to Live With and Without It*. New Jersey: Citadel.

Essex, S., Gumbleton, J. & Luger, C. (1996). Resolutions: working with families where responsibility for abuse is denied. *Child Abuse Review*, 5, 191–201.

Fonagy, P., Steele, M., Steele, H., Higgit, A. & Target, M. (1994). The theory and practice of resilience. *Journal of Child Psychology and Psychiatry*, 35(2), 231–257.

Foucault, M. (1975). *The Archaeology of Knowledge*. London: Tavistock.

Gergen, K. (1997). *Realities and Relationships: Soundings in Social Construction*. Cambridge, MA: Harvard University Press.

Gergen, K. J. & Davis, K. E. (eds) (1985). *The Social Construction of the Person*. New York: Springer-Verlag.

Goldner, V. (1985). Warning: family therapy may be hazardous to your health. *Family Therapy Networker, Nov.–Dec.*, 19–23.

Goldner, V., Penn, P., Scheinberg, M. & Walker, G. (1990). Love and violence: gender paradoxes in volatile attachments, *Family Process*, 29(4), 343–364.

Haley, J. (1963). *Strategies of Psychotherapy*. New York: Grune and Stratton.

Harré, R. & Secord, P. F. (1972). *The Explanation of Social Behaviour*. Oxford: Blackwell.

Herr, J. & Weakland, J. H. (1979). *Counseling Elders and their Families*. New York: Springer.

Houston, J. (1998). *Making Sense with Offenders: Personal Constructs, Therapy and Change*. Chichester: John Wiley & Sons.

Kelly, G. A. ([1955] 1991). *The Psychology of Personal Constructs*, (vols 1 and 2). New York: Norton.

Livingstone, L. (2001). An application of attributional models of helping to the care of elderly residents with dementia who manifest aggressive resistance during intimate care. Unpublished doctoral thesis, University of Plymouth.

Main, M., Kaplan, N. & Cassidy, J. (1985). Security in infancy, childhood and adulthood: a move to the level of representation. In I. Bretherton & E. Waters (eds), *Growing Points of Attachment Theory and Research, Monographs of the Society for Research in Child Development*, 50: (1–2) Serial No. 209.

McCoy, M. (1977). A reconstruction of emotion. In D. Bannister (ed.), *New Perspectives in Personal Construct Theory*. London: Academic Press.

Miles, B. S. & Southwick (2000). *Asperger's Syndrome and Difficult Moments: Practical Solutions for Daily Challenges*. London: Jessica Kingsley.

Minuchin, S. (1974). *Families and Family Therapy*. London: Tavistock.

Novaco, R. W. (2000). Anger, In A. E. Kazdin (ed.), *Encyclopaedia of Psychology*. Washington, DC: American Psychological Association and Oxford University Press.

Oram, H. (1982). *Angry Arthur*. London: Red Fox.

Piaget, J. (1955). *The Child's Construction of Reality*. London: Routledge and Kegan Paul.

Procter, D. A. (1996). An analysis of the Free Distribution Theory in the Platty. Unpublished BSc thesis, John Moores University, Liverpool.

Procter, H. G. (1981). Family construct psychology: an approach to understanding and treating families. In S. Walrond-Skinner (ed.), *Developments in Family Therapy*. London: Routledge.

Procter, H. G. (1985). A construct approach to family therapy and systems intervention. In E. Button, *Personal Construct Theory and Mental Health*. Beckenham: Croom Helm.

Procter, H. G. (1996). The Family Construct System. In D. Kalekin-Fishman & B. Walker (eds), *The Construction of Group Realities: Culture, Society and Personal Construct Psychology*. Malabar, FL: Krieger.

Procter, H. G. (2001). Personal Construct Psychology and autism. *Journal of Constructivist Psychology*, *14*, 107–126.

Procter, H. G. (2002). Constructs of individuals and relationships. *Context*, *59*, 11–12.

Ravenette, A. T. (1999). *Personal Construct Theory in Educational Psychology*. London: Whurr.

Schachter, S. & Singer, J. E. (1962). Cognitive, social and physiological determinants of emotional state, *Psychological Review*, *69*, 379–399.

Schildkraut, J. J. & Kety, S. S. (1967). Biogenic amines and emotion. *Science*, *156*, 21–30.

Shotter, J. (1987). The social construction of us: problems of accountability and narratology. In R. Burnett, P. McGhee & D. D. Clarke (eds), *Accounting for Relationships*. London: Methuen.

Stern, D. (1998). *The Interpersonal World of the Infant: A View from Psychoanalysis and Developmental Psychology*. London: Karnac.

Trevarthen, C. (1992). The function of emotions in early infant communication and development. In J. Nadel & L. Camioni (eds), *New Perspectives in Early Communicative Development*, London: Routledge.

Watzlawick, P., Beavin, J. & Jackson, D. D. (1968). *Pragmatics of Human Communication: A Study of Interactional Patterns, Pathologies and Paradoxes*. London: Faber and Faber.

White, M. & Epston, D. (1990). *Narrative Means to Therapeutic Ends*. London: Norton.

Young, J.E. (1999). *Cognitive Therapy for Personality Disorders: A Schema-Focused Approach*. Sarasota, FL: Professional Resources Press.

10

GENDER AND ANGER

*Bhavisha Dave, Dina Pekkala, Diane Allen
and Peter Cummins*

When the 'Working with Anger' groups started in Coventry it was apparent that fewer women than men were referred for anger (a ratio of 3:1). By contrast, our colleagues working with deliberate self-harm reported an infinitely higher referral rate of women than men (at least 10:1). Despite our endeavours to run mixed anger groups, we have often ended up with all-male groups. We thought of taking advantage of this and comparing an all-male and an all-female group, so we set out to form an all-female group. We did not realise how difficult this would be, and to date we have not managed to run one, though we have had some interesting experiences from comparing the all-male and mixed gender groups.

This chapter explores gender differences in the expression and experience of anger, societal expectations and the impact of those expectations and norms on clients.

The language of Kelly ([1995] 1991) is always masculine. The fundamental postulate talks of the way in which 'HE' anticipates events. Five of his 11 corollaries specify that it is:

> 'for *his* convenience' (Organization Corollary)
> 'a person chooses for *himself*' (Choice Corollary)
> 'as *he* successively construes' (Experience)
> '*his* psychological processes' (Commonality)
> '*he* may play a role' (Sociality)

Where this is acknowledged, it is simply assumed that this is just a reflection of the societal expectations of the time that Kelly was writing in (in the late 1940s/early

Working with Anger: A Constructivist Approach.
Edited by Peter Cummins. © 2006 John Wiley & Sons, Ltd.

1950s). It follows from this that, in response to current societal expectations, we just have to alter to *him/her*. An example of this approach is explained by Leitner and Dunnett (1993 in their preface p. x):

> A great deal of discussion has gone into maintaining gender neutrality while avoiding awkward phrasing. In approximately the first half of each chapter we assume a female therapist and a male client; we reverse these in the second half of each chapter. When discussing people in general, the male gender is used for approximately the first half of each chapter; the female gender for the second half. Of course in situations where specific clinical illustrations are being discussed we have maintained the genders as they were in the therapy room.

This demonstrates how some personal construct pychology (PCP) writers aim 'to maintain gender neutrality'. In contrast, in the clinical field working with angry clients, the issue is more controversial.

GIRLS CONSTRUE DIFFERENTLY

There is a small but consistent PCP literature which suggests that there are gender differences in construing in general. Landfield (1971) found that females tended to use more complex sets of constructs to describe people, for example using multiple descriptions whereas males tended to use single constructs. He summarised this as women construing more holistically. Chetwynd (1976) showed that men and women had different stereotypes of the role of wife and mother. In comparing the two, women saw little difference between 'wife' and 'mother' but the men saw a wide contrast. Chetwynd reviewed the literature on the development of these constructs and suggested that the critical differences in perception between male and female occur in the years between adolescence and early adulthood. Phillips (1985, p. 282) examined adolescents' (aged 13/14) process of construing in the classroom. She found a 'marked difference' between the boys' and the girls' constructs. The boys' constructs tended to have logical opposites as poles while the girls tended to use more 'complex constructs'. Sypher and Sypher (1987) found, when they looked at the construct systems underlying liked and disliked co-workers, that women typically display significantly more differentiated construct systems. Sypher and Zorn (1988, p. 41) note that 'gender differences in construct system content are . . . important in understanding communicative choices but they have been . . . ignored'. Sypher and Zorn's conclusion was that the research may imply that females are more likely to see both sides of a person. This appears to echo Landfield's (1971) suggestion that women 'are more adept at construing other people and also tend to perceive them in more holistic ways'. This is a good example of sociality in action (see Chapter 1).

This difference in gender construing is reinforced by Campbell and Muncer (1987) who concluded that men and women have very different implicit models of aggression. They propose that in America gender is an important part of understanding what anger and aggression mean to the individual. Howells and Day (2002) concur and highlight the failure to address the anger management programmes possible different needs of women has been neglected'. Robertson (2005) addresses this issue in a chapter that outlines a way of providing anger treatment for women with developmental difficulties. She was able to find only two previous strands of research which focused on female anger. One of these strands was a series of studies, all of which were within the forensic setting. The other strand was a series of case reports from within a private psychodynamic practice. Robertson's (2005) comment that 'this is not an approach which lends itself to treatment with our clinical population' is equally true of the population we work with.

To address this issue within our Coventry 'Working with Anger' group, we decided to look at the gender differences in construing anger within our groups. We realised yet again the truth of the classic Kelly ([1995] 1991) quote, 'If you want to know what's going on . . . ask the patient he just might tell you' . . . and SHE might tell you too.

BOYS VERSUS GIRLS

Steve's experiences epitomise many of the experiences of our male anger clients: 'When I was growing up, my father used to hit me. Out on the street I'd often come off worse from fights. If I went home crying, my father would hit me for being such a wimp and send me back out. "Boys don't cry, they fight" was his motto. My tears meant I wasn't a real man. "Don't be such a girl" he would berate me as he smacked me around and told me "It'll toughen you up"'.

Julie's anger is also rooted in her childhood, but by contrast Julie was expected to 'Shut up and put up'.

'I used to get angry when my father used to abuse me. When I'd go and talk to mum about it, she would ignore it and tell me to be quiet and go off and play. I became a sex toy for my father and a punch bag for my brothers, and she wonders why I'm so pissed off with her now'.

> What are little boys made of?
> Frogs and snails and puppy dogs' tails
> That's what little boys are made of!
> What are little girls made of?
> Sugar and spice and all things nice
> That's what little girls are made of!

This nursery rhyme reflects different societal expectations of boys and girls. Boys should be tough. They should compete and challenge. If they experience emotions of hurt or sadness, they should not show it to others, as it's not a 'manly' thing to do. Men are expected to be rough, tough, independent, competitive and macho. Masculine attitudes develop as boys internalise cultural norms and expectations about gender-appropriate behaviour (Thompson & Pleck, 1995). Studies show fathers stimulate their sons to engage in aggressive activities from about 18 months (Miller, 1991). By 3 years of age boys are more likely to kick, shove, wrestle and hit more than girls (Fagot, Leinbach, & Hagan, 1986). Pollack (2000) describes how a boy code itself consists of a policy whereby boys must exhibit toughness and deny any fear and weakness. (See Chapter 12 for a further discussion of male construing.)

Girls, on the other hand, should be nice and pleasant, offering support and kindness to others. Emotions (as long as they are harmonious) are acceptable but anger is not. Traditionally, women are expected to be passive, empathic, forgiving, homely and nurturing. Women are of the 'weaker sex'. Birnbaum (1983) and Fuchs and Thelen (1988), as cited in Kring (2000), have found that children view the expression of anger as being more acceptable from boys than girls. Sharkin (1993) (also cited in Kring, 2000) maintains that while male anger is construed as a socially acceptable emotion, it is also pathologised as a masculine potential for lack of control and failure to moderate emotional expression according to the requirements of the situation.

The Expression of Anger

Women are more likely to suppress their anger or express it through somatic symptoms than men (Haynes, Levine, Scotch, Feinleib, & Kennel, 1978). Men's responses to angry situations are reported to be more verbally or physically aggressive in nature than women's (Harris, 1992a). Most researchers attribute this difference to gender role socialisation and not to biological sex (Brody & Hall, 1993). Kring (2000) is critical of this, citing Deaux and Major's (1990) comment that using a socialisation argument is not much more circular than saying that people are different because they are different. Gender roles do, however, appear to play a major part in the decision to refer people for anger management. In our experience, although fewer women are referred to our service for anger than men, women often seek help for their anger themselves as they are concerned about the possible impact this may have on their family, particularly if children are involved. Men, however, tend to be coerced into seeking help, either by their partners, who are threatening to leave unless they do something about their anger, or they are encouraged to seek help by social services or probation services.

This reluctance by men may be linked to the observation that men consider anger as acceptable, even when expressed physically (Courtenay, 2000). This acceptance of anger as appropriate is often what is articulated in our anger groups and it can be quite difficult to challenge.

Men are more likely to feel that behaving aggressively will improve their mood, while women see distraction as a means of improving their mood (Harris, 1992b). Howells and Day (2002) propose that anger is perceived as more appealing than depression. Tiedens (2001), as cited in Howells and Day (2002), suggests there are greater perceived benefits of anger for men than women. In our 'Working with Anger' group when we look at the benefits of anger (see Cummins, Chapter 2) the men often express the opinion that anger is seen as sexually attractive to women. Similarly, Taylor and Novaco (2005) report three main areas of gender differences. They affect the expression of anger (males are more physical, while females are more verbal); the situation (males are more likely to express anger outside the home and to people they are not connected to, while females are more likely to express anger in the home and to loved ones); and the antecedent for the anger (males are more likely to respond angrily to behaviour causing harm and to physically aggressive females, while females are more likely to respond angrily to verbal aggression and insensitive or condescending behaviour). Milovchevich, Howells, Drew & Day (2001) found that gender role identification rather than gender was a factor in anger scores on the STAXI-2, with both males and females who identified with a masculine role having higher Trait-Anger scores, while males and females who identified with a feminine role, having higher Anger-In scores.

Measuring the Expression of Anger

Studies investigating the expression of anger using State Trait anger scales (e.g. Kopper, 1991; Deffenbacher et al., 1996) have largely been unable to identify gender differences. Kring (2000, p. 223) suggests that what is needed is 'theoretically derived hypotheses about how and when women might differ in their anger response'. There is also no gender difference between men and women when studying what triggers anger, for example, Frodi (1977) found both men and women expressed feelings of anger when incited by the opposite sex. Campbell and Muncer (1987) (as cited in Kring, 2000) also found no differences between men and women in anger antecedents. What is evident from our quantitative assessment of men and women referred for anger is the similarity in their anger profiles on the STAXI-2 (see Chapter 14 in this volume by Pekkala and Dave). Both men and women tend to score within the higher quartile on Anger Expression Out and Anger Expression In dimensions and overall anger scores, while scoring within the lowest quartile on Anger Control Out and In. However, while men often score on the 99 percentile on the majority of anger dimensions, women are barely within the clinical population (see Figure 10.1). This suggests that the referred women, the system surrounding the women and their referrers are less tolerant of women's anger.

The lower referral threshold for women suggests that when women express anger it is seen as problematic and requiring management at a much lower level than would be the case for male expressions of anger. This pattern may illuminate the summary by Kring (2000, p. 221) who argued that 'the accumulated evidence does not allow us to conclude that men are more angry than women, or that women are more angry

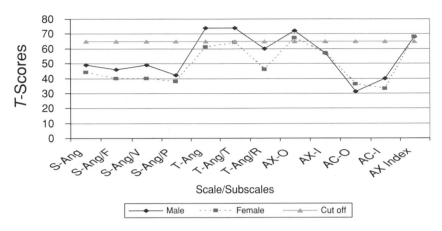

Figure 10.1   STAXI-2 Score Profile of male and female members of the Coventry 'Working with Anger' group

than men or that men and women do not differ'. Men may not be more angry but they would appear to be allowed to express far more anger than women. Our experience would suggest that women who are invalidated demonstrate a much lower level of anger expression than men. This pattern begins in childhood and continues on into adulthood. As McLaughlin, Maras, Reiger & Paternite suggest in Chapter 12 of this volume, male invalidation is often not acknowledged until it is expressed by violence. By contrast, many of the women we have worked with are referred because of levels of anger expression that would not have been noticed within the male population.

We looked at this within our anger groups by asking group members to give us their perspective on how their gender expresses anger, and how they think the opposite sex expresses anger. We found clear distinctions between men's expression of anger and women's expression of anger. Here are some examples of their responses:

- *Men's perspective on men's anger:* Lash out, threaten, goad, do not forgive nor forget and play physical games to get their own back, hold grudges.
- *Women's perspective on men's anger:* sulks, physical, threaten, sarcastic, go drinking, they will make you stay and listen, drive the car fast.
- *Men's perspective on women's anger:* the bigger the problem the louder they will argue, they will bring up things from the past, little things will annoy them, they will give you the silent treatment, will cry, they'll refuse to cook for you.
- *Women's perspective on women's anger:* ignore the other person, talk with friends about the situation, withdraw sex, self-harm, scream, pull hair/scratch, bring irrelevant issues into the situation, and spend on his credit card.

We have repeated this exercise every time we go to talk to groups about anger by asking them for their opinions about gendered expression of anger and found that the same examples (as within a clinical population) were reiterated by other clients, colleagues and university students.

Many women in our groups relied upon social support (for example, from family and friends) as a means of responding to their anger. Conversely, the male members of our groups reported an inability to discuss their angry feelings and experiences with family and friends. Without exception, male group members cite the opportunity that the group gave them to discuss their feelings and experiences as being one of the most valuable aspects of the group experience. In contrast, women have a propensity to discuss their angry event more often than men (Haynes, Levine, Scotch, Feinleib & Kennel, 1978; Thomas, 1991).

Our experience has been that groups can be run single-gendered (all male) or mixed. Irrespective of the group, the same gender issues arise. We have observed that groups are most effective when the group consists of both male and female members. They then have the opportunity to listen to the views and experiences of the opposite sex which encourages clients to hear how the other gender construes their constructions of the world (see section on sociality in Chapter 1). A good example of this was a recent interchange in the group when a female group member said, 'You can't rely on men' then turned to the male group members saying, 'Nothing personal, guys'.

POSSIBLE NEUROLOGICAL BASIS FOR GENDER DIFFERENCES IN EMOTIONAL BEHAVIOUR

Gur, Gunning-Dixon and Gur (2002) looked at sex differences in temporo-limbic and frontal brain volumes of healthy adults. They found that women had larger orbital frontal cortices than men. Part of this cortex is associated with regulating emotion and monitoring behaviour. This may suggest an explanation of neurological influence for sex differences and behaviour such as aggression.

Researchers have also observed gender differences in two areas in the frontal and temporal lobes connected to language, the Broca's and Wernicke's areas. Schlaepfer et al. (1995) found these areas were significantly larger in women than men, suggesting a possible explanation for gender differences in the ability to verbally express emotions.

THE 'WORKING WITH ANGER' GROUP

Anna, aged 32, was a victim of physical abuse as a child. Her dreams and hopes of going into a sporting profession were shattered by her father who used to say 'It's not a woman thing'. Constantly discouraged from her ambition, Anna then reluctantly decided to give it up. As one of four siblings and the only female among them she was often forgotten or rather 'left out' from the 'lads' time' her father used to have with her three brothers, which often took the form of going to football matches or going for a drink together. Anna would look for support from her mother but her mother (also a victim of abuse by Anna's father) chose not to see what was happening. Anna grew up searching for acceptance and inclusion, someone who would not take her for granted. This, however, did not transpire in her relationships. Anna found herself vulnerable, searching for acceptance, love and attention but time and time again becoming involved in abusive relationships. Her main way of defending herself and to be noticed was to use her physical attributes i.e., her tall, strong, feminine frame. The problem was that when she felt invalidated, she would become very upset and angry often becoming verbally and, at times, physically aggressive.

Adam, a 36-year-old, was often let down by people and soon grew to expect this from everyone. A hard tough bloke is what he was brought up to be. In a fight or flight situation, Adam was taught to always fight. 'Flight is what girls do' is the voice that always haunted him. Adam was a man who always believed that actions speak louder than words. He described the familiar experience of wanting to talk to someone, because he was scared and upset about being bullied, only to be laughed at and called a 'wimp' by people he trusted.

Anna and Adam both repeatedly talked of behaving the way their parents, partners and society expected of them and sometimes going against what they wanted for themselves. While they were aware of this conflict, they initially did not link it with their expression of anger. Using a constructivist framework we have been able to explore Adam and Anna's anger in depth. This approach enables them to understand the origins of their anger and the implications this can have for their family network. These implications are almost always seen as destructive and requiring containment.

More recently, researchers have begun to look into the concept of constructive anger (Davidson, MacGregor, Stuhr, Dixon & MacLean, 2000). Constructive anger can be used to make others aware of how the person is feeling and attempting to resolve the problem. We often commence our anger groups by clearly stating, that we are not there to teach people to 'manage' their anger, nor do we wish to turn all our group members into 'door mats' or 'pussy cats'. We are adamant that anger is a useful emotion, when expressed to the appropriate degree, to the appropriate person, at the appropriate time. This is a framework which was first suggested by Aristotle (see Chapter 13 by Warren in this volume).

CONCLUSION

While much of the constructivist literature is gender neutral, there is common agreement, supported by research, that some aspects of construing, and many of society's expectations regarding anger, differ between the two genders. Some of this may relate to neurological differences between the sexes. Taylor and Novaco assert that women's anger has been given credence, both in relation to their discontent with social inequality and in the breaking of the social stereotype that anger was a male province. They conclude that anger has become 'an equal opportunity product' (2005, p. 77). This is validated by Robertson's (2005, p. 180) comment that 'few differences were found between the anger experienced by the women and that experienced by the men'. This may be true in forensic settings, but our findings are consistently different. We have repeatedly compared the STAXI-2 scores of women referred with anger to men referred with anger; our findings suggest that while men and women's *profiles* are similar, men referred score within the atypical population, while women are scoring within the typical anger population. Our research suggests that women get referred for help with their anger at much lower levels of anger expression than men, and that they are themselves much more likely than men to seek such help. The women referred to us would not be defined as having an anger problem according to quantitative measures. However, according to the women, their families and their referrers, the level of anger expressed by these women justifies referral to a tertiary psychological service. This pattern is linked to societal expectations of anger expression which are reflected by our group participants. There appear to be some clinical gains to be made from exploiting these differences, by mixing the sexes in therapy groups, in order to promote the development of greater sociality as a way of challenging societal expectations.

REFERENCES

Brody, L. & Hall, J. (1993). Gender and emotion. In M. Lewis & J. M. Haviland (eds), *Handbook of Emotions*. New York: Guilford, pp. 447–460.

Campbell, A. & Muncer, S. (1987). Models of anger and aggression in the social talk of women and men. *Journal of the Theory of Social Behavior*, *17*, 489–511.

Chetwynd, J. (1976). Sex differences in stereotyping the roles of wife and mother. In P. Slater (ed.), *The Measurement of Intrapersonal Space by Grid Technique*. Vol. 1: *Explorations of Intrapersonal Space*. London: John Wiley & Sons, pp. 142–152.

Courtenay, W. H. (2000). Engendering health: a social constructionist examination of men's health beliefs and behaviors. *Psychology of Men & Masculinity*, *1*, 4–15.

Davidson, K., MacGregor, M. W., Stuhr, J., Dixon, K. & MacLean, D. (2000). Constructive anger verbal behaviour predicts blood pressure in a population-based sample. *Health Psychology*, *19*, 55–64.

Deffenbacher, J. L. et al. (1996). State-Trait Anger Theory and the Utility of the Trait Anger Scale. *Journal of Counseling Psychology*, *43*(2), 131–148.

Fagot, B. I., Leinbach, M. D. & Hagan, R. (1986). Gender labelling and the development of sex-typed behaviours. *Developmental Psychology*, *22*, 440–443.

Frodi, A. (1977). Sex differences in the perception of a provocation: a survey. *Perceptual and Motor Skills*, *44*, 113–114.

Gur, R. C, Gunning-Dixon, F. & Gur, R. E. (2002). Sex differences in temporo-limbic and frontal brain volume of healthy adults. *Cerebral Cortex*, *12*(9), 998–1003.

Harris, M. (1992a). Sex and ethnic differences in past aggressive behaviour. *Journal of Family Violence*, *7*, 85–102.

Harris, M. (1992b). Beliefs about how to reduce anger. *Psychological Reports*, *70*, 203–210.

Haynes, S. G., Levine, S., Scotch, N., Feinleib, M. & Kannel, W. B. (1978). The relationship of psychosocial factors to coronary heart disease in the Framingham study: I. Methods and risk factors. *American Journal of Epidemiology*, *107*, 362–383.

Howells, K. & Day, A. (2002). Readiness for anger management: clinical and theoretical issues. *Clinical Psychology Review*, *584*, 1–20.

Kelly, G. A. ([1955] 1991). *The Psychology of Personal Constructs* (vols 1 and 2). London: Routledge.

Kopper, B. A. & Epperson, D. L. (1991). Women and anger: sex and sex-role comparisions in the expression of anger. *Psychology of Women Quarterly*, *15* (1), 7–14.

Kring, A. M . (2000). Gender and anger. In A. H. Fischer (ed.), *Gender and Emotion: Social Psychological Perspectives*. Cambridge: Cambridge University Press, pp. 212–231.

Landfield, A. W. (1971). *Personal Construct Systems in Psychotherapy*. Chicago: Rand-McNally.

Leitner, L. M. & Dunnett, N. G. M. (1993). *Critical Issues in Personal Construct Psychotherapy*. Melbourne, FL: Krieger.

Miller, J. B. (1991). The construction of anger in women and men. In J. Jordan, A. Kaplan, J. B. Miller, I. Stiver & J. Surrey (eds), *Women's Growth in Connection: Writings from the Stone Center*. New York: Guilford, pp. 181–196.

Milovchevich, D., Howells, K., Drew, N. & Day, A. (2001). Sex and gender role differences in anger: an Australian community study. *Personality & Individual Differences*, 31, 117–127.

Phillips, E. M. (1985). Using the repertory grid in the classroom. In N. Beail (ed.), *Repertory Grid Technique and Personal Constructs: Applications in Clinical and Educational Settings* London: Croom Helm, pp. 275–294.

Pollack, W. S. (2000). The Columbine syndrome: boys and the fear of violence. *National Forum: The Phi Kappa Phi Journal*, *80*(4), 39–42.

Robertson, A. (2005) Anger treatment for women with developmental disabilities. In J. L. Taylor & R.W. Novaco (eds). *Anger Treatment for People with Developmental Disabilities*. Chichester: John Wiley & Sons.

Schlaepfer, T. E., Harris, G. J., Tien, A.Y., Peng, L., Lee, S. and Pearlson, G.D. (1995). Structural differences in the cerebral cortex of healthy female and male subjects: a magnetic resonance imaging study. *Psychiatry Research*, *61* (3), 129–35 *(Medline)*.

Sypher, H. E. & Sypher, B. D. (1987). Communication and affect. In R. L. Donohew, H. E., Sypher & E. T. Higgins (eds), *Communication, Social Cognition and Affect*. New Jersey: Lawrence Erlbaum, pp. 81–92.

Sypher, B. D. & Zorn, T. E. (1988). Individual differences and construct system content in descriptions of liked and disliked co-workers. *International Journal of Personal Construct Psychology*, *1*, 37–51.

Taylor, J.L. & Novaco, R. W. (eds) (2005). *Anger Treatment for People with Developmental Disabilities*. Chichester: John Wiley & Sons.

Thomas, S. P. (1991). Toward a new conceptualization of women's anger. *Mental Health Nursing*, *12*, 31–49.

Thomas, S. P. (2001). *Healthy Anger Management: A Manual for Trainers*. Knoxville, TN: S. P. Thomas.

Thompson, E. H. & Pleck, J. H. (1995). Masculinity ideologics: a review of research instrumentation on men and masculinities. In R. F. Levant & W. S. Pollack (eds) *A New Psychology of Men*. New York: Basic Books, pp. 129–163.

11

PATHWAYS IN THE DEVELOPMENT OF ANGER

APPRAISAL, ACTION AND REGULATION

Michael F. Mascolo, James C. Mancuso and Tammy Dukewich

This chapter is dedicated to the memory of Dr James C. Mancuso—devoted mentor, engaging colleague, and trusted friend—who passed away just as this chapter was going into press.

In recent years, there has been a great deal of research on emotion and aggression (Petitt, 1998; Tremblay, 2000). However, there has been comparatively little research on the development of anger, presumably because of difficulties of assessing affective states. In this chapter, we adopt the view that anger, like all emotional states, is composed of multiple constituent processes (Mascolo, Fischer & Li, 2002). These include (1) *appraisals* that perceived events are not only *unwanted* but also contrary to the way in which they should or ought to be (de Rivera, 1981; Roseman, 1984; Smith & Ellsworth, 1985; Shaver, Schwartz, Kirson & O'Connor, 1987). We call such appraisals *ought violations* (Mascolo & Mancuso, 1990; Mascolo & Griffin, 1998). Ought violations involve the attribution of blame to agents that can be held responsible for their actions (Lazarus, 1991). In addition, anger involves (2) an affective or phenomenal component that people describe using metaphors such as "heat", "pressure" or "tension". De Rivera (1981) has suggested that the affective component of anger involves the experience of the strengthening of will to move against and remove a violation. Anger also involves (3) action tendencies directed toward removing ought violations (de Rivera, 1981; Mascolo & Griffin, 1998; Mascolo, Harkins & Harakal, 2002) which consist of instrumental actions (e.g., verbal or physical attack;

Working with Anger: A Constructivist Approach.
Edited by Peter Cummins. © 2006 John Wiley & Sons, Ltd.

indirect or passive aggression; retribution; retaliation; symbolic aggression) as well as facial (e.g., furrowed brow; square mouth), vocal (e.g., increased volume, pace) and bodily (e.g., tightening muscles; flailing arms) actions. Finally, anger involves (4) self-regulatory processes through which individuals inhibit, manage or otherwise control the display of their anger. In this chapter, we examine developmental changes in appraisal, action and self-regulatory components of anger.

Theorists have traditionally held that aggression functions as one manifestation of anger. As such, it is possible to use research on the development of aggression to inform a model of the development of anger. Much work on the development of aggression has been spurred by social cognitive models of anger. Dodge (1980, 1986; Crick & Dodge, 1994) has maintained that children exhibiting aggressive dispositions (1) fail to use the full range of social cues available in a social situation (encoding); (2) attribute hostile intent to social cues of others; (3) generate fewer alternative ways of responding to social situations; and (4) anticipate that their aggressive actions will produce positive social outcomes. Recent research building on this model has allowed discrimination among *reactive* and *proactive* and *normative* forms of anger and aggression. Research suggests that children who display a tendency toward reactive aggression hold a hostile attribution bias (Crick & Dodge, 1994; Zelli, Dodge, Lochman & Laird, 1999; Yoon, Hughes, Cavell & Thompson, 2000). Such children are more likely to attribute hostile intent to a peer's negative or ambiguous social actions. From this view, appraisals that a peer's unwanted actions result from hostile intent mediates the production of angry aggression toward the other.

In contrast, children who show proactive aggression are more likely to have beliefs about the legitimacy and utility of aggression in social situations (Olweus, 1979; Erdley & Asher, 1998; Yoon, Hughes, Cavell & Thompson, 2000). Such beliefs are thought to mediate the use of aggression as a strategy to advance personal goals. Research suggests that relative to normative and proactively aggressive samples, children with a tendency toward reactive aggression, are more likely to exhibit difficult temperament organized around angry affect (Pettit, 1998); a history of punitive, hostile or abusive parenting (Dodge, Pettit, Bates & Valente, 1995); insecure attachment (Pettit, 1998); peer rejection (Zelli, Dodge, Lochman & Laird, 1999; Yoon, Hughes, Cavell & Thompson, 2000); and indiscriminant or enabling reactions to aggression in the home (Dumas, LaFreniere & Serketich, 1996). Hubbard et al. (2004) have shown that reactive aggression is more strongly associated with observational, physiological and self-report indices of anger than is proactive aggression.

PATHWAYS IN THE DEVELOPMENT OF ANGER

In what follows, we use Fischer's (1980) model of skill development to chart developmental transformations in appraisal, action and self-regulatory components of normative, reactive and dominating forms of anger. Fischer's (1980) model specifies a series of 13 levels in the development of particular skills as they change from infancy through adulthood. What changes in development is the particular *emergent structure* of an action and meaning as it is deployed within a particular context. Following this model, appraisal, action and regulatory components of anger develop through four broad tiers: *reflexes*, *sensori-motor actions*, *representations* and *abstractions*. *Reflexes* (emerging after birth) consist of innate action elements that require stimulation for their evocation (e.g., distress-related facial actions to painful stimuli). *Sensori-motor actions* (emerging around 4 months of age) consist of the proactive execution of actions directed toward persons or objects in one's immediate environs (e.g., pushing away an obstacle to a goal-directed action); *representations* (emerging around 18–24 months of age) consist of symbolic meanings that represent concrete aspects of persons, objects or internal states (e.g., "that dolly is mine!"); *abstractions* (emerging around 10–11 years of age) consist of generalized meaning structures that represent intangible, abstract or general aspects of persons, events, or experiences (e.g., "You don't care about me the way a father should"). Within each of these broad tiers, appraisal, action and regulatory skills develop through four levels: *single sets*, *mappings*, *systems* and *systems of systems*. Higher-level skill structures emerge from the successive differentiation and inter-coordination of lower-level skills or skill components. In what follows, drawing upon existing research, we use Fischer's (1980) neo-Piagetian framework to trace developmental changes in appraisal, action and regulatory components through these various levels and tiers of development.

Figure 11.1 depicts a developmental web describing structural changes in the development of *normative*, *defensive-reactive* and *proactive-dominating* trajectories of anger. The normative path is defined in terms of the capacity to move against violations of personal motives while still preserving social relationships with others (Mascolo & Margolis, 2004). The normative path is mediated by appraisals that are defined with reference to increasingly complex socio-moral standards for interpreting relations between self and others. The reactive pathway involves the deployment of anger as a strategy toward defending the self against physical or psychological attack. The dominating pathway involves the proactive use of anger as a strategy for advancing one's personal goals through intimidation. In what follows, drawing upon Fischer's scheme, we outline 10 selected steps in the development of anger.

ORIGINS OF ANGER IN THE REFLEX AND SENSORI-MOTOR TIERS OF DEVELOPMENT

Anger begins to develop early in infancy within the *reflex* (0–4 months) and *sensori-motor* (4–18 months) tiers of development. Step 1 in the development of anger involves the use of single reflexes—simple elements of action that require stimulation for their evocation (e.g., sucking a nipple). Using operant techniques, researchers have shown

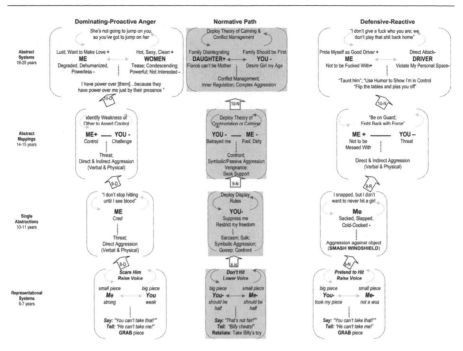

Figure 11.1 Developmental web of structural changes in the development of anger trajectories

Note: Each step identified   in each trajectory of Figure 11.1 depicts the structure of appraisal, action and self-regulatory components of anger. The central segment of each diagram describes the structure of a typical motive-relevant appraisal for the step in question. Each appraisal reflects an assessment if the relation between a motive and perceived events. The lower segment of the diagram describes emerging action tendencies that develop in tandem with appraisal activity. The top portion of each diagram depicts the structure of emerging strategies for regulating the appraisal, affective and action components of anger. It is important to note that rather than seeing reactive and dominating forms of anger as inherently less developed than normatively developing anger, we have suggested that each from of anger has its origins though a common affective core and then develops through its own trajectory.

the disruption of simple reflex-outcome contingencies results in negative emotional reactions in young infants. Infants younger than about 6 weeks of age respond to such disruptions with facial and vocal actions that mix anger- (e.g., furrowed brows) and distress-related (e.g., closed eyes) acts. At Step 2, more unambiguous signs of anger emerge around 2 months of age with the onset of reflex mappings. Using reflex mappings, a child can connect one simple element of action (e.g., a swipe of the arm) to another (seeing the onset of an audiovisual display in front of the face).

Lewis, Alessandri & Sullivan (1990) made the appearance of an audiovisual display contingent upon arm pulling in infants as young as 2 months of age. Violations of this contingency brought about negative affects, including increased instrumental action

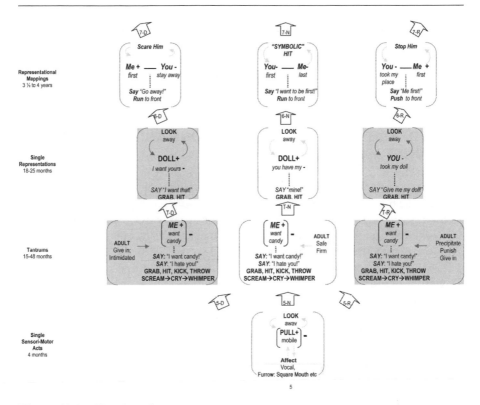

Figure 11.1   *(Continued)*

(e.g., increase the vigor of arm pulling) and anger-related facial (e.g., furrowed brows; square mouth) and vocal activity. At around this same point in time, if a caregiver gazes expressionless for several minutes at a 2-month old, the infant will evince signs of distress and anger (Trevarthen, 1984). Such unusual actions violate the history contingent interaction developed between adult and infant.

Anger continues to develop as infants acquire the capacity to proactively deploy sensori-motor acts around 4 months of age. Unlike skills in the reflex tier, sensori-motor actions are acquired and coordinated behaviors that do not require physical stimulation for their evocation. At Step 3 at the level of single sensori-motor actions, an infant is able to bring action under the proactive control of simple motor goals that exist from the onset of acting (e.g., actively reaching for a seen rattle or face). Disruption of such goal-direction actions brings about anger-reactions (Lewis, Alessandri & Sullivan, 1990). Beginning around 7–8 months of age (Step 4), an infant is capable of constructing *sensori-motor mappings* in which the infant coordinates the relation between two single sensori-motor acts (e.g., removing a cover in order to retrieve an object). This skill underlies an infant's protest when a wanted adult leaves a child's field of vision. At this level, the parent's act of leaving cues the formation of an image of the absent parent. The cued capacity to represent the wanted but absent parent in action constitutes a goal violation. The resulting anger state activates the sensori-motor action of seeking the absent parent.

THE TRANSITION TO REPRESENTATIONS AND THE ONSET OF OUGHT VIOLATIONS

While forms of normative, defensive, and dominating anger take on earlier forms in infancy, the transition to the representational tier brings forth greater divergence in anger trajectories. Figure 11.1 documents changes in normative, reactive and dominating forms of anger throughout the representational and abstract tiers of development. At Step 5, in the transitional period *prior* to the onset of single representations at 18–24 months of age, toddlers begin to exhibit temper tantrums (Potegal, Kosorok & Davidson, 1996). The transition to the representational tier is marked by a rudimentary capacity to represent and communicate desires (e.g., "Candy!"). Tantrums result because the child does not command the resources to regulate the affective reactions that occur when adults refuse such requests. How adults respond to a child's negative affect in contexts that involve tantrums and other forms of anger is crucial in the development of anger regulation strategies in the child. In North American and Western European societies, a bias toward the normative pathway is fostered by parenting styles that involve emotionally responsive but firm control of the enactment of anger. In the context of a tantrum, this style involves providing both firm enforcement of the prohibition in question (not "giving in" to the child) while also providing a physically and emotionally safe environment for the child throughout the course of the tantrum. After the tantrum, the parent is able to use inductive explanation (Mancuso & Lehrer, 1985) and provide alternative strategies for handling refusals in the future. Such practices enable children not only to develop strategies for bringing anger under control; they also teach children that their anger enactments will not be successful. By providing children with alternative strategies for making requests and delaying gratification, children can acquire skills for negotiating their needs without anger.

Punitive and permissive tantrum regulation strategies are important determinants of unregulated tantrums. Patterson's (Patterson, Reid & Dishion 1992) concept of *coercion cycle* describes the processes by which children's anger escalates and ultimately proves successful in parent–child interaction. Given an angry episode or tantrum by a child, the parent makes efforts to forestall the outburst. If a parent fails (because of temperamental biases or ineffective discipline), he or she might punish the child. In some families, punishment may take the form of physical or hostile aggression. Research has consistently demonstrated that such forms of punishment fail to forestall aggression in the long run. Continued repetition of tantrums prompts the parent to "give in" to the child's demands as a way to end the outburst. Such practices not only fail to promote the development of effective emotional regulation, they have the effect of perpetuating the use of aggression as a strategy for social problem solving.

Three styles of temper tantrums are depicted in Step 5 of Figure 11.1. In the normative path (Step 5-N), refusal of a child's request produces a series of cycles of anger and calming as described above. Children who consistently receive punitive reactions in the context of tantrums, especially physical punishment, show a defensive mix of inhibition and escalation of anger as reactions to punishment (Step 5-R). Tantrums of children whose parents repeatedly "give up" or "give in" may be short-lived; however, such practices lead to rapid escalation of aggression as a mode of advancing the child's personal agenda (Step 5-D).

Beginning around 18–24 months of age, children enter the *representational* tier of development. Representations consist of concrete symbolic meanings. The use of representations allows children to go beyond the here-and-now of sensori-motor experience and cued recall adult experiences of anger are mediated by appraisals that events violate conditions that the adult believes *ought* to exist. As a moral concept, an *ought* requires the capacity to compare what currently exists to some preferred or idealized way an event should be. This requires a capacity to form signs and symbols. Within the representational tier, children's skills move through four levels. Using single representations, children can begin to construct single social categories for representing self, objects and desires. This includes the symbolic construct of a sense of agency (I), identity (me), and possession (mine) (Mascolo & Fischer, 1998). At Step 6, the first genuine ought violations emerge as intrusions on a child's symbolic boundaries or sense of agency. At this level, a child can appraise the playmates' actions violating the child's sense of mine. In the normative path (Step 6-N), the child makes an appraisal like "you have my doll!" In reactive anger, a child may construct an appraisal like "You *took* my doll" or, with further development, "You took my doll *on purpose!*" In contrast, in dominating anger, using anger as a means to advance personal goals, a child may construct an appraisal such as "*I want* that doll." At this age, the child's capacity for anger regulation is limited to inhibiting aggression in the presence of adults or looking away from the violator. As such, children's anger can involve acts of physical aggression (grabbing the doll; hitting the playmate).

The next step (Step 7) emerges at around $3\frac{1}{2}$ to 4 years of age with the capacity to coordinate two single representations into a representational mapping. In so doing, a child can understand different types of relations between two or more single representations (e.g., cause and effect; sequential order; reciprocity, etc.). Using representational mappings, children begin to construct motives based on social comparisons. For example, at Step 7-N, $4\frac{1}{2}$ year-old Jack had developed a consistent desire to be the "first one" to go in or out of a door. This motive requires a capacity to order the actions of self and other. One day, an older girl raced Jack to the door. With an angry face and voice (action), Jack said "I want to be first" (motive-relevant appraisal) and forced himself in front of the girl (action tendency). In anger, the boy symbolically "hit" the girl by making a hitting gesture and pulling it just prior to contact. This act shows a rudimentary capacity to regulate angry actions.

Unlike the normative form, the reactive version (Step 7-R) involves a focus on the hostile intent of the violator. As such, rather than focusing on the outcome *per se* ("I want to be first!"), a child can make an appraisal implicating negative intent on the part of the violator (e.g., "*You took my place* in front!"). Rather than simply forcing his way forward, this appraisal might be accompanied by a more aggressive action (e.g., pushing the violator out of the way). The appraisal that mediates the dominating version (Step 7-D) can involve an accentuation of the self's intent to assert his rightful place in line (e.g., "I won't let you get in front of me"), complete with a display of anger intended to frighten the other away. At this level, without inhibiting anger, reactive or dominating anger can involve attempts to regulate the display of anger strategically for purposes of forestalling or scaring a violator.

The next step (Step 8) emerges around the age of 6–7 with the capacity to coordinate two representational mappings into a representational system. Representational systems underlie the child's capacity to perform traditional Piagetian concrete operational tasks (e.g., conservation, seriation, etc.). Whereas mappings allow children to represent simple relations, systems allow children to generalize across mappings to form concrete and systematic rules. Rule-based representations (e.g., social reciprocity, fairness) are central to the development of moral feeling. Thus, along the normative pathway, (Step 7-N) appraisals that another child has violated concrete expectations or rule involving fairness or reciprocity begin to emerge. For example, if a friend were to take the largest piece of pizza at a party, a child can make an appraisal like: "That's not fair; your piece is bigger than mine; we should both get the same!" Such an appraisal requires representational systems; the child must not only be able to compare the relative size of the pieces, but also must assert that each piece should be equal. At this step, children can exhibit action tendencies that are directed toward restoring or acknowledging the violated rule, retribution or retaliation. In addition, more complex forms of indirect and symbolic aggression begin to emerge. Children can also begin to regulate their anger using concrete rules such as "never hit", "she won't like me if I raise my voice," etc.

Appraisals that mediate reactive (Step 8-R) and dominating (Step 8-D) forms of anger can also invoke rule-based representations; albeit different rules or justifications may be advanced. Appraisals that mediate reactive anger can be framed in terms of the violator's intentions to do harm to the self and/or self-image, "You took the big piece and left me the small one on purpose; I'm not gonna let you do that!" Reactive appraisals motivate action tendencies involving threatening acts, use physical or verbal aggression, or an entitled grab for the big piece of pizza. Appraisals that mediate dominating anger can be framed in terms of the self's strength or status in comparison to the violator. Note again that reactive and dominating modes of anger need not be uncontrolled; children can develop rule-based regulation strategies for presenting anger in defense or dominating ways.

ABSTRACTIONS AND VIOLATIONS OF HIGHER-ORDER MOTIVES AND VALUES

Beginning around 10–11 years of age, older children begin to be able to construct skills in the abstract tier of development. Abstractions consist of representations of generalized and intangible aspects of meaning. Using abstractions, children can begin to form generalized identity-related motives and abstract values. Using abstractions, a child can begin to develop abstract rules that apply to a wide variety of concrete social situations. Beginning around 10–11 years of age, children gain the capacity to construct single abstractions. Using a single abstraction, children can begin to appraise motive-inconsistent events in terms of violations of enduring identity- and relational-motives (Step 9). For example, a male college student described the following normative instance of anger (Step 9-N):

> I am paying my way through school, so I feel that what I do here is my own choice. My parents are constantly asking where I've been every weekend, and my usual reply is that I stayed at [school]...They try to invoke the 'If you live under my house, you live by my rules' approach. I am not asking to...be totally on my own, just a little freedom.

In this scenario, the individual has represented his desire in terms of the single abstraction "[I am asking for] just a little freedom." As such, the appraisal that mediates his anger involves a violation of this morally-tinged motive-relevant abstraction. At this level, informed by a more generalized understanding of social relations and expectations, young adolescents gain the capacity to use direct confrontation as well as indirect (e.g., sarcasm) and passive displays of anger (e.g., sulking). They are also able to begin to develop abstract conceptions of their own anger and ways to regulate anger. For example, the individual above indicated "My anger just brews, rather than just dissipating with time, and they try to handle the situation day by day rather than confront the whole issue and settle it."

The following reconstruction describes an instance of reactive-defensive anger mediated by appraisals involving single abstractions (Step 9-R):

> I was [with my] ex-girlfriend... in a car... and I was teasing about her school life and everything... just busting her balls to how easy [her school] was and how a lot of people are losers... she got all pissed off and yelling and everything... and she slapped me, right in the face, she just cold-cocked me, and I was like, wow, and right then and there I just snapped and don't want to, never hit a girl, I know that, and... I was like ahhh, smashed the windshield with my fists... I got sacked... I did not feel I should've got slapped.

In this reconstruction, the young man appraised his girlfriend's slap in terms of a set of vaguely defined single abstractions, being unjustifiably "sacked" or "cold-cocked." This event motivated an act of physical violence toward an object other than the violator (the shattering of the windshield). Despite the violence of the act, it was nonetheless moderated through an act of self-control that was itself mediated by a generalized rule against "hitting a girl." This illustrates an act of reactive anger that is both mediated and regulated at the level of single abstractions.

Step 9-D depicts an example of dominating anger in a 10-year-old girl, Natasha, identified by her teacher as a "bully." In discussions about her tendency to use aggression in peer interactions, Natasha indicates the importance of being *cred* in the eyes of others. To be *cred* is to be *credible*, powerful, to be known as someone who can back up what she says. Natasha uses her anger to ward off challenges to her sense of being *cred*. Her actions take the form of fighting and other acts of physical aggression. Natasha is explicit about the conceptions that regulate her use of anger to intimidate: "I don't stop hitting until I see blood."

Beginning around age 14–15, adolescents gain the capacity to construct abstract mappings, which consist of coordinated relations between two or more single abstractions. At this level, an adolescent's or young adult's anger can be mediated by appraisals of violations of relations between enduring values or motives (Step 10). At this level, in anger, an individual can coordinate generalized representations of both the self's thwarted identity-related motives and the nature of the other's blameworthy violation. For example, at Step 10-N, a young woman described the following incident:

> My boyfriend and I were extremely close and shared everything . . . Until one day he informed me that he had slept with another girl at his college. I was so angry because of his lying to me and because of the betrayal . . . I felt like a fool . . . He was the only person I trusted with all my heart and he lied to me. I felt betrayed because of the close bond that we had. I felt like a fool because I felt like the joke was on me. I also in a way felt dirty thinking that someone else had shared the same things with this man as I did.

The appraisal that mediates this woman's reconstruction of anger involves violations of relations among abstract morally-tinged motives. More specifically, this is represented as a mapping between the woman's abstract conception of being "betrayed" and "lied to" and the consequential effect of feeling "dirty" and "used." At this level, an individual's action-tendencies function in the service of these higher-order abstract relations. A person is capable of performing sophisticated acts of retaliation, revenge, indirect and passive aggression. In addition, with the formation of abstract mappings, with training and experience, individuals become increasingly able to reflect upon and develop generalized models of anger, social interaction and conflict management. Such abstract models can provide the basis of constructive strategies for regulating anger that are guided by an awareness of relations between the generalized needs of both parties.

As before, dominating and reactive forms of anger differ primarily in the motivational dispositions that the self takes in relation to the violator. At this level, individuals are able to fully differentiate generalized self- and other-related values and motives. For example, in Step 9-D, an individual can represent violations in terms of the generalized relations between an attempt to be in control over a series of events and the ways in which the actions of others challenge one's sense of dominance or control. In reactive anger (Step 9-R), rather than experiencing others as potential challenges to one's proactive dominance, others are experienced reactively as threats to one's higher-order boundaries. At this level, individuals are capable of regulating their enactments in terms of higher-order conceptions of the demands of the situation (e.g., knowing an opponent's weaknesses and exploiting them in direct or indirect ways).

Step 10, which consists of violations of abstract systems of values, is made possible by the emergence of the capacity to construct abstract systems at around 19–20 years of age. Abstract systems arise from the coordination of at least two abstract mappings. Using abstract systems, one can represent violations to a set of relations among higher-order values or motives. A normative example (Step 10-N) of such violations involves the situation of a 22-year-old daughter whose 44-year-old father became engaged to a 25-year-old woman. In this case, the daughter viewed her father's actions as in violation of a system of personal values. To the daughter, the father violated standards of propriety by being desirous of a woman "who is just a few years older than me." The father, while not expecting his children to treat his fiancé as their mother, nonetheless had hoped that the children would "come to her for advice once in a while." The daughter felt that she and her siblings could not "treat her like a mother" and thus that the family was "disintegrating." From her view, the father "should put his family first" before his fiancé. In this context, as part of the action of her anger, the daughter requested counseling with the father in order to explore their differences in the presence of an impartial third party. The daughter, while disagreeing vehemently with her father, nonetheless desired a way to reconcile their incompatible belief systems. This action tendency was regulated by higher-order beliefs about the need to seek peaceful resolutions to conflicts, no matter how disturbing they might be.

Step 10-D depicts a particularly articulate example of dominating anger at the level of abstract systems. The example is based on an interview with a rather articulate 22-year-old man who discussed his feelings about the possibility of committing rape (Beneke, 1982):

> Let's say I see a woman and she looks really pretty and really clean and sexy, and she's giving off very feminine, sexy vibes. I think, "Wow, I would love to make love to her," but I know she's not really interested. It's a tease. A lot of times a woman knows that she's looking really good and she'll use that and flaunt it, and it makes me feel like she's laughing at me and I feel *degraded*. I also feel dehumanized, because when I'm being teased I just turn off, I cease to be human . . . If I were actually desperate enough to rape somebody, it would be from wanting the person, but it would be a very spiteful thing, just being able to say, "I have power over you and I can do anything I want with you," because really I feel that *they* have power over *me* just by their presence.

This abstract system is composed of the coordination of two abstract mappings. Women regarded as sexy or attractive cause feelings of lust and the desire to make love. However, these women are unavailable. Unavailable sexy women have power over the man because they can withhold something that he wants. The man thus feels humiliated and dehumanized simply by the presence of sexy and rejecting women. The action tendency is a desire to rape framed in terms of the desire to balance the scales of social power: "I [want] power over you ... because they have power over me just by their [humiliating] presence." Again, in this case, the man's spiteful appraisal is not uncontrolled, it is regulated by the awareness that "if I go with my human emotions I'm going to want to put my arms around her and kiss her, and to do that would be unacceptable"; at the same time, sexual relations between men and women are guided by the principle that "if you're not aggressive with a woman, then you've blown it. She's not going to jump on you, so *you've* got to jump on *her*."

The following consists of a description of reactive anger (Step 10-R) mediated by appraisals at the level of abstract systems:

> I was pulling out of a toll and ... a car was coming across two lanes of traffic and ... flashed its high beams at me. And I went ... I can't fucking believe this. *Who the fuck does this person think they're dealing with? ...* I don't give a fuck where you're at, we don't play that shit back home ... [when] he flashed his high beams at me from behind ... as if to say ... "I have the right of way," you know, sort of like, why did you cut me off; and that was almost an instinct trigger because I *guess I pride myself on being a good driver and ... he had violated my personal space by doing that.*

In this situation, the young man's anger was mediated by an appraisal like "I pride myself as a *good driver* and I am *not be fucked with*; your actions *violated my personal space* and are a *direct attack on me*." Describing his actions, the individual said, "I taunted him ... [I wanted] to mouth off and then go out of my way to confront the person not necessarily physically, but to let them know you shouldn't have done that and it was wrong what you did, now I'm going to flip the tables and piss you off; you want to play games, we'll play games and I'll piss you off and I'll really piss you off and I'll get you too." As a result, the individual flashed his lights back while shouting epithets to the person. When the violator pulled ahead and revealed a badge, the angered individual "stuck my [college] ID out the window." For the angered person, this was an act of irony as the violator "didn't expect [my response] and too it was humorous because I felt like I controlled the situation." Although the angered individual did not inhibit his anger, he nonetheless controlled his enactment relative to his explicit values about moving against challenges to the self: "I'm the type of person that'll go, if you challenge me and you want to fuck with me, you should be prepared to have your life fucked with ... there are many ways in confrontation that you can aggravate another person and make them see your side of it or make their life uneasy without ... physical violence."

CONCLUSION

Working with anger in children and adults requires an awareness of how the various components of anger come together and affect each other in any given angry episode. Such experiences are mediated by appraisals that develop gradually over time and take multiple forms in ontogenesis. A structural analysis of the specific form that appraisal, action and regulatory components of normative, reactive and dominating anger take in development can inform the practical task of working toward modifying those elements.

REFERENCES

Beneke, T. (1982). *Men on Rape*. New York: St. Martin's Press.

Bierman, K. L., Smoot, D. L. & Auiller, K. (1993). Characteristics of aggressive-rejected, aggressive (nonrejected), and rejected (nonaggressive) status. *Child Development, 64*, 139–151.

Camras, L. A. (1992). Expressive development and basic emotions. *Cognition and Emotion, 6*, 269–283.

Crick, N. & Dodge, K. A. (1994). A review and reformulation of social information-processing mechanisms in children's adjustment. *Psychological Bulletin, 114*, 74–101.

de Rivera, J. (1981). The structure of anger. In J. H. de Rivera (ed.), *Conceptual Encounter*. Washington, DC: University Press of America, pp. 35–82.

Dodge, K. A. (1980). Social cognition and children's aggressive behavior. *Child Development, 51*, 162–170.

Dodge, K. A. (1986). A social information processing model of social competence in children. In M. Perlmutter (ed.), *The Minnesota Symposia on Child Psychology*. Vol 18: *Cognitive Perspectives on Children's Social and Behavioral Development*. Hillsdale, NJ: Erlbaum, pp. 77–125.

Dodge, K. A., Pettit, G. S., Bates, J. E. & Valente, E. (1995). Social information processing patterns partially mediate the effect of early physical abuse on later conduct problems. *Journal of Abnormal Psychology, 104*, 632–643.

Dumas, J. E., LaFreniere, P. J. & Serketich, W. J. (1996). "Balance of Power": A transactional analysis of control in mother–child dyads involving socially competent, aggressive, and anxious children. *Journal of Abnormal Psychology, 104*, 104–113.

Erdley, C. A. & Asher, S. R. (1998). Linkages between children's beliefs about the legitimacy of aggression and their behavior. *Social Development, 7*, 321–339.

Fischer, K. W. (1980). A theory of cognitive development: the control and construction of hierarchies of skills. *Psychological Review, 87*, 447–531.

Hubbard, J. A., Parker, E. H., Ramsden, S. R., Flanagan, K. D., Relyea, N., Dearing, K. F., Smithmyer, C. M., Simons, R. F. & Hyde, C. T. (2004). The relations among observational, physiological and self-report measures of children's anger. *Social Development, 13*, 14–39.

Lazarus, R. S. (1991). *Emotion and Adaptation*. New York: Oxford University Press.

Lewis, M., Alessandri, S. & Sullivan, M. W. (1990). Expectancy, loss of control and anger in young infants. *Developmental Psychology, 26*, 745–751.

Mancuso, J. C. & Lehrer, R. (1985). Cognitive processes during reactions to rule violation. In R. Ashmore & D. Broozinsky (eds), *Thinking About the Family: Views of Parents and Children* (p. 67–93). Hillsdale, New Jersey: Lawrence Erlbaum Associates.

Mascolo, M. F. & Fischer, K. W. (1998). The development of self through the coordination of component systems. In M. Ferrari & R. Sternberg (eds), *Self-awareness: Its Nature and Development*. New York: Guilford, pp. 332–384.

Mascolo, M. F., Fischer, K. W. & Li, J. (2003). The dynamic construction of emotion in development: a component systems approach. In R. J. Davidson, K. Scherer, & H. H. Goldsmith (eds), *Handbook of Affective Science*. Oxford: Oxford University Press.

Mascolo, M. F. & Griffin, S. (1998). Alternative trajectories in the development of anger. In Mascolo, M. F. & Griffin, S. (eds) *What Develops in Emotional Development?*. New York: Plenum, pp. 219–249.

Mascolo, M. F., Harkins, D. & Harakal, T. (2000). The dynamic construction of emotion: varieties in anger. In M. Lewis and I. Granic (eds), *Emotion, Self-Organization and Development*. New York: Cambridge University Press, pp. 124–152.

Mascolo, M. F. & Mancuso, J. C. (1990). The functioning of epigenetically-evolved emotion systems: a constructive analysis. *International Journal of Personal Construct Theory*, *3*, 205–222.

Mascolo, M. F. & Margolis, D. (2005). Social meanings as mediators of the development of adolescent experience and action: a coactive systems approach. *European Journal of Developmental Psychology*, *1*, 289–302.

Olweus, D. (1979). Stability of aggressive reaction patterns in males: a review. *Psychological Bulletin*, *86*, 852–875.

Olweus, D. (1993). *Bullying at School: What We Know and What We Can Do*. Cambridge, MA: Blackwell Publishers.

Patterson, G. R., Reid, J. & Dishion, T. (1992). *Antisocial Boys*. Eugene, OR: Castalia.

Pettit, G. S. (1998). The developmental course of violence and aggression: Mechanisms of family and peer influence. *Anger, Aggression and Violence*, *20*, 283–299.

Potegal, M., Kosorok, M. R. & Davidson, R. J. (1996). The time course of angry behavior in the temper tantrums of young children. In C. F. Ferris & T. Grisso (eds), *Understanding Aggressive Behavior in Children*. New York: Annals of the New York Academy of Sciences, pp. 31–45.

Roseman, I. J. (1984). Cognitive determinants of emotions: a structural theory. In P. Shaver (ed.), *Review of Personality and Social Psychology* (Vol. 5, pp. 11–36). Beverly Hills, CA: Sage.

Shaver, P., Schwartz, J., Kirson, D. & O'Connor, C. (1987). Emotion knowledge: further exploration of a prototype approach. *Journal of Personality and Social Psychology*, *52*, 1061–1086.

Smith, C. A. & Ellsworth, P.C. (1985). Patterns of cognitive appraisal in emotion. *Journal of Personality and Social Psychology*, *48*, 813–838.

Tremblay, R. E. (2000). The development of aggressive behaviour during childhood: what have we learned in the past century? *International Journal of Behavioural Development*, *24*, 124–141.

Trevarthen, C. (1984). Emotions in infancy: regulators of contact and relationships with persons. In K. R. Scherer & P. Ekman (eds), *Approaches to Emotion*. Hillsdale, NJ: Erlbaum, pp. 129–157.

Yoon, J. S., Hughes, J. N., Cavell, T. A. & Thompson, B. (2000). Social cognitive differences between aggressive-rejected and aggressive-nonrejected children. *Journal of School Psychology*, *38*, 551–570.

Zelli, A., Dodge, K. A., Lochman, J. E. & Laird, R. D. (1999). The distinction between beliefs legitimizing aggression and deviant processing of social cures: testing measurement validity and the hypothesis that biased processing mediates the effects of beliefs on aggression. *Journal of Personality and Social Psychology*, *77*, 150–166.

12

CHALLENGING TRADITIONAL APPROACHES TO SCHOOL VIOLENCE
ALTERNATIVE CONSTRUCTIONS OF YOUTH ANGER AND AGGRESSION

Marc D. McLaughlin, Melissa A. Maras, Christopher J. Reiger and Carl E. Paternite

INTRODUCTION

In the late 1990s, a series of highly publicized school shootings in seemingly un-likely white middle-class communities across the United States profoundly changed how Americans think about schools, and the youth that they serve. These ostensibly senseless acts of extreme violence brought unprecedented attention to youth anger and violence. Parents, educators, police, mental health professionals, legislators, and the public at large sought explanations for these events. Some asserted that negligent gun-control laws were to blame (Klein & Chancer, 2000). Others reproached the parents of the assailants or linked the violent attacks to traumatic events in the lives of the perpetrators (Seltzer, 1997). Others chose to believe that the youth (all boys) who committed these atrocities were "born defective" (Glassner, 1999), that they were aberrations who could be differentiated from the rest of society's children (e.g. "Superpredators", see Garbarino, 2001a). In the end, however, the conclusions seemed similar—each boy had *personal problems*, as is the case with predominant popular explanations for youth suicide (see Gaines, 2000). The general public succeeded in distancing itself and avoiding analyses of cultural and systemic problems.

Working with Anger: A Constructivist Approach.
Edited by Peter Cummins. © 2006 John Wiley & Sons, Ltd.

Perhaps most fundamentally, the public evaded the reality that American boys are socialized to perceive anger as one of a small handful of acceptable emotions and that destructive aggression (i.e. violence) is the only acceptable way in which to express it (Pollack, 1998, 2000). Indeed, society typically fails to teach boys that anger is just one of a wide array of emotions, each of which can be expressed in a variety of ways. More importantly, because society poorly understands the intricate connections between emotions and behavior, the public fails to recognize that anger does not always lead to violence, and that violence, when it occurs, is not simply the direct product of anger. It is our intention to raise awareness of the complex connections between youth anger, potential for violence, and the developmental quality of various relationships, activities, and locales in which youth socialization takes place. We argue that such awareness can prompt schools and communities to pursue systemic changes that promote healthy development while simultaneously decreasing youth anger and violence.

HOW SCHOOL VIOLENCE HAS BEEN DEALT WITH AND WHY

In reference to extreme school violence, Raywid and Oshiyama (2000) and others have suggested that blaming guns, death metal music, violent movies, poor parenting, etc., reflects a shirking of responsibility by those who interact regularly with youth. Blaming the National Rifle Association or violent video games is more palatable than turning a sharp eye on our schools, our communities, and ourselves.

Simple Solutions

In the wake of school shootings, simplistic solutions were proposed, including pro-filing to identify characteristics of "Killer Kids," dress codes, metal detectors, clear backpacks, video surveillance, and on-site police (Pollack, 2000; Bender, Shubert, & McLaughlin, 2001; Leisner, 2001; Webber, 2003). Mulvey and Cauffman (2001) concluded that the public was eager to try virtually anything to combat the perceived dangers at school. Unfortunately, these efforts focused on decreasing the behavioral manifestations of students' emotions (especially anger) rather than building a school culture that directly addresses emotions and fosters students' competence in handling them appropriately.

The Superpredator

Spina (2000) observed that when critique was turned inward on schools, it typically was not school culture that was examined, but instead specific students—in every trench-coat shrouded outsider hid the next "killer kid." Some schools even turned to students to help them uncover the identity of potential shooters. Spina (2001) expressed concern that this new "leadership role" for students encouraged reporting of classmates whose behavior, attire, and/or interests deviate from the unstated norm for the school, with many eyes bringing the situation under control.

In 2002, the U.S. Secret Service and U.S. Department of Education issued a report based on analysis of 37 incidents of targeted school shootings that had occurred over a three-decade period, concluding that no useful "profile" can be derived to describe the student perpetrators, other than the fact that they were white, disgruntled teenage boys. Similarly, Mulvey and Cauffman (2001) concluded that such profiling is not empirically supported and that for every "killer kid," there are *many* students with the same behaviors or attitudes who do not come close to killing or seriously harming their peers.

Beyond its ineffectiveness, the consequences of such profiling are of concern to the extent that they have fueled commitment to cultural norms that enforce a strict code of conduct for all students, especially boys. The impacts likely fall most directly on the shoulders of boys who are outcast. For example, as Pollack observed:

> Because the Columbine killers were outcast boys, spiteful, non-conforming boys who were estranged from their peers, society has now rushed to the conclusion that adolescent boys who seem "different"—especially those who seem quiet, distant, and in pain—are likely the perpetrators of the next ghastly Columbine-like crime.
>
> (2000, p. 201)

Such fear has been solidified through the use of profiling. Further, we have been distracted from important efforts to understand school culture and the larger societal culture propagating stereotypes of heroism, masculinity, and dominance (Pollach, 2000). The pseudo-solution of profiling "killer kids" simply masks underlying social issues.

Acts of containment

Containment measures also have become popular. Many schools have adopted "zero tolerance" policies intended to scare sense and obedience into every student bringing potential weapons (even nail clippers) to school (Skiba, 2000; Browne, 2003; Sughrue, 2003). Perlstein (2000) suggested that, by reacting in these ways, schools have overemphasized rules rather than empathy, and stricter security instead of open hearts and ears. Webber (2003) argued that containment policies have unwittingly exposed students to harmful influences. Zero tolerance, monitoring, and surveillance, and general diffidence about such strategies, have not decreased violence in school, but have increased paranoia (Black, 2001; Mulvey and Cauffman, 2001; Webber, 2003). Pollack (2000) further suggested that such policies send a particularly unfortunate message to boys, communicating blanket expectations of anger and destructive aggression. Pollack observed that containment policies and strategies (e.g., gun detectors, armed guards) goad boys into the very aggression we, and they, fear—with expectations for anger and dangerousness pushing boys to fulfill the prophecies.

ANGER, VIOLENCE, AND THE SOCIALIZATION OF BOYS

American culture adheres to a well-defined conceptualization of masculinity. Behavioral expectations of what it means to be male are clearly identified, especially during the middle/high school years when youth are experimenting with their personal identities. These behavioral expectations rest on the fundamental belief that boys and men should be largely emotionally inhibited, with the only exceptions being anger and lust. The expression of emotions associated with vulnerability and the display of submissive behaviors commonly connotes femininity (see Miedzian, 2002). For this reason, their expression is avoided.

In general, deviations from such well-defined, socially scripted behaviors reduce a boy's positioning in the social hierarchy, which can be critically wounding to a boy with a developing sense of self. Boys who depart from the rigid script suffer repercussions in status (Klein & Chancer, 2000). Because the social construction of masculinity accentuates heterosexuality often to the degree of homophobia (Herek, 1987), boys who more fully subscribe to the masculine script feel compelled to harass those who less fully do so. Several perpetrators of recent school shootings reported that they were frequently called names that implied that they were homosexuals (Klein & Chancer, 2000). Insulting one's masculinity is potentially detrimental because it is a direct threat to one's sense of autonomy. Because hegemonic masculinity is the form of masculinity that is most sought after and revered in American society (e.g., military figures, corporate executives, and influential politicians), if a male is accused of being feminine, then the implication is that he will fail in both school and society (Klein & Chancer, 2000; Webber, 2003).

Being told repeatedly that one is a deviation from what one "should" be no doubt causes significant pain. Because the expression of vulnerability is culturally unacceptable for males, boys eventually question whether or not the accusations are accurate. At this point pain is exchanged for anger and rage—emotions that *are* culturally appropriate for males. Outward expressions of anger and rage are signs of masculinity; therefore, these violent attacks are—by youth's estimation—unmistakable acts of masculinity (Miedzian, 2002).

REVENGE FOR HAVING ONE'S MASCULINITY ATTACKED

Garbarino (2001b) described the boys who have perpetrated extreme school violence as decent students, most of whom had little or no previous involvement with the juvenile justice system. Some of the boys received mental health services. All were described by their peers as isolated and ostracized. Most experienced extensive and chronic harassment or bullying. Consequently, it is not surprising that revenge was the most common explanation offered by the boys.

Such acts of violence almost always mask what are commonly deemed as unacceptable emotions for males. Garbarino elaborated that:

> such behaviors may be warped and distorted and difficult to fathom from the outside, but if we dig deeply enough and listen openly enough, we may hear the need to restore justice by personally acting on the feelings of shame that come from being rejected, denied, abused, and deprived.
>
> (2001a, p. 85)

Seemingly only about anger and rage, these attacks hide pain and vulnerability (Cintron, 2000).

The perpetrators believe that their retaliation is justified; their acts contain some element of moral conviction (Cintron, 2000). When an individual or a group believe that they have suffered a significant degree of oppression, it becomes easier for them to reproach the advantaged group and justify their violent behavior. These boys believe that a violent attack is a means to restore order to an unjust world (i.e. school). The desperate need to restore order explains why such violent attacks often are directed at nonspecific people. If someone is not a bully, he or she is either a follower of the bully, a supporter, a disengaged onlooker, or a potential defender (Olweus, 2003). Everyone plays a part. Consequently, these boys perceive everyone as being guilty and deserving of punishment.

Maintenance of Socially-Constructed Scripts by Schools

Schools in the USA portray themselves as safe and open environments but commonly promote ideals of denial, hurt, and victimization; some students count and others do not. Environmental factors within schools (e.g. the attitudes, behavior, and routines) assume a critical role in determining the degree to which bullying and harassment occur in the classroom and hallway (Olweus, 2003).

School personnel routinely take little notice when they hear youth calling others "faggots" or "pussies," and they silently, and unwittingly, endorse the extreme stratification of students by doing nothing to prevent it. Students who participate in school-sponsored activities (e.g. football, honor societies) receive attention and praise. Students who don't or can't participate in such activities receive less attention and encouragement from educators. In effect, the message that is internalized is that they matter less. When the students who are praised by school faculty harass those who are not, it is often tolerated and, at times, even endorsed—almost as if the staff believe that the "good" students are doing their peers a favor by "encouraging" them to conform to the expectations of the school.

Although schools might intend to teach their students to be critical thinkers and active participants in democratic processes, structures that are valued and maintained encourage the contrary. Most schools express a commitment to produce individuals who are competent in making decisions based on consideration of their interests and those of others, while in reality they tend to manufacture "thinkers" that are driven largely by final causes (e.g. grades, proficiency test scores) and rely nearly exclusively on passive, transmission strategies of instruction and rote memorization to achieve the academic goals (see Kohn, 1999; Webber, 2003).

Rather than encourage students to engage in mature decision-making, schools too often attempt to regulate both thought and behavior. For example, most classrooms are structured to convey the idea that the teacher is the expert dispenser of knowledge and that the students are passive recipients. Clearly, current approaches to classroom instruction and to school behavior management (e.g. zero tolerance, metal detectors) are less than ideal—given the predominant emphasis on psychological (and physical) control unbalanced by an emphasis on warmth, engagement, attachment, and participation in learning and decision making (Lesser, 1985; Leondari & Kiosseoglou, 2002).

Social Cultivation of Violence

Violence in the media has long been considered by social scientists and commentators to be a contributing factor to the violence of boys. However, Klein and Chancer (2000) identified a critical element of this argument that commonly is omitted; rather than mere exposure to acts of violence, it is exposure to acts of violence when they are depicted as being the *defining* behaviors of *effective* men, that breeds violence among youth (especially boys). In the absence of alternative models, these images of "successful manhood" will prevail in the minds of youth.

The glorification of violence, and its portrayal as the hallmark of successful masculinity, unfortunately also can be instilled via curricula in our schools to the extent that violence is espoused as an effective method of problem solving without critically analyzing reliance on its use; for example, if violence is taught as if it were inevitable and the only effective solution to a myriad of historical problems. Concern has been expressed that history is too often rewritten and taught to glorify violence as the only effective method of intervention, what Jacoby (1975) calls "social amnesia" and Chomsky (2000) calls "historical engineering." The glorification of violence without critical analysis is dangerous and contributes to a growing mentality that its use is natural and reasonable.

POSITIVE YOUTH DEVELOPMENT

The Positive Youth Development (PYD) perspective suggests a critical role for schools and communities in promoting the development of important youth *competencies*. Arguably, the important issue with youth is not so much that they can be angry or violent, but rather that they lack emotional, relational, and vocational *competencies* requisite for success in adolescence and adulthood (Benson, Leffert, Scales, & Blyth, 1998; Larson, 2000). The PYD perspective advocates a focus on strengths and skills (rather than problems and deficits) as both predictors and outcomes describing youth functioning (Leffert, Benson, Scales, & Sharma et al., 1998; Scales & Leffert, 1999; Scales, Benson, Leffert, & Blyth, 2000). PYD encourages the cultivation of inter-locking family/school/community resources that nurture youths' socio-emotional strengths and skills; and it emphasizes a view of prevention/attenuation of specific problems as an indirect benefit of nurturing youths' overall competencies, rather than the central goal of intervention (Catalano, Berglund, Ryan, Lonczak & Hawkins, 2002). In other words, it is apparent that society's focus on the "problem" of youth anger and violence diverts us from a fundamental responsibility to foster a compre-hensive set of developmental competencies in youth—strengths that lead to fulfilling lives and, concurrently, prevent problems such as unfettered anger and violence.

POSITIVE YOUTH DEVELOPMENT IN CHILDHOOD AND ADOLESCENCE

From a PYD perspective, early interventions can impact a broad set of *competencies* in later life—such that interventions should be justified not simply as a means to prevent destructive aggression, but rather as a means to enhance well-being *and* prevent a host of problems (see Ramey and Ramey, 1998; Masten & Coatsworth, 1998). Strengthening development-enhancing resources begins very early in life.

The most fundamental resource impinging on early childhood development is the child's experience in a home with competent, nurturing parents (see Masten & Coatsworth, 1998). Thus, efforts to optimize early childhood environments should fo-cus on maximizing the proportion of youth who are born into competent environments and fortifying new parents who substantially lack child-rearing assets.

From a PYD perspective, preventing accidental teen pregnancies represents an integral component in comprehensive violence prevention strategies. Teen pregnancy is one of the strongest predictors that offspring will grow up in a compromised environment, with limited resources, and without access to a competent, involved father figure to aid in socializing non-violent conflict resolution. Even with substantial intervention, many of the offspring of teen parents will remain at risk for engagement in (and being the victim of) violence (see Coley & Chase-Lindsdale, 1998; Alan Guttmacher Institute, 2001; Horn & Sylvester, 2002).

Convincing schools and broader communities to focus intently on teen pregnancy also is important from a PYD perspective because such focus forces schools/communities to confront interlocking youth risk factors, interconnected youth protective factors, the positive correlations between youth competencies, and the cumulative impacts of risk and protective factors on youth outcomes (Jessor et al., 1995; Benson et al., 1998; Kirby, 2001). In short, schools/communities that are serious about preventing teen pregnancy inevitably must confront the need to attend to the competency-development of the "whole child"; in so doing, they will concurrently prevent youth violence *and* teen pregnancy, while also promoting student well-being and school success.

Maximizing youth exposure to competent parents must also attend to increasing parents' ability to provide their offspring with fundamental developmental resources that Brazelton and Greenspan (2000) refer to as the "irreducible needs of children." For example, one of the best ways to enhance the human capital of parents is to employ evidence-based interventions such as the Nurse-Family Partnership program (NFP) (Olds, Hill, Mihalic, & O'Brien, 1998). In this program, a nurse home visitor works with an at-risk family in their home during pregnancy, and during the first two years of the child's life. The program has been tested in ethnically diverse populations with 15-year longitudinal studies. Findings include dramatic reductions in adolescent run away, juvenile arrests, and adolescent alcohol use. Such asset-building interventions contribute to the prevention of youth violence, by creating a youth culture marked by fewer problematic behaviors and issues. Positive outcomes create a culture/context less ripe for youth anger and violence (c.f. Benson, 1997).

Relationship/Socialization-based Interventions with Children and Adolescents

There is a need to foster *relational* competencies among youth in school and community settings. Building these relational competencies can concurrently prevent anger, violence and a host of other problems. For example, when done well, preschool interventions (e.g. Head Start) build a broad set of cognitive/academic/social competencies while simultaneously reducing the short-term and long-term likelihood of specific problematic behaviors; they also support parents by amplifying their capacity to nurture youth (McLoyd, 1998; Ramey & Ramey, 1998). In this sense, they are ideal examples of a PYD approach to preventing youth violence.

There are a number of PYD-oriented interventions applicable to later childhood, as well. Miedzian (2002), for instance, described a school-based infant-caretaking/familiarization program for young boys. This program involved exposing young boys to infants and teaching them about tending to infants' needs. Over multiple years, the boys and infants maintained contact until the infants reached preschool. This intervention was posited as an effective way to start very early to separate masculinity from violence. Young boys learn from these types of asset-enhancing experiences that their identities as men are heavily tied to caretaking and responsible/dependable engagement with their offspring (Parke, 2002). They are taught the value of care, and the powerful experience of being needed/wanted by another human being—both important protective factors against destructive expression of anger (cf. Garbarino, 1999).

Experience with PYD interventions among adolescents confirms that there is a need to focus on the strength of positive relationships. Indeed, it is futile to encourage youth to turn away from maladaptive anger management and from violence unless they are offered more constructive, rewarding alternatives. There is a strong positive relationship between adolescents' assets and decreased youth anger and violence. This is especially evident in the cumulative effect of youth assets—the aggregate number of assets youth possess is correlated negatively with youth engagement in violence (Leffert & Benson et al., 1998). Such assets are developed in the context of trusting relationships with adults in schools and across a variety of other contexts (see Benson et al., 1998; Scales & Leffert, 1999).

Unfortunately, the USA is a high-paced, work-driven society that has difficulty fostering development-enhancing relationships between adults and youth (c.f. Spina, 2000; Webber, 2003; Miedzian, 2002). This is compounded by the massive proportion of Americans who live in poverty—working long hours, never quite able to make ends meet, and living in perpetual stress and frustration (McLoyd, 1998; Ehrenreich, 2002).

In many cases, parents respond to their hectic lifestyles by allowing youth to be mentored by peers or by the television (Jordan & Nettles, 1999). American teens, on average, watch an estimated 28 hours of TV per week (see Rich, 1999). One result is bored, unchallenged, socially underdeveloped youth (Larson, 2000). Little wonder, then, that the introduction of TV into numerous world societies has been followed by marked increases in aggression and violence (U.S. Department of Health and Human Services, 2001). Regardless of TV content, it remains a poor substitute for the real-life social interactions—with friends, loved ones, and other mentors—that build developmental assets.

Given the context described above, it is important to stress that schools offer unparalleled public access as a point of engagement with youth for promotion of their positive development, including enhancement of developmental assets, well-being and school success. In the USA over 52 million youth attend 114,000 schools, and over 6 million adults work in schools. Combining students and staff, one-fifth of the US population can be reached in schools (President's New Freedom Commission, 2003).

Meaningful youth–adult relationships in school (and broader community contexts) have relevance for reducing levels of anger, violence prevention and a host of asset-building outcomes. Youth benefit greatly when they are thoroughly exposed to adults who take a real interest in them, spend time with them, talk to them about their problems and concerns, help them identify their strengths and weaknesses, coach them on appropriate social skills, and assist them in developing a true vision of their potential (cf. Benson, 1997; Benson, Leffert, Scales, & Blyth, 1998).

In this regard, examination of outcome data for the Big Brothers Big Sisters of America (BBBSA) mentoring program—one of the most rigorous and most pragmatic evidence-based interventions for at-risk youth—is instructive. BBBSA targets youth age 6 to 18, typically from single parent homes. Controlled 18-month follow-up studies have documented that, compared to control group youth, BBBSA youth were: 46 % less likely to initiate drug use; 27 % less likely to initiate alcohol use; almost one-third less likely to hit someone; were better in academic behavior, attitudes, and performance; were more likely to have higher quality relationships with their parents or guardians; and were more likely to have higher quality relationships with their peers (McGill, Mihalic, & Grotpeter, 1998).

Fortunately, community planners and policy-makers increasingly demonstrate an understanding of the potency of focusing on interventions that build social competencies in a real-life fashion—not merely through a curriculum, not only through an instructional video, not solely in an individual "therapy" session once a week, but within the context of genuine, trusting relationships across diverse community settings. They are increasingly realizing that a wide array of assets crucial to life result from a pragmatic relationship that focuses broadly on coaching; social skills modeling; the development of intimacy, trust, and dependable support; and identification with a respectable adult figure (Larson, 2000; Hansen, Larson, & Dworkin, 2003; Catalano et al., 2002).

Unfortunately, *school* policy-makers and reformers have not widely embraced this realization. Given their primary mission of educating students, schools have tended to focus quite narrowly on the fact that academic success promotes well-being, and they have not adequately acknowledged (and responded accordingly to) the well-documented fact that youth well-being (and the enhancement of developmental assets) promote academic/school success (Klern & Connell, 2004; Paternite & Johnston, 2005). In challenging this practice and advocating for more meaningful school–community–family partnerships to promote positive youth development (including youths' healthy management of anger), it is important to stress that "most educators, parents, students, and the public support a broader educational agenda that also involves enhancing students' social-emotional competence, character, health, and civic engagement" (Greenberg et al., 2003, p. 466).

Fathers and Men as Integral Mentors in Socializing Non-Violent Youth

Notwithstanding the essential and well-documented importance of women in nurturing and guiding the development of youth, in the USA there is a dearth of competent male role models thoroughly invested in fostering youths' overall development. When it comes to raising non-violent youth, perhaps the most troublesome form of relational absence in America is to be found in many fathers' failure to provide for their children's developmental needs.

Placing aside all debates about "essentiality" and diverse family forms (Silverstein & Aurebach, 1999; Popenoe, 2000), our youth live in a rather "fatherless America" (see Blankenhorn, 1995). Approximately 24 million children (34 %) live absent from their biological father (see Horn & Sylvester, 2002). Many of these biological-father-absent children have not seen their father during the past year; a substantial portion reside far distances away from their father, and many have never set foot in their father's home (Braver, 1998). And, as Horn and Sylvester summarize:

> Children with involved, loving fathers are substantially more likely to do well in school, have healthy self-esteem, exhibit empathy and pro-social behavior, and avoid high-risk behaviors such as drug use, truancy, and criminal activity, compared to children who have uninvolved fathers.
>
> (2002, p. 15)

Further, while impoverishment is more prevalent among "father-deprived" children (Silverstein & Auerbach, 1999, 2000; McLoyd, 1998), socioeconomic status does not account for all of the variance in youth outcomes between father-deprived and non-father-deprived youth (Hetherington, Bridges & Insabella, 1998; Horn & Sylvester, 2002).

As with formally assigned community-based mentors, fictive kin networks (especially among urban minority families) can appreciably compensate for the absence of predictable, competent fathers (Masten & Coatsworth, 1998; McLoyd, 1998; Jayakody & Kalil, 2002). However, these networks don't fully account for the intra-family and community effects of father absence, particularly in terms of creating non-violent youth (see Popenoe, 1996). This is especially true because where there is father absence, there are heightened frequencies of family transitions and other stressors on youth (Hetherington et al., 1998; McLoyd, 1998). For instance, currently over 3.3 million children live with an unmarried parent and the parent's cohabiting partner, and the number of cohabiting couples with children has nearly doubled since 1990, to approximately 1.7 million today (see Horn & Sylvester, 2002). Cherlin and Formby's (2002) study of cohabiting "parent-figure" (i.e., boyfriend/girlfriend) households among impoverished populations found that only 42 % of the couples studied at Time 1 were still together a year later.

In homes in which the turnover of men is *very* frequent, youth can be *particularly* stressed (Hetherington, 1998). Also, it is difficult for *these* youth, in particular, to internally construe adult males as *responsible, predictable, caring, and trustworthy* role models. Consider, for example, the anger evident in the rhyme from the murdered, assaultive rapper, Tupac Shakur: "Take a look at my family/A different father every weekend/Before we get to meet him they break up before the weekends/I'm getting sick of all the friendships/As soon as we kick it he done split and whole [thing] ends" (as quoted in Sylvester, 2002).

The deleterious impact of transient males extends beyond the family. Intact family structures are one of the best predictors of urban violence, with the concentration of intact families correlating with decreased violence, even when many other variables are controlled (e.g., Sampson, 1995). Smith and Jarjoura (1988), for example, found that the proportion of single-parent households in a community predicted its rates of violent crime and burglary, but the community's poverty level did not. These findings complement those of Brooks-Gunn, Duncan, Klebanov, and Sealand (1993), who noted how the prevalence of single-mother households in a neighborhood with few middle-class neighbors influenced rates of drop-out and teenage childbearing. Additional research is needed to more clearly delineate the unique contribution of father absence to these outcomes, but the current findings warrant serious consideration during an era in which many youth—particularly boys—are deprived of substantial positive contact with dependable, responsible, nurturing males (cf. Miedzian, 2002).

In the absence of trustworthy/caring men, male teens in deprived communities can take drastic measures to acquire male friends that will be loyal to them, even if the tasks associated with such loyalty are developmentally immature and violent (Thornberry, 2001). For this and other reasons, many of the answers to unhealthy expression of youth anger and to violence are largely to be found in strong male mentoring (by fathers and/or community males, *including in schools where youth spend a great deal of their time*) of young boys as they grow into men (cf. Miedzian, 2002). This sentiment is largely shared by Robert Bly (1996), who argued that the absence of strong, nurturing male involvement in young boys' lives contributes to the "Sibling Society"—a society in which underdeveloped, boys-in-men's-bodies fail in their attempts to fill the adult roles of parenting and community caretaking, thereby perpetuating an intergenerational cycle of destructive aggression and overall underdevelopment.

Bly's espousal of male mentoring as initiation is intriguing in light of the nation's current, myopic focus only on extreme school violence afflicting the sliver of white, middle-class, suburban youth who are in fact exposed to a more robust set of development-enhancing relational resources than less-privileged youth. Such a narrow focus allows our nation to ignore the decline of American culture into a "sibling society"—particularly our male culture and perhaps particularly among our less privileged members. It begs the question of whether policies aimed at violence prevention spend sufficient funds on father training programs, male-teacher mentoring programs in schools, and transition programs for the hundreds of thousands of fathers who are currently incarcerated in our nation's prisons (Mumola, 2000). And it leads us to inquire as to whether the media's attention to high-profile youth-violence protests are sufficiently complemented by large-scale attention to proactive initiatives to amplify male competence in nurturing the development of youth in school, community, and family contexts.

CONCLUSION

Because aggregate youth anger and violence are manifestations of a broad set of fundamental issues demanding society's attention, middle-class America's obsession with school violence in particular—arriving only after it occurred among white, suburban schools—serves to divert society's attention away from more pressing issues that impact American youth. In addition, the problem-focused, problem-specific thrust of proposed remedies is unfortunate. Youth are not merely beings that warrant splicing into disparate problems, particularly not in response to agendas focused on devising new interventions for alleviating a single, identified problem, such as anger or violence. Promoting positive youth development has more to do with acquiring competencies than it has to do with simply helping youth avoid problem behaviors (cf. Benson et al., 1998; Catalano et al., 2002).

It is the case that much of the anger experienced and violence perpetrated by youth happens outside of school and therefore attention must be paid to the experiences, relationships, and development-enhancing resources available to youth across a variety of community contexts. Nonetheless, interpersonal conflict and aggression are palpable in schools (e.g., bullying). In addition, schools are one of the most important contexts of youth life—unrivaled as a public setting within which to engage youth for promotion of their well-being. While we must look *in and beyond* schools for the causes of youth anger violence and effective positive youth development interventions, *schools are ideal settings for exposing youth to development-enhancing resources* (e.g., many of their potentially closest and most salient role models are adults in schools, schools are the primary setting in which youth interact and socialize with their peers), thereby promoting competencies that will improve their life chances in a number of contexts beyond the school walls.

As proposed by analysis of PYD interventions, youth competencies integral to violence prevention are best conveyed in the context of positive adult–youth relationships (cf. Benson et al., 1998). This is a change from the conventional attention to negative relationships with adults and peers. Indeed, the PYD perspective seeks to amplify relationships that grow strengths rather than prevent relationships that foster problems.

Hopefully, school and community planners and policy-makers will increasingly invest in asset-enhancing interventions aimed at creating competent, successful adults, rather than merely investing in disparate programs aimed at preventing school violence and an innumerable set of other "problems." When we make this conceptual shift, youth will rise to the standard to which we hold them—to become active, successful contributors to an evolving and improving society, not merely to become problem-avoidance statistics (cf. Benson et al., 1998; Larson, 2000).

REFERENCES

Alan Guttmacher Institute (2001). *Teenage Sexual and Reproductive Behavior in Developed Countries*. Washington, DC: Alan Guttmacher Institute.

Bender, W. N., Shubert, T. H. & McLaughlin, P. J. (2001). Invisible kids: preventing school violence by identifying kids in trouble. *Intervention in School and Clinic, 37*, 105–111.

Benson, P. L. (1997). *All Youth Are Our Youth: What Communities Must Do to Raise Caring and Responsible Children and Adolescents*. San Francisco: Jossey-Bass.

Benson, P. L., Leffert, N., Scales, P. C. & Blyth, Dale A. (1998). Beyond the 'village' rhetoric: creating healthy communities for children and adolescents. *Applied Developmental Science*, 2, 138–159.

Black, N. (2001). After a shooting. *The New York Times*, 8 March. p. A23.

Blankenhorn, D. (1995). *Fatherless America: Confronting Our Most Urgent Social Problem*. New York: Basic Books.

Bly, R. (1996). The Sibling Society. Reading, MA: Addison-Wesley.

Braver, S. (1998). *Divorced Dads: Shattering the Myths: The Surprising Truth about Fathers, Children, and Divorce*. New York: Tarcher/Putnam.

Brazelton, C. T. & Greenspan, S.I. (2000). *The Irreducible Needs of Children: What Every Child Must Have to Grow, Learn, and Flourish*. New York: Perseus.

Brooks-Gunn, J., Duncan, G. J., Klebanov, P. & Sealand, P. (1993). Do neighborhoods influence child and adolescent development? *American Journal of Sociology*, 99, 353–395.

Browne, J. A. (2003). *Derailed! The Schoolhouse to Jailhouse Track*. New York: Rockefeller Foundation.

Catalano. R. F., Berglund, M. L., Ryan, J. A. M., Lonczak, H. S. & Hawkins, D. J. (2002). Positive youth development in the United States: research findings on evaluations of positive youth development programs. *Prevention & Treatment*, 5, Article 15. Available at: http://journals.apa.org/prevention/volume5/pre0050015a. Accessed 2/14/03.

Cherlin, A. & Fomby, P. (2002). *A Closer Look at Changes in Children's Living Arrangements in Low-Income Families*. Baltimore, MD: Johns Hopkins University. Available at: http://www.jhu.edu/~welfare/19837BriefLivingArrang.pdf. Accessed 2/7/03.

Chomsky, N. (2000). *Chomsky on Miseducation*. Lanham, MD: Rowman & Littlefield.

Cintron, R. (2000). Listening to what the streets say: vengeance as ideology? T*he Annals of the American Academy*, 567, 42–53.

Coley, R. L. & Chase-Lansdale, L. C. (1998). Adolescent pregnancy and parenthood: recent evidence and future directions. *American Psychologist*, 53, 152–156.

Ehrenreich, B. (2002). *Nickel and Dimed: On (Not) Getting By in America*. New York: Henry Holt.

Gaines, D. (2000). America's dead-end kids. In S. U. Spina (ed.), Smoke and Mirrors: The Hidden Context of Violence in Schools and Society. New York: Rowman & Littlefield Publishers, Inc.

Garbarino, J. (1999). *Lost boys: Why Our Sons Turn Violent and How We Can Save Them*. New York: Free Press.

Garbarino, J. (2001a). Making sense of senseless youth violence. In J.M. Richmna & M.W. Fraser (eds), *The Context of Youth Violence*. Westport, CT: Praeger.

Garbarino, J. (2001b). Making sense of school violence: why do kids kill? In M. Shafii & S.L. Shafii (eds), *School Violence*. Washington, DC: American Psychiatric Publishing, Inc.

Glassner, B. (1999). *The Culture of Fear: Why Americans Are Afraid of the Wrong Things*. New York: Basic Books.

Hansen, D. M., Larson, R. W. & Dworkin, J. B. (2003). What adolescents learn in organized youth activities: A survey of self-reported developmental experiences. *Journal of Research on Adolescence*, 13(1), 25–55.

Herek, G.M. (1987). On heterosexual masculinity. In M.S. Kimmel (ed.), *Changing Men: New Directions in Research on Men and Masculinity*. Thousand Oaks, CA: Sage.

Hetherington, M.B., Bridges, M. & Insabella, G.M. (1998). What matters? What does not?: Five perspectives on the association between marital transitions and children's adjustment. *American Psychologist*, 53, 167–184.

Horn, W. H. & Sylvester, T. (2002). *Father Facts*. 4th edn. Gaithersburg, MD: National Fatherhood Initiative.

Jacoby, R. (1975). *Social Amnesia*. Boston: Beacon Press.

Jayakody, R. & Kalil, A. (2002). Social fathering in low-income, African American families with preschool children. *Journal of Marriage and Family, 64*, 504–516.

Jessor, R., Van Den Bos, J., Vanderryn, J., Costa, F. M., & Turbin, M. S. (1995). Protective factors in adolescent problem behavior: Moderator effects and developmental change. *Developmental Psychology, 31*, 923–933.

Jordan, W. J. & Nettles, S. A. (1999). *How Students Invest their Time out of School: Effects on School Engagement, Perceptions of Life Chances, and Achievement.* Baltimore, MD: Center for Research on the Education of Students Placed At Risk (CRESPAR). Available at: www.csos.jhu.edu/crespar/techReports/Report29.pdf. Accessed 2/24/03.

Kirby, D. (2001). *Emerging Answers: Research Findings on Programs to Reduce Teen Pregnancy.* Washington, DC: National Campaign to Prevent Teen Pregnancy.

Klein, J. & Chancer, L.S. (2000). Masculinity matters: the omission of gender from high-profile school violence cases. In S. U. Spina (ed.), *Smoke and Mirrors: The Hidden Context of Violence in Schools and Society.* New York: Rowman & Littlefield Publishers, Inc.

Klern, A. M. & Connell, J. P. (2004). Relationships matter: linking teacher support to student engagement and achievement. *Journal of School Health, 74*, 262–273.

Kohn, A. (1999). *The Schools Our Children Deserve: Moving Beyond Traditional Classrooms and "Tougher Standards."* New York: Houghton Mifflin Co.

Larson, R. W. (2000). Toward a psychology of positive youth development. *American Psychologist, 55*, 170–183.

Leisner, H. (2001). No blanket security measures. *School Construction News, 4*, 31–33.

Leondari, A. & Kiosseoglou, G. (2002). Parental, psychological control and attachment in late adolescents and young adults. *Psychological Reports, 90*(3), 1015–1030.

Leffert, N., Benson, P. L., Scales, P. C., Sharma, A. R., Drake, D. R. & Blyth, D. A. (1998). Developmental assets: measurement and prediction of risk behaviors among adolescents. *Applied Developmental Science, 4*, 209–230.

Lesser, H. (1985). The socialization of authoritarianism in children. *The High School Journal, 68*(3), 162–166.

Masten, A. & Coatsworth, J. D. (1998). The development of competence in favorable and unfavorable environments: lessons from research on successful children. *American Psychologist, 53*, 205–220.

McGill, D. E., Mihalic, S. F. & Grotpeter, J. K. (1998). *Blueprints for Violence Prevention, Book Two: Big Brothers Big Sisters of America.* Boulder, CO: Center for the Study and Prevention of Violence.

McLoyd, V. C. (1998). Socioeconomic disadvantage and child development. *American Psychologist, 53*, 185–204.

Miedzian, M. (2002). *Boys Will Be Boys: Breaking the Link Between Masculinity and Violence.* New edition. New York: Latern Books.

Mulvey, E. P. & Cauffman, E. (2001). The inherent limits of predicting school violence. *American Psychologist, 56*, 797–802.

Mumola, C. J. (2000). *Bureau of Justice Statistics Special Report: Incarcerated Parents and their Children* (No. NCJ 182335). Washington, DC: Department of Justice, Office of Special Programs.

Olds, D., Hill, P., Mihalic, S. & O'Brien, R. (1998). *Blueprints for Violence Prevention, Book Seven: Prenatal and Infancy Home Visitation by Nurses.* Boulder, CO: Center for the Study and Prevention of Violence.

Olweus, D. (2003). A profile of bullying at school. *Educational Leadership, 60*(6), 12–17.

Parke, R. D. (2002). Fathers and families. In M. H. Bornstein (ed.), *Handbook of Parenting.* Vol. 3: *Being and Becoming a Parent.* 2nd edn. (pp. 27–73).

Paternite, C. E. & Johnston, T.C. (2005). Rational and strategies for central involvement of educators in effective school-based mental health programs. *Journal of Youth and Adolescence, 34*, 41–49.

Perlstein, D. (2000). Failing at kindness: why fear of violence endangers children. *Educational Leadership, 57*, 76–79.

Pollack, W. W. (1998). *Real Boys: Rescuing Our Sons from the Myths of Boyhood.* New York: Random House.

Pollack, W. S. (2000). *Real Boys' Voices.* New York: Penguin Group.

Popenoe, D. (1996). *Life Without Father: Compelling New Evidence that Fatherhood and Marriage are Indispensable for the Good of Children and Society.* New York: The Free Press.

Popenoe, D. (2000). Ideology trumps social science. *American Psychologist, 55*(6), 678–679.

President's New Freedom Commission on Mental Health (2003). *Achieving the Promise: Transforming Mental Health Care in America.* Final Report for the President's New Freedom Commission on Mental Health (SMA Publication No. 03–3832). Rockville, MD: Author.

Ramey, C. T. & Ramey, S. L. (1998). Early intervention and early experience. *American Psychologist, 53*, 109–120.

Raywid, M. A. & Oshiyama, L. (2000). Musings in the wake of Columbine: What can schools do? *Phi Delta Kappa, 81*, 444–6.

Rich, M. (1999). Pediatricians should educate parents, youths about media's effects. *AAP News: The Official News Magazine of the American Academy of Pediatrics* (September, 1999). Available at: http://www.aap.org/advocacy/rich999.htm. Accessed 9/23/04.

Sampson, R. J. (1995). Unemployment and imbalanced sex rations: race-specific consequences for family structure and crime. In M. Belinda Tucker and C. Mitchell-Kernan, *The Decline in Marriage among African Americans.* New York: Russell Sage Foundation, pp. 229–254.

Scales, P. C., Bernson, P. L., Leffert, N., & Blyth, D.A. (2000). Contribution of developmental assets to the production of thriving among adolescents. *Applied Developmental Science, 4*(1), 27–46.

Scales, P. C. & Leffert, N. (1999). *Developmental Assets: A Synthesis of the Scientific Research on Adolescent Development.* Minneapolis: Search Institute.

Seltzer, M. (1997). Wound culture: trauma in the pathological public sphere. *October, 80*, 3–26.

Silverstein, L. B. & Auerbach, C. F. (1999). Deconstructing the essential father. *American Psychologist, 54*, 397–407.

Skiba, R. J. (2000). *Zero Tolerance, Zero Evidence: An Analysis of School Disciplinary Practice.* Policy Research Report #SRS2. Bloomington, IN: Indiana Education Policy Center.

Smith, D. A. & Jarjoura, G. R. (1988). Social-structure and criminal victimization. *Journal of Research in Crime and Delinquency, 25*(1), 27–52.

Spina, S. U. (2000). *Smoke and Mirrors: The Hidden Context of Violence in Schools and Society.* New York: Rowman and Littlefield.

Sughrue, J. A. (2003). Zero tolerance for children: two wrongs do not make a right. *Educational Administration Quarterly, 39*, 38–58.

Sylvester, T. (2002). When is a parent not a parent? *Fatherhood Today, 7* (2), 5. Available at: www.fatherhood.org/ftoday.

Thornberry, T. P. (2001). Risk factors for gang membership. In J. Miller, C. L. Maxson, & M. W. Klein (eds), *The Modern Gang Reader.* Los Angeles: Roxbury Publishing Company.

U.S. Department of Health and Human Services (2001). *Youth Violence: A Report of the Surgeon General.* Washington, DC: Author.

Webber, J. A. (2003). *Failure to Hold: The Politics of School Violence.* New York: Rowman and Littlefield.

13

PHILOSOPHICAL WRITING ON ANGER AND VIOLENCE AND ITS RELATION TO PERSONAL CONSTRUCT PSYCHOLOGY

Bill Warren

This chapter is a selective but hopefully reasonably comprehensive and usefully illustrative review of anger as it has been discussed by philosophers. The aim is to background discussion of anger in personal construct psychology and to identify congenial philosophical perspectives.

SOME OBSERVATIONS ON ANGER IN PHILOSOPHY

Anger is dealt with in philosophy as part of the much bigger question of emotions and feelings, where a wide variety of emotions is considered in terms of a variety of theories, none of which on its own has been considered satisfactory to explain this human experience. Across different theories there is overlap in terms of the essential characteristics and the emphasis to be placed on each, as well as conceptual difficulties. Thus, as to essential characteristics, cognition, bodily sensations, action potential, and some sort of 'disturbance' of an otherwise less-disturbed functioning of mind, are highlighted. In terms of conceptual matters, 'feeling' and 'emotion' are used of different things ranging from more or less fixed *attitudes* to particular things (men/women, race, politics), of enduring tendencies to *act* in certain ways (generously, humbly, caringly), and, again, of relatively temporary *states* (irritation, fear, reactively depressed mood state).

Working with Anger: A Constructivist Approach.
Edited by Peter Cummins. © 2006 John Wiley & Sons, Ltd.

The particular emotion identified as 'anger' has been given some but not extensive specific scrutiny by individual philosophers. What is revealed in a review of philosophical treatment of anger, however, is the manner in which this concept, this human experience, is more problematic than others, often standing out in a particular consideration as more puzzling or difficult to account for than other emotions. This difficulty is reflected in the different definitions of anger, as well as in judgements concerning it. It is complicated also by the different terms used in the ancient world to describe 'anger' and related emotions, and by the puzzle of why it was felt necessary to control it (Harris, 2001). In regard to the control of anger – 'anger management' – Harris (2001, p. 25) makes a point that the writings of the philosophers were primarily directed to the moral life and education of the social elites, a point that might give pause for thought in regard to the likely clients for much of the anger management engaged in by psychologists!

Plato, in the *Philebus*, for example notes that anger is one of the 'mixed pleasures' in that it blends pleasure and pain, and is entirely a mental experience; in contrast to, for example, *relief* that follows the bodily sensation when an itch (which is in the body) is scratched, and *hope* that is associated with the predicted arrival of a meal (which is jointly related to mind and body). Thus, Socrates says, we speak of anger, fear, envy, and the like, as pains which belong only to the soul and which are full also of 'the most wonderful pleasures', anger, for example, 'which stirs even a wise man to violence, and is sweeter than honey' (*Philebus*, 47e; Jowett, 1953, p. 606).

Aristotle, in his discussion of the 'mean', that is, the standard by which actions are judged when choice is available to a person, instances anger as one emotion where this principle ought to be applied:

> [M]oral excellence is a mean . . . between two vices, the one involving excess, the other deficiency, and that it is such because its character is to aim at what is intermediate in passions and in actions . . . so, too, any one can get angry – that is easy – . . . ; but to do this to the right person, to the right extent, at the right time, with the right aim, and in the right way, *that* is not for everyone, nor is it easy; that is what goodness is both rare and noble.
>
> (1984a, II.9, 20–30)

Whatever its relationship to the good life, Aristotle had considered the specific nature of anger in his *Rhetoric*, adopting there a device of juxtaposing terms to describe some fifteen feeling states such as love and hate, pity and resentment, fear and confidence, and, more pertinent here, anger and placability. He defined anger as 'a desire accompanied by pain, for a conspicuous revenge for a conspicuous slight at the hands of men who have no call to slight oneself or one's friends' (1984b. II.2, p. 2195). For Aristotle, too, anger is always attended by pleasure, 'that which arises from the expectation of revenge'. The three significant types of slighting are *contempt, spite*, and *insolence*, and the objects of anger are always other, particular people who treat us with contempt, spite, or insolence. In turn, *calm* is the opposite or the settling of anger, and this can occur 'naturally' as, for example, when we are long removed in time from the slight against us, from pity at seeing our revenge lead to a greater suffering than was appropriate, or from a change in our mood to amusement or some other satisfaction. Interestingly, again, Aristotle thinks that we cannot be angry with people we fear or respect: 'you cannot be afraid of a person and also at the same time angry with him'. Again, he thinks that we feel no or little anger with a person who commits a slight against us out of anger, for 'we do not feel that they have done it from a wish to slight us, for no one slights people when they are angry with them'.

The Roman philosopher, Seneca (3 BCE – 65 CE) was a follower of the philosophy known as Stoicism, a philosophy consolidated initially by the Greek philosopher Zeno, drawing on the ideas of the great philosopher of *process*, Heraclitus. Seneca suffered a similar fate as had Socrates, and died in a similarly calm fashion. Stoicism changed over the years from the ideas taught by Zeno, but essentially it is a philosophy which has its chief significance in the field of ethics where it stresses the importance of living in accord with the benevolence and orderliness that the universe itself exhibits. In that form of life or behaviour, one would achieve well-being and inner, spiritual peace. The tactic suggested for living such a life was less focused on action or behaviour as it was in developing a particular way of approaching the world, a particular attitude which encompassed all of the virtues: knowledge (of what is good and bad), bravery (knowing what to fear), justice (giving what is due to others), and self-control. In this approach to the world one was enjoined to approximate the outlook of the person who was wise, was 'undisturbed' in their manner of dealing with life. These ideas encompass a notion of natural law, and also an egalitarianism in that every individual had the same prospects of applying that feature which every individual regardless of rank or status shared, that is, *reason*. Seneca, in three long treatises on anger begins by characterising it as 'madness':

> [A]nger is temporary madness. For it is equally devoid of self-control, forgetful of decency, unmindful of ties . . . closed to reason and counsel, excited by trifling causes, unfit to discern the right and true. . . . you have only to behold the aspect of those possessed by anger to know that they are insane.
>
> (1958, p. 107)

He finds anger contrary to nature, serving no good purpose, not – as he says Aristotle had suggested – necessary in battle, inappropriate, because it itself is a wrong, to right a wrong, devoid of reason, and careless of the truth. There is nothing in anger that is great or noble and it has no place in the mind of a wise person. De Botton (2000) puts Seneca's views in a more accessible fashion, citing Seneca as the classic exponent of a sensible, prudent, rational position in response to that 'ultimate infantile collision' that is anger. He notes Seneca's view of anger as a kind of madness and how he refused to allow that when it had passed one might apologise and explain in terms of one's rational faculty having been temporarily turned off. Anger was not akin to that involuntary action that is a shiver from contact with cold water or a blink that follows a finger-flick close to our eyes. It was a result of the operation of certain rationally held *ideas* which must be changed if we are to change our propensity to anger. What makes us angry are overly optimistic ideas of what other people are like and how they should behave; we are angry not because of a failure to get what we want but because 'we believe ourselves entitled to obtain' what we want (De Botton, 2000, p. 83).

The medieval period saw a reduced need for individual reflection in the face of a well-articulated 'revealed truth', but one of the great thinkers of the Roman Church, Saint Thomas Aquinas, did address the matter of anger. In his monumental work, *Summa Theologia*, Aquinas offers a similar classification of the passions as had Aristotle and other Greek thinkers, dividing them into those which involve the body primarily, leading then to an impact on the 'soul' (for example, a wound), and those which are connected with the body only secondarily, though usually and always in a way that is deleterious for the body (for example, fear or anger). Within his system of classification he distinguishes passions which are associated 'naturally' with goodness (and evil) and those where effort is required to realise goodness and avoid evil. In the first category is Love and Hate, Desire and Aversion, and Pleasure and Pain; the second has Hope and Fear, Despair and Courage, and, with no opposite, Anger. He discusses this lack of an opposite specifically, noting Aristotle's view (Aristotle is 'the Philosopher' in Aquinas' writings) that 'calm is contrary to anger' but disagrees. Anger, Aquinas believes, is one possible response when there is 'already a difficult evil present' in the mind; anger is the movement of attack against that evil. The other possible response is to succumb to that evil, which is *sadness*. The opposite of anger is not calm, which would be to withdraw from the evil and not combat it, but to attack the evil; the removal of that evil is both a move toward goodness and a dissipation of anger (1981, Question 23, 3). Further, as with the ancient Greeks, anger is a passion that is made up of contradictory passions, and he contrasts anger with love and with hate (1981, Question 46, 2). An individual might love or hate a particular food, someone who loves will wish good on both him or herself and their beloved, and someone who hates will wish evil on another and be expressing evil in their hatred. With anger, however, the individual wishes both good and evil: 'Whereas anger regards one object under the aspect of good, viz., vengeance, which it desires to have; and the other under the aspect of evil, viz., the noxious person, on whom it seeks to be avenged. Consequently it is a passion made up of contrary passions' (1981, Question 46, 2).

Descartes' ([1649] 1985) account is interesting because of the manner in which it highlights the so called mind–body problem that has to be faced by physiological accounts of anger; also, perhaps because of the element of 'mystery' that might be cynically suggested to endure into such explanations of human psychological distress that focus on brain chemistry and psychopharmacological treatments. Descartes offered a perspective that was rooted in a 'biological' and mechanical understanding of human beings. That complex system of bodily organs that was the human being was somehow orchestrated through the soul (located in the pineal gland) and emotions arose in the soul – it was the soul which loved, hated, and was angry – even though the experiences related to these emotions were physical ones. In relation specifically to anger, this was a 'kind of hatred or aversion that we have towards those who have done some evil or who have tried to harm not just anyone they happen to meet but us in particular' ([1649] 1985, p. 399). There are two sorts of anger, according to Descartes, and anger is distinguished from *indignation* which is the hatred or aversion we feel to those who *generally* do evil, as distinct from doing it to us, *personally*. One sort, to which 'the most kind-hearted persons are most prone', flares up quickly 'is quite evident in external behaviour, but it has little effect and is easy to assuage'. The other is less apparent, gnaws away at the heart, involves hatred and sadness, and it is the 'weakest souls who most allow themselves to be carried away' by this type. In any event, the strength of this second sort of anger grows by the agitation which is stirred in the blood, and 'the blood, being mixed with the bile driven to the heart from the lower part of the liver and spleen, produces a very keen and piercing heat there' ([1649] 1985, p. 400).

Spinoza ([1677] 1967), too, dealt with anger in his comprehensive account of the passions. The passions were 'confused ideas', ideas which are generated by external events or happenings that act *on* the individual, where the mind does not have a clear idea or is mistaken of the source of an idea. For Spinoza, anger was one of the 30 or so passions: 'Anger (*ira*) is the desire whereby through hatred we are incited to work evil to him whom we hate' (Definition 36). In turn, Hatred (*odium*) is 'pain accompanied by the idea of an external cause' (Definition 7). His account was within a theory which centred the notion of '*conatus*', a principle that described an impulse to self-perpetuation, a striving for the maintenance of each individual thing's own existence. In this striving, the primary aspect is 'desire' which is coupled with pleasure and pain, of which all the passions are derivative or compounded.

Hobbes' ([1640] 1969; [1651] 1991) account of anger is equally tied in with a wider project, one focused on an understanding of human nature sufficient to allow him to develop principles of social life and government. The passions provide the dynamism for human life in all of its aspects and are summarised in a notion of 'endeavour'; this manifests as appetite/desire (endeavour towards), or aversion (endeavour away from). Anger, is, perhaps curiously, 'sudden courage' which is:

> the appetite or desire of overcoming present opposition. It hath been commonly defined to be grief proceeding from an opinion of contempt; which is confuted by the often experience we have of being moved to anger by things inanimate and without sense, and consequently incapable of contemning us.
>
> ([1640] 1969, pp. 38–39)

Herbart's ([1816] 1901) thinking is also of interest here. His general position in relation to feelings is that they are indications of harmony or disharmony between ideas. For example, we perceive something and an idea is aroused or generated in the 'apperceptive mass'. That idea comes to consciousness but also, related ideas come with it. When there is harmony between the ideas, positive feelings ensue, when disharmony, negative feelings ensue; the intensity of the feelings is related to the degree of harmony or disharmony. Thus, the sight of some object might generate memories of similar objects and raise a variety of harmonious memories concerning them, generating pleasant feelings; whereas memories of a friend who has died, generated, for example, by an object that was precious to the dead friend, would lead to unpleasant feelings. Herbart notes a distinction between emotions (transitory variations from equanimity) and the passions ('rooted desires'; [1816] 1901, p. 80), one that was noted above at the outset to generate the different senses in which the term 'anger' can be used and the difficulty this causes. He also discusses the connection between physiology and psychology in regard to the emotions, accepting Kant's classification of the emotions into 'melting' ('paralysing to activity') and 'stirring' ('arousing of activity'); 'mental shock, sadness, fear' belong to the former class, 'joy and anger' to the latter ([1816] 1901, p. 80). His discussion here takes a turn reminiscent of Descartes, but he also notes the manner in which different bodily conditions belong to different emotions: 'For example, shame drives the blood to the cheeks, fear makes one pale, anger and despair increase the strength of the muscles' ([1816] 1901, p. 81).

With the existentialists and phenomenologists, reflection on the emotions turns even more 'inward'. The phenomenologists argued that anger is always anger about something, is always 'anger about X or Y'. If the object of my anger were a state of affairs in the world – the X or the Y – then what would it say concerning a mistaken belief concerning X or Y? What sense would it make to say that the state of the affairs in the world was the basis of my anger if that state of affairs was not as I took it to be? Anger must therefore lie in my belief, for example, that such and such was the case or had happened, rather than in the fact of it happening. The so-called 'object' of my anger must be a belief, a mental state, that the object of my anger did exist. The phenomenologists called this an 'intentional object' and the general principle in operation here, *intentionality*.

An analysis of anger, however, is not a core focus of phenomenology which is addressed to other matters, particularly to epistemological ones, but the principle of intentionality was taken up more specifically in regard to the emotions by the Existentialists; even though it is *angst* that is perhaps more interesting for them. Their general perspective is captured in a most illustrative adage expressed by C.J. Chesterton and cited by Wilson (1966, p. 43) that: 'an adventure is an inconvenience rightly considered, an inconvenience an adventure wrongly considered'. In this vein, Sartre ([1943] 1966), in particular, takes up this theme arguing against the view that emotions like jealousy or fear or anger are merely features or facts of our individual existence, arguing to the contrary that these are rather *choices* we make. More specifically, Sartre suggests that anger 'of all the emotions, is perhaps the one whose functional role is most evident' (1948. p. 68). While Fell (1965) has suggested that Sartre took over from other theorists (particularly Kurt Lewin and Tamara Dembo, but also Pierre Janet) an explanation of anger that he generalised as a theory of the emotions as such – a notion of 'tensions' caused by the 'blocking' of desired action by the demands of reality – the location of anger is in the interaction between the individual and the world, not somehow 'in' the world or 'in' the person (Fell, 1965, p. 120).

Finally, it is also of interest to note a social-philosophical perspective in one of the few thinkers to write in a positive or accepting mode concerning violence, the French Syndicalist, Georges Sorel (1847–1922). Sorel ([1906] 1950) added a social philosophical dimension, arguing that violence was the manner by which the State – the bourgeois State particularly, but any State more generally – maintained its control. Thus, the preparedness to use violence had to be established in the working people. Significantly here, Sorel, like Marx and also the Anarchists, draw attention to the manner in which ideas get 'fixed in the head' – for example, the rejection of violence, and judgements concerning anger as an 'evil' or at least a 'wrong' – but that fixedness and the prohibition it effects are only in place because of the propaganda of the ruling class or power.

In summary, the foregoing selective review suggests that anger has proven most difficult for the philosophers to fit into their schemes for understanding the emotions more generally. That it is 'different' is evidenced in Plato who early identified its contradictory character as involving both pleasure and pain, and in Aquinas who found it had no easily identifiable opposite. For some it arises toward people, for others it can also arise towards things. Some are judgemental, as with Seneca, while others seek to apply the same standards to anger as to any other human action, for example, Aristotle's admonition to strive toward the 'mean'. Sometimes it is seen as settling of its own account (through time, distraction, or death of the person who has slighted us), sometimes it needs to be confronted in some way. In most analyses it is placed squarely in 'the mind', and in some thinkers this is done in a way which emphasises dynamism, whether that is done in terms of intentionality or social consequences.

PERSONAL CONSTRUCT PSYCHOLOGY AND ANGER IN PHILOSOPHY

There are three perspectives in our review that appear better suited to a personal construct psychology understanding of anger. These are the views of Spinoza, Seneca, and the Existentialists. In relation to Spinoza, what is of value is his insistence that the functioning of the mind not be divided into separate activities which were cognitive, emotional, and conative. Cognition and emotion were not opposed aspects of mind but complementary ones, inherently connected. Thus, Spinoza has been suggested as a congenial thinker in relation to Kelly's ([1955] 1991) insistence that the threefold division of mind into cognitive, affective and conative processes was unhelpful (Warren, 1998). Spinoza helps us circumvent unhelpful debates about distinctions between 'thoughts' and 'feelings', and a personal construct psychology view of anger needs to be developed with this clearly in view.

Seneca, is congenial, too, with his focus on the role of ideas and the need to change them in dealing with anger, we might say, 'at its source'. Personal construct psychology would say that it is our constructions that we must change, but in general could see resonance with De Botton's gloss on Seneca: 'Rage is caused by a conviction, almost comic in its optimistic origins (however tragic in its effects), that a given frustration has not been written into the contract of life' (2000, p. 84). Such a view is, consciously or otherwise, coincidentally recognised some time ago in Rational Emotional Therapy, Ellis entitling a chapter of his book 'The Insanity of Anger' (1977).

Finally, the idea of intentionality, of a mind reaching out into the everyday 'life-world' of people and interpreting events, is congenial for personal construct psychology. That activity which Sartre had centred in what it was to be an authentically functioning human being, that is, *choice*, is itself a core feature of personal construct psychology. Anger would thus be 'chosen' and personal construct psychology moved to look for the inner logic – the 'psychologic' – of this choice, and what was thought to be achieved by such a response, and for what was being, validly or invalidly construed as a slight against one.

The task of developing a comprehensive understanding of anger from within personal construct psychology is left to other contributors to this volume, but the foregoing discussion can be drawn together by way of focusing the threads of the discussion on this psychology.

Significant in this focusing is the idea of anger, indeed emotion more generally, as 'moving out of' the mind into the world, as centred in the mind not in the world. Equally significant is the role of ideas, of interpretation. Central to personal construct psychology is that it is the psychology of the 'inner outlook' and central to the process of psychological functioning is the interpretation of events, the development of understanding, the making of meaning.

This said, personal construct psychology will do well if the three dimensions noted at the outset can be accommodated. That is, first, that anger involves some degree of cognition, bodily sensations, a tendency to act, and a disruption of an otherwise optimally functioning system. Second, it will need to differentiate concepts: *hostility* is not *anger*, and neither might it lead to *aggression*. Moreover, anger, for example – but perhaps not aggression – might be compatible with *love*: 'one can fully, without interruption and alteration, love someone despite periods of anger' (Saul, 1956, p. 3). And, third, it must accommodate that anger, like other feeling words is used of different things ranging from more or less fixed attitudes to particular things, enduring tendencies to act in certain ways, and of relatively temporary states.

By way of conclusion, it is useful to adapt an observation made by Broad in his conclusion to his critical survey of five types of *ethical* theory. He said that if one thing was clear from that survey it was the complexity of the topic and the 'paradoxical position of man, half animal and half angel . . . too refined to be comfortable in the stable and too coarse to be at ease in the drawing-room' (1930, p. 284). Thus may it be with both the fact and the understanding of human anger.

REFERENCES

Aquinas, T. (1981). *Summa Theologia*. Vol. II. Trans. the Fathers of the English Province. Westminister, MD: Christian Classics.

Aristotle (1984a). *Nicomachean Ethics*. In *The Complete Works of Aristotle*. Revised Oxford translation (2 vols), J. Barnes (ed.). Princeton, NJ: Princeton University Press.

Aristotle (1984b). *Rhetoric*. In *The Complete Works of Aristotle*. Revised Oxford translation (2 vols), J. Barnes (ed.). Princeton, NJ: Princeton University Press.

Broad, C. D. (1940). *Five Types of Ethical Theory*. London: Kegan Paul, Trench, Trubner and Co. Ltd.

Descartes, R. ([1649] 1985). *The Passions of the Soul*. In *The Philosophical Writings of Descartes*. 2 vols. trans. J. Cottingham, R. Stoothoff, and D. Murdoch. Cambridge: Cambridge University Press.

Ellis, A. (1977). Anger: How to Live With and Without It. Melbourne: The Macmillan Co. of Australia.

Fell, J.P. (1965). *Emotion in the Thought of Sartre*. New York: Columbia University Press.

Harris, W. V. (2001). *Restraining Rage: The Ideology of Anger Control in Classical Antiquity*. Cambridge, MA: Harvard University Press.

Herbart, F. ([1816] 1901). *Textbook in Psychology*. Trans. M.K. Smith. New York: D. Appleton and Co.

Hobbes, T. ([1651] 1991). *Leviathan*. Edited by R. Tuck. London: Cambridge University Press.

Hobbes, T. ([1640] 1969) *The Elements of Law*. 2nd edn. London: Frank Cass and Co.

Kelly, G. A. ([1955] 1991) *The Psychology of Personal Constructs*, (vols 1 and 2) London: Routledge.

Plato (1953). *Philebus*. In *The Dialogues of Plato*. 4 vols. Trans. B. Jowett. Oxford: The Clarendon Press.

Sartre, J. P. ([1943] 1966). *Being and Nothingness*. Trans. H.E. Barnes. New York: Philosophical Library.

Sartre, J. P. (1948). *An Outline of a Theory of the Emotions*. Trans. B. Frechtman. New York: Philosophical Library.

Saul, L. J. (1956). *The Hostile Mind: Sources and Consequences of Rage and Hate*. New York: Random House.

Seneca (1958). *Moral Essays*. 3 vols. Trans. J. W. Basore. London: William Heineman.

Sorel, G. ([1906] 1950). *Reflections on Violence*. Trans. T. E. Hulme and J. Roth. London: Collier-Macmillan Ltd.

Spinoza, B. ([1677] 1967). *Ethics*. London: J.M. Dent and Sons Ltd.

Warren, B. (1998). *Philosophical Dimensions of Personal Construct Psychology*. London: Routledge.

Wilson, C. (1966). *Introduction to the New Existentialism*. London: Hutchinson.

14

EVALUATION

Dina Pekkala and Bhavisha Dave

More and more in these days of evidence-based practice there is an emphasis on, and pressure for, clinical practitioners to draw on interventions that are 'proven' to be effective, and in turn, to evaluate their own interventions. However, as highlighted by the UK Department of Health, 'There is a wide gap between research on psychological therapies and its everyday practice' (DOH, 2004, p. 4).

GAP BETWEEN RESEARCH AND CLINICAL INTERVENTION

Anger seems to be an extreme version of this paradox. Clinicians and researchers alike have long neglected anger. Searching published articles from 1985 to 1997, DiGiuseppe (1999) found one-tenth the number of articles relating to anger, in comparison to depression and one-seventh in comparison to anxiety. However, as many clinicians now find, anger is one of the most common referrals to forensic out-patient services (Munro & Macpherson, 2001) and to adult clinical psychology departments (O'Loughlin, Evans & Sherwood, 2004; Cummins, see Introduction). At present, criteria for diagnosis of an anger disorder do not exist within the *Diagnostic and Statistical Manual of Mental Disorders* (DSM-IV) (American Psychiatric Association, 1994) or the *International Classification of Mental and Behavioural Disorders* (ICD-10) (World Health Organisation, 1994). However, anger is often a component of many mental disorders in both DSM-IV and ICD-10 (e.g. borderline personality disorder, antisocial personality disorder, post-traumatic stress disorder). Finally, as highlighted by Laming in Chapter 3, anger is invariably a component of domestic violence. However, as Laming further proposes, anger may be more a *phurfee*, a red herring, in effect an excuse or justification for violent or abusive behaviour.

Working with Anger: A Constructivist Approach.
Edited by Peter Cummins. © 2006 John Wiley & Sons, Ltd.

Hence, there appears to be a mis-match between clinicians' inclination to evaluate and publish articles on anger interventions, and the referral rate of anger. Possibly this discrepancy can be accounted for by both a *clinicians component* and a *clients component*. This is not to say that these two elements are not intrinsically interrelated.

CLINICIANS' COMPONENTS

1. Anger was for a long while an embarrassing emotion. Bry (1976) proposed that clients were infinitely more reticent to discuss their anger problems than their sexual problems. Just as we clinicians may initially find addressing clients' sexual problems difficult, we may also experience a parallel discomfort with clients' anger problems. As clinicians, we are very aware of transference and counter-transference, however, drawing on neuroscience Rothschild argues convincingly that we are *hardwired* to respond to others' emotions, and as therapists we are exquisitely vulnerable to *catching* our clients depression, rage and anxiety' (2004, p. 48). Thus, our innate ability to empathise, mirror and resonate with our clients' anger may be a profoundly uncomfortable experience for us.

2. Anger is often not construed as a mental health problem. When the first author (DP) was pursuing employment post-clinical training, she was told by several trusts that of course she would not be able to specialise in working with anger, as, after all, it was not a mental health issue. Informally, psychologists have told us, 'We don't do anger'.

3. Further, we speculate as to whether there is also a *scare* factor, which contributes both to the reticence to address anger within mental health services and a reticence to discuss clients' experiences of their anger.

CLIENTS' COMPONENT

1. The employment and evaluation of interventions with out-patient anger populations are habitually difficult, as attendance rates for clients referred with anger are invariably low. Munro and Macpherson (2001) report an attendance rate of 35 % from 600 referrals for anger. This poor attendance may be due to the nature of referrals. In our experience of running the Tuesday Group (see Cummins, Chapter 2), all too often, clients' attendance at psychological services to *deal* with their anger is either due to coercion (i.e. their partners have told them to 'get it sorted, or they and the kids are out of it') or is mandatory, in that Social Services or the Probation Service have erroneously endeavoured to make *treatment* for the individual's anger, intrinsically linked with the individual: (1) continuing to have access to their children; (2) the return of their children; or (3) a component of rehabilitation. There is a comprehensive discussion of these issues in Howells and Day's (2002) paper on the issues relating to *treatment readiness*.

2. In addition to low initial attendance, this client group has a high attrition rate. Hird, Williams and Markham (1997) ran anger control groups for violent offenders in the community over a 3-year period; they report that only 18 % completed treatment. This, too, may be inherently linked to the 'external' as opposed to 'internal' motivations of this client group to seek help. However, another aspect of this client group that often seems to be overlooked is their low literacy level. We have frequently found in our Tuesday groups that group members have had difficulties reading and writing and often felt humiliated, shamed and consequently angry about their school experiences (Cummins, 2005). Unfortunately, being a profession very orientated to the written word, clinicians can often compound those early mortifying experiences of school. In effect, many anger programmes are educational not collaborative; O'Loughlin et al. (2004) reported that they could not administer post-measures due to the high attrition rate of anger group members. They also describe telling group members during the first session that they would be given a 20-page handout in the second session. Ironically, this handout was described by O'Loughlin et al. as 'a reward for coming back' (2004, p. 18).

3. Finally the long-term effectiveness of interventions is difficult to establish with any client group, but particularly so with clients with anger. After we administered post-group measures at the end of our first Tuesday 10-week 'Working with Anger' group, we gave the group members graphs displaying their pre-group anger scores. We advised the group members, that once we had scored their post-group questionnaires we would send them the scores to plot on their graphs, enabling them to see how they had got on (progressed hopefully). This prompted our group members to unanimously ask us to send out the questionnaires again; enabling them to see if they had maintained their improvements, improved further, or slipped back since ending the group; a researching clinician's dream! Not too surprisingly, when we sent out the questionnaires three months after the group ended, only one of the seven group members returned his completed questionnaire; a researching clinician's reality!

THE BENEFITS OF EVALUATION

Often the treatment of many disorders, such as depression, anxiety and obsessive compulsive disorder has been dominated by psychiatry and pharmacology. Consequently, the designs and outcomes of psychological interventions with people within these client groups are then compared with the designs and outcomes of randomised control trials of psychiatry. Kraemer, Wilson, Fairburn and Agras (2002) propose that randomised clinical trials (RCTs) are the *gold standard* for evaluating the efficacy and effectiveness of psychiatric treatments. However, research conducted with psychological therapies in clinical settings often has difficulty adhering to the strict requirements of RCTs. Our local ethics board, for example, is adamant that we cannot deny one group of clients a therapeutic intervention for the purpose of a control group. Thus, the efficacy of psychological interventions and the dissemination of the findings of those interventions are often at a disadvantage in comparison to studies undertaken by pharmaceutical companies.

In an attempt to address that disadvantage, The Task Force of the American Psychological Association (1995) established criteria by which the methodology of psychological treatment studies could be evaluated and categorised into: *well-established treatments* and *probably efficacious treatments*. They further proposed that those treatments not meeting the criteria for the aforementioned categories be considered as *experimental treatments*. This framework enables clinical psychology to evaluate interventions and disseminate information as to the effectiveness of those interventions, enabling psychology to 'survive in this heyday of biological psychiatry' (American Psychological Association, 1995, p. 3).

NO PILL FOR ANGER

Many general practitioners and psychiatrists will prescribe medication in an attempt to ameliorate many of the components of anger. Selective Serotonin Reuptake Inhibitors (SSRIs), such as Fluoxetine and Sertraline are often prescribed to reduce impulsivity. Antipsychotics, such as Risperidone, Haloperidol and Chlorpromazine are often prescribed to take the edge off aggression and violence. Antimanic drugs, such as Lithium and Carbamazepine are particularly used in forensic settings to stabilise mood. However, there is no pill specifically designed to address anger. This *oversight* by pharmacological companies does, in effect, leave *talking therapies* with a clear field. To date, it is questionable as to whether effective and efficacious treatments for anger have been established.

RESEARCH TO DATE

Reviews and meta-analysis of anger interventions indicate that interventions with anger clients are effective (Beck & Fernandez, 1998; DeGiuseppe & Tafrate, 2003; Del Vecchio & O'Leary, 2004). Beck and Fernandez (1998) proposed 'moderate treatment gains', with an effect size of .70, from their meta-analysis of 50 CBT interventions with children, adolescents and adults. However, of the 50 studies within the paper, 24 of the studies were conducted with students, not clinical populations. Further, Beck and Fernandez do not clarify if the studies' populations had clinically significant levels of anger prior to intervention.

The meta-analysis of anger interventions with adults, conducted by DeGiuseppe and Tafrate (2003), concluded that the moderator variable of 'subject type' had no bearing on effect size; which was .71 for between-group studies, and .99 for within-group studies. However, it is unclear how many of the 57 studies within their meta-analysis were conducted with non-clinical populations or how many studies were conducted with participants with an anger disorder. The authors state that they did not require the studies in their meta-analysis to have defined 'an anger disorder *a priori*' as 'such a strategy would have excluded most existing studies' (2003, p. 72).

Del Vecchio and O'Leary (2004) applied much stricter criteria for inclusion in their meta-analysis; i.e. all studies were RCTs whose participants scored within the clinical range on standardised anger measures, prior to intervention. The criteria set by Del Vecchio and O'Leary resulted in 88 studies being excluded, leaving a final sample of 23 studies. The authors report mean weighted effect sizes ranging from .61 to .90 depending on the treatment intervention (.90 for relaxation therapy; .82 for cognitive therapy; .68 for cognitive behaviour therapy; and .61 for therapies that did not fall within the previous categories).

However, the overall effect sizes were inflated by the success of the eight studies conducted with populations with driving anger as measured by the Driving Anger Scale (DAS) (Deffenbacher, Oetting & Lynch, 1994), which made up 34%) of the studies. Effect sizes with the DAS were between 1.07 and 2.10 depending on treatment intervention. Conversely, effect sizes on sub-scales of the Spielberger State-Trait Anger Expression Inventory (STAXI) (Spielberger, 1996) showed much smaller effect sizes; the STAXI subscales of AX-O (measuring anger expression) showed effect sizes of between .38 and .61, whilst the AX-I (measuring internal experience and suppression of anger) showed effect sizes of between .16 and .64.

Yet again, as with the previous meta-analyses by Beck and Fernandez (1998) and DeGiuseppe and Tafrate (2003), the majority of the studies (73%) in Del Vecchio and O'Leary's (2004) meta-analysis, were conducted with college students. As highlighted by DiGiuseppe back in 1999, a major limitation of the anger outcome research is that the majority of studies have used volunteer participants, invariably student populations. Clients with anger problems are often very resistant to treatment due to their impatience, reticence to engage and deficit in both social and cognitive skills (Novaco, 1996). Thus, it is unlikely that college students, volunteering for participation in research studies, are reflective of the clients who present for treatment to psychological services and forensic services. Harris sums this up by commenting 'one therefore hopes to read no more universal pontifications about anger founded on questionnaires administered to well-fed middle-class American or British 20-year-olds' (2001, p. 409).

This gap between the findings of the majority of published research on anger, and the clinical application of successful interventions is encapsulated by the reality, that both of the forensic services in our nearby major city have abandoned group work with anger clients, as they concluded it is ineffective.

ANGER INTERVENTIONS

Published research into the treatment of anger is often a manualised cognitive be-havioural form of intervention, with many clinical practitioners finding its practical application stiff, unwieldy, dismissive of the idiosyncrasies of their individual clients and unrealistic within the demands of a busy clinical setting. In effect, many of these interventions propose *one size fits all*, resulting in a tension between manual-based intervention and intervention based on individual formulation. Taylor and Novaco highlight that 'even researchers describing highly successful structured manual-based therapy seem unable to resist a *clinician's reaction* to justify deviation from protocol' (2005, p. 154).

EVALUATING THE TUESDAY ANGER GROUP

'Working with Anger' groups, in one format or another, have taken place at Psycho-logical Services in Coventry for the past seven years. The original Tuesday Group was an open group, with group members joining throughout the year, attending for varying numbers of sessions and indicating they had got what they needed either by a nego-tiated ending or by no longer attending. Hence, quantitative evaluation of the change and effectiveness of the group was difficult to ascertain. However, effectiveness of the groups was tangible both from how the group members interacted with each other, indicating their increased capacity to construe how others construe (an augmenting of their capacity for *Sociality*), and from reports of their day-to-day experiences, where evidence of *second-order change* was apparent, as the group members' *alternative view of reality* no longer produced the anger responses of before (Ecker & Hulley, 1996).

We decided that, rewarding as these reports and displays of change were, we should evaluate the change quantitatively to ascertain just how effective the Tuesday Anger groups were. The onset of the 10-week 'Working with Anger' group afforded us the opportunity to do this.

Measures used

CORE – Clinical Outcomes in Routine Evaluation (Core System Group, 1998)

In the UK, the need for practitioners to use similar outcome measures to evaluate routine effectiveness and efficacy has been acknowledged (Department of Health, 1996; 1999). The CORE was developed as a result of that need.

The CORE contains 34 simply worded statements answered on a five-point scale, ranging from 'not at all' to 'most or all the time'. The items cover four domains:

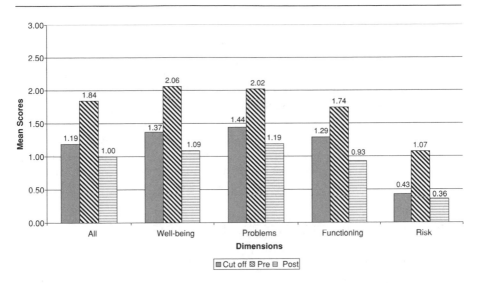

Figure 14.1 The integrated results of the last three 'Working with Anger' groups' CORE scores
Note: n = 21.

subjective well-being (4 items), problems/symptoms (12 items), life functioning (12 items) and risk to self and to others (6 items) (Evans et al., 2002). The mean of all 34 items can be used as a global index of distress. The measure defines people as being either within a clinical or non-clinical population.

Integrating the results from the last three anger groups, the administering of the CORE indicated a *clinically significant* reduction (Jacobson & Truax, 1991) i.e. the group members had moved from the clinical population into the normal population, on all four dimensions (see Figure 14.1).

The use of the CORE as a tool to evaluate the change in anger group members enables us to compare our outcome with the outcome of interventions with other clinical populations. However, as DiGiuseppe and Tafrate (2003) highlight, measures that most closely relate to the core constructs of anger are more likely to capture change and show effect. Thus a questionnaire specific to anger was also required.

STAXI-2 – State-Trait Anger Expression Inventory-2 (Spielberger, 1996)

The STAXI-2 and its predecessor STAXI were found to be the most common psychometric measures used to define when anger is a problem in DiGiuseppe and Tafrate's (2003) examination of 92 treatment interventions, incorporating 1,841 participants.

The normative data for the STAXI-2 is standardised into male and female normal and psychiatric populations in three age groups: 16 to 19 years, 20 to 29 years, and 30 years and above.

The 57 items questionnaire yields scores for six scales, five subscales and the Anger Expression Index. Scales and subscales are:

> S-Ang – State Anger
> > S-Ang/F – Feel Angry
> > S-Ang/V – Feel like Expressing Anger Verbally
> > S-Ang/P – Feel like Expressing Anger Physically
> T-Ang – Trait Anger
> > T-Ang/T – Angry Temperament
> > T-Ang/R – Angry Reaction
> AX-O – Anger Expression-Out
> AX-I – Anger Expression-In
> AC-O – Anger Control-Out
> AC-I – Anger Control-In
> AX-Index – Anger Expression Index

Raw scores are converted into percentile scores and T-scores. Percentile scores between 25 and 75 % are considered as falling within the normal range, while scores above 75 % are classified as a-typical anger, and are indicative of anger within the clinical range. T-scores have a mean of 50 with a standard deviation of 10, scores above 65 are classified as a-typical anger. Most clients referred to our anger group are well above the 75th percentile on all the scales and subscales other than Anger Control-Out and Anger Control-In, in which they often score around the 1st percentile. However, women referred with anger seldom reach the 75th percentile (see Chapter 7 in this volume on gender by Dave et al.). Invariably, our objective was to lower the elevated scores and increase the depressed scores.

Integrating the results from the last three anger groups, the administering of the STAXI-2 indicated a clinically significant decrease from a-typical anger into the normal range on the Trait Anger scale and subscales, the Anger Expression-Out, Anger Expression-In and the Anger Expression Index; in addition both the Anger Control-Out and Anger Control-In scales increased, see Figure 14.2.

Note: we do not include the State anger scales and subscales within the graph as these scales measure how somebody is feeling at the time they completed the questionnaire, hence they can be somewhat transitory.

Prior to intervention, many of our anger clients score on the 99th percentile on the Trait Anger scale and subscales and the Anger Expression-Out, Anger Expression-In and Anger Expression Index. This has led us to wonder if there is too low a ceiling on the

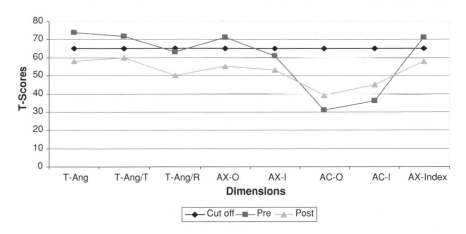

Figure 14.2 The integrated T-scores from the last three, ten-week 'Working with Anger' groups' STAXI-2 scores
Note: n = 21.

STAXI and STAXI-2. Similarly, DiGiuseppe and Tafrate (2003) have hypothesised that the definition of 75th percentile may present too low a floor of anger problems, resulting in insufficient power to detect differences in effective treatment. With this in mind we have started to administer a second anger questionnaire and will compare the results of the STAXI-2 with that second questionnaire, the NAS-PI (Novaco, 2003).

NAS-PI – the Novaco Anger Scale and Provocation Inventory (Novaco, 2003)

The NAS-PI was standardised on a sample of 1,546 normal and clinical samples aged between 9 and 84. Standardised norms are provided for 9–18 years old and 19 years and older.

This 2-part, self-report questionnaire yields scores for 6 scales. Part-one, the Novaco Anger Scale (NAS), contains 60 questions and yields scores for 5 scales:

Cognitive
Arousal
Behavioural
Anger Regulation
NAS total score

The Provocation Inventory contains 25 questions and yields a single PI score which provides insight into the degree of anger experienced with regard to potentially provocative situations. Definitions are given for the NAS-PI T-score ranges. The

NAS-PI contains an 'Inconsistency Responding Index' (INC), which, as Novaco points out, is unlikely to uncover sophisticated falsifiers, but may help to identify unusual levels of inconsistency. Correlation of the 'NAS Total' and the 'PI Total' with the 'STAXI-2 Total' on clinical populations was .77 and .67 respectively. Correlation of the 'NAS Total' and the 'PI Total' with the 'STAXI-2 Total' for forensic inpatients was .81 and .85 respectively. Correlation statistics are given for each of the scales within the NAS-PI with each of the scales within the STAXI-2.

At the last 'Working with Anger' group, the group members unanimously voted a preference for the NAS-PI. They particularly liked the second part of the questionnaire (the PI), which they felt really captured situations/provocations where they are likely to respond with anger. However, the caveat should be added that this is a small number of clients. For this reason we have not included a graph indicating the pre- and post-scores on the NAS-PI, however, the trend was very similar to the STAXI-2.

Of note is that the group members of the last three groups have generally had few literacy difficulties in comparison with previous group members. When group members have reported that they have difficulties with either reading or writing (this is something we ascertain at assessment), we ensure during group sessions that one of the facilitators is on hand when reading or writing skills are required. If necessary, a subtle and relaxed offer to scribe for the individual, dyad or triad where group members may struggle ensures that the group members do not feel humiliated or experience further invalidation. We also restrict the need for reading and writing to the minimum necessary for evaluation; we do not routinely use written material.

In addition to the standardised measures of group members' overall well-being and anger, we have two other measures of the efficacy of these groups. The first of these is the drop-out rate. In total we have offered 29 places in the last three 'Working with Anger' groups. In each group, two members attended for assessment and then dropped out prior to the first session. Of the remaining 23 group members 13 (57 %) attended the full 10-week course. Of the remaining 10 group members, 3 (13 %) attended for 9 of the 10 weeks, 4 (17 %) attended for 8 of the 10 weeks, 1 (4 %) attended for 7 of the 10 weeks, 1 was offered individual therapy as he proved to be unable to control his anger in the group setting, and 1 member dropped out after the third week. This means that 70 % attended 9 or more sessions, and 87 % attended 8 or more sessions. This is a marked contrast with other researching clinicians' experiences; Siddle, Jones and Awenat (2003) report that only 11 (16 %) of those clients invited to join a 6-session CBT anger group attended the full course, and only 34 (49 %) attended one or more sessions. Other researchers have reported similar attrition rates to Siddle et al. (Hird et al., 1997; Munro & Macpherson, 2001; O'Loughlin et al., 2004).

Our second measure was a qualitative evaluation of the group. This enabled group members to rate each component of the group on a 5-point Likert scale and to ponder and report on both the good and bad of their experiences of the group. We also asked them questions about how their behaviour and thinking had changed since starting the group. These questions afforded us some insight into whether *first-order change*, or *second-order change* has occurred (Ecker & Huckley, 1996). The omnipotent value of the group dynamic is apparent in the group members' evaluation of their experiences, when they answer our question: 'What was the most beneficial part of the group?'

> Talking about the problems within me and hearing about other people's problems.

> Realising that I wasn't alone.

> Sharing, listening and the feeling of being listened to.

> Being part of it, listening to others.

> Knowing I wasn't the only one.

These comments are understood by us to indicate that we have been successful in producing the conditions that enable the persons' invalidation to be addressed. Their shifts from the clinical population to the non-clinical population (as described above) are part of their revalidation. The significant changes demonstrated by the STAXIs are a further indication of the success of this approach in effecting real change in a population that is traditionally viewed as difficult to work with. As one group member so succinctly put it: 'We're not the bastards we're made out to be'.

CONCLUSION

In the writing of this chapter, (DP) contacted the authors of the other chapters within this book who had written about clinical interventions. Although many of the authors had administered questionnaires at assessment, few had evaluated the outcomes of their interventions. The exceptions were Laming and Adelman.

Laming (Chapter 3) uses a variety of measures to evaluate the effectiveness of the SHED project. Using self-assessment, the men rate themselves on broad continuums of abusive behaviour, between the contrasting poles of 'equality' and 'power and control'. In addition, an Abusive Behaviour Checklist is used, which covers a variety of behaviours, such as: 'anger and intimidation', 'coercion and threats', 'physical abuse' and 'emotional abuse'. The men score themselves on a scale of 1–5 (where 1 = never and 5 = constantly) and their partners also independently rate them on the same scales. In the last session, the men also evaluate each other's growth, participation in the group and areas that still need work. As Laming proposes, effectiveness of the group is measured by what is important to the men and their wives.

Adelman (Chapter 12) administers the Adolescent Treatment Outcome Package (TOP, Behavioural Health Laboratories, 1992-2005). The TOP in America, like the CORE in Britain, was designed as a universal core battery that could be used as a common outcome tool across all outcome studies (Kraus, Seligman & Jordan, 2005). The TOP covers a wide range of mental health symptoms, such as depression, mania, suicidal ideation, violence and substance abuse.

Evaluating outcomes of interventions can be time-consuming to set up and administer, but has often been very rewarding in enabling us to see how effective our interventions have been. An ineffective outcome is probably not so rewarding, but is just as useful in informing and enhancing psychological interventions.

REFERENCES

American Psychiatric Association (1994). *Diagnostic and Statistical Manual of Mental Disorders*. 4th edn. Washington, DC: APA.

American Psychological Association. Task Force on Promotion and Dissemination of Psychological Procedures (1995). Training in and dissemination of empirically-validated psychological treatments. Report and recommendations. *The Clinical Psychologist*, 48(1), 3–24.

Beck, R. & Fernandez, E. (1998). Cognitive-behavioural therapy in the treatment of anger: a meta-analysis. *Cognitive Therapy Research*, 22(1), 63–74.

Bry, A. (1976). *How to Get Angry Without Feeling Guilty*. New York: Signet.

Core System Group (1998). *CORE System (Information Management) Handbook*. Leeds: Author.

Cummins, P. (2005). The experience of anger. In D. Winter & L. Viney (eds), *Personal Construct Psychotherapy*. London: Whurr.

Deffenbacher, J. L., Oetting, E. R. & Lynch, R. S. (1994). Development of driving anger scale. *Psychological Reports*, 74, 83–91.

Del Vecchio, T. & O'Leary, K. D. (2004). Effectiveness of anger treatments for specific anger problems: a meta-analytic review. *Clinical Psychology Review*, 24, 15–34.

Department of Health (1996). *NHS Psychotherapy Services in England: Review of Strategic Policy*. London: HMSO.

Department of Health (1999). *A National Service Framework for Mental Health*. London: Stationery Office.

Department of Health (2004). *Organising and Delivering Psychological Therapies*. London: Department of Health Publications.

DiGiuseppe, R. (1999). End piece: reflections on the treatment of anger. *Psychotherapy in Practice*, 55 (4), 365–379.

DiGiuseppe, R. & Tafrate, R. C. (2003). Anger treatment for adults: a meta-analytic review. *Clinical Psychology: Science and Practice*, 10(1), 70–84.

Ecker, B. & Hulley, L. (1996). *Depth Oriented Brief Therapy*. San Francisco: Jossey-Bass.

Evans, C., Connell, J., Barkham, M., Margison, F., McGrath, G., Mellor-Clark, J. & Audin, K. (2002). Towards a standardised brief outcome measure: psychometric properties and utility of the CORE-OM. *British Journal of Psychiatry*, 180, 51–60.

Harris, W. V. (2001). *Restraining Rage: The Ideology of Anger Control in Classical Antiquity*. Cambridge, MA: Harvard University Press.

Hird, J. A., Williams, P. J. & Markham, D. M. H. (1997). Survey of attendance at a community-based anger control group treatment programme with reference to source of referral, age of client and external motivating features. *Journal of Mental Health*, 97(6), 1, 47–54.

Howells, K. & Day, A. (2002). Readiness for anger management: clinical and theoretical issues. *Clinical Psychology Review*, 584, 1–20.

Jacobson, N. S. & Truax, P. (1991). Clinical significance: a statistical approach to defining meaningful change in psychotherapy research. *Journal of Consulting and Clinical Psychology, 59, 1,* 12–19.

Kraemer, H. C., Wilson, G. T., Fairburn, C. G. & Agras, W. S. (2002). Mediators and moderators of treatment effects in randomized clinical trials. *Archives of General Psychiatry, 59*(10), 877–883.

Kraus, D. R., Seligman, D. A. & Jordan, J. R. (2005). Validation of a behavioural health treatment outcome and assessment tool designed for naturalistic settings: The Treatment Outcome Package. *Journal of Clinical Psychology, 61*(3), 285–314.

Munro, F. & Macpherson, G. (2001). Anger management fast-track: a waiting list initiative utilizing a large group format. *Clinical Psychology Forum, 147,* 30–34.

Novaco, R. W. (1996). Anger treatment and its special challenges. *NCP Clinical Quarterly, 6,* 3. Retrieved April 22, 2005 from Department of Veterans Affairs, World Wide Web: http://ncptsd.va.gov/publications/cq/v6/n3/novaco.html

Novaco, R. W. (2003). *The Novaco Anger Scale and Provocation Inventory.* Los Angeles: Western Psychological Services.

O'Loughlin, S., Evans, J. & Sherwood, J. (2004). Providing an anger management service through psychoeducational classes – and avoiding therapy. *Clinical Psychology, 33,* 17–20.

Rothschild, B. (2004). Mirror. *Psychotherapy Networker, September/October,* 46–51.

Spielberger, C. D. (1996). *State-Trait Anger Expression Inventory, Research Edition: Professional Manual.* Florida: Psychological Assessment Resources.

Taylor, J. L. & Novaco, R. W. (2005). *Anger Treatment for People with Developmental Disabilities.* Chichester: John Wiley & Sons.

World Health Organisation (1994). *ICD-10 Classification of Mental and Behavioural Disorders.* 10th edn. London: Churchill Livingstone.

INDEX